FAMILY TREATMENT
In Social Work Practice

Family Treatment In Social Work Practice

Curtis Janzen and Oliver Harris

School of Social Work and Community Planning

University of Maryland at Baltimore

F. E. PEACOCK PUBLISHERS, INC.
ITASCA, ILLINOIS 60143

To our families . . .
from whom we have learned so much

Preface

After treating families in practice and teaching family treatment for several years, we have undertaken in this book to address the needs of helping professionals, especially social workers, in finding effective ways to deal with family problems encountered in practice. This effort was generated by our perceptions of what is involved in treating families within the context of a social work agency and the need expressed by many students and practicing social workers for more direction in their work with families.

Much of the family treatment literature addresses families and family problems that are not frequently encountered in the day-to-day practice of social workers in agency settings. This book, therefore, extrapolates from existing theory and technique to provide an approach to treatment that more readily conforms to the specific constraints of social work agencies.

In many situations agency constraints have a tremendous impact on the social worker's treatment activities. In some agencies contact with families is often of short duration, requiring immediate assessment of the problem and brief treatment to alter dysfunctions. Many times the tasks are specific, as in helping a family to make the shifts and realignments required by the illness of one of its members or to adapt to the return of a family member after a period of absence. The family struggling to reconstitute after breakups and remarriage, the family in which children are abused, the minority family, and the family of low socioeconomic background are typical of the practice encounters of the agency-based social worker. At issue in these situations is sufficient understanding by the social worker of the way family transactions relate to the problem in question and the impact intervention is likely to have on the family's pattern of operation.

In response to the needs of social workers with regard to treating families within the agency context, this book accomplishes two critical objectives. First, it introduces the use of family treatment in a variety of problem situations. This is realized through the identification of a focus for assessment of various family problems and for addressing the necessary realignments for improved family functioning.

Second, a "family system" understanding is brought to the work with each kind of family and family problem. This will assist the worker in organizing the existing variables as they relate to various situations, which should be of special value to those who have to relate to families of identified clients or patients with limited perception of the events taking place. Families are often perceived as having a negative effect on the identified problem person, but helping professionals have less often been aware of the effects that families and identified problem persons produce in each other and their reaction to each other's reactions. Still less frequently are helping professionals aware of the mechanisms and rules which govern such transactions, and of the effects of the presence and behavior of other family members on transactions within a dyad. Effective intervention may frequently have occurred without conscious knowledge of the family as an organized system, but knowledge does aid the professional both in understanding what has been done and in planning what is to be done in producing change in families.

This book is directed to undergraduate social work students and graduate social work students who are beginning to study and familiarize themselves with the theory and technique relative to family functioning and family treatment. It is also directed to the practitioner who is beginning the transition from treating individuals to treating families as a unit.

We would like to thank the many practitioners, students, client families, and colleagues who have reinforced our recognition of the need for this book and stimulated our thinking in many ways. Our thanks go to Judith Fine, M.S.W., University of Maryland Hospital, who is the author of Chapter 9; John Goldmeier, Ph.D., University of Maryland, School of Social Work and Community Planning, who is the author of Chapter 10; and Pallassana R. Balgopal, D.S.W., University of Illinois, Jane Addams School of Social Work, for his contribution to Chapter 7. We are also very grateful to Mrs. Virginia Peggs, whose patience and undying efforts in typing the manuscript will never be forgotten, and to Tom LaMarre, editor, and the F. E. Peacock Publishers staff, who were extremely helpful to us in writing this book.

Curtis Janzen
Oliver Harris

Table of Contents

Conjoint Family Sessions
Engaging the Family in Treatment
Opening Procedures
Summary
References

Chapter

Introduction
Poverty Families as Problem Families
External System/Family System Operations
Internal Family System Operations
Family Problems and Family Problem Solving
Conjoint Family Treatment
Beginning Treatment
Interventions in Family Communications
Interventions in Family Structure
Work with the Extended Family
Reducing Family Isolation
Reorienting External Systems
Notes about Co-Workers and Agencies
Treatment Program Effectiveness
Summary
References

Attitudes toward the Aged
The Aging Process
Losses Experienced by the Aged
Working with the Family
Summary
References

Part I

Theoretical Framework

The purpose of Part I is to introduce the field of family treatment and some of the most widely accepted support for the study and treatment of the family. Because no single theoretical structure for treating families has yet been developed, there are several approaches to family treatment. All of these approaches, however, recognize the existence of a systems format within which the family operates to achieve growth and resolve problems. It is in this context that this part of the book has been written. Each of the three chapters contributes to building an understanding of family functioning and suggests ways to plan appropriate strategies for changing interactional patterns when families become dysfunctional.

The first chapter gives a brief overview of family treatment in social work practice and presents theory and concepts, with emphasis on a systems view of family processes. This presentation is centered on the content of the communicative-interactive and structural approaches to work with families, though it also considers the work of individual clinicians who have contributed to the existing body of knowledge relative to family treatment. The family's struggle to maintain a balance in relationships and to cope with being close and being separate is discussed. Developmental cycles of the family and processes that contribute to growth and dysfunction are

1

presented, in order to explore the interior of family transactions and provide in part a base upon which change strategies can be organized.

Chapter 2 continues the task of building a framework for the study and treatment of families by examining the impact of various problems on the organization and functioning of the family. It also emphasizes the kinds of realignments and changes necessary to resolve problems when they occur. Meeting the material needs of the family, adapting to role changes, resolving conflict between family goals and individual goals, and communication and negotiation around changed circumstances are among the issues discussed in this chapter. The interrelatedness of a family's problems and its problem-solving efforts is demonstrated, with examples of the intimate relationship between the persistence of family problems and the ineffectiveness of problem-solving methods.

Chapter 3 completes our suggested framework for assessing family functioning and planning intervention. This chapter moves into the social worker's process of intervention with families. The ways in which the systems view of the family affects beginning the treatment and engaging the family are delineated. The use of conjoint sessions with families; the task of actually engaging the family; procedures for beginning with the family; the social worker's role in treatment; and contracting with the family are among the topics discussed. A major emphasis is the worker's concurrent efforts in solving the problems presented by the family and changing the way in which the family goes about solving those problems.

CHAPTER 1

An Introduction to Family Treatment

The idea of involving the entire family in resolving a problem expressed by one of its members is still relatively new. Prior to the 1950s when the family was first perceived as the client system, more traditional ways of changing dysfunctional patterns of behavior were favored. Most therapists, including social workers, approached problem solving from the viewpoint of changing an individual; the person who expressed the problem, usually through behavior unacceptable to others, was seen as the target for change. It was believed that the reason for the maladaptive behavior was somehow located within the individual, and reaching the locus of the innermost seat of the problem was necessary if problem-solving efforts were to be effective. And this task could best be achieved through a one-to-one relationship between therapist and patient or worker and client.

These beliefs were discounted during the 1950s, as therapists began to work with more than one member of the family. The reasons for this movement away from the concept of individual therapy as the primary mode of intervention are not clear, as Haley (1971) points out. Various disciplines were involved, and all accepted this new way of affecting change as offering some advantages.

During the late 1950s and early 1960s parallel movements toward

3

working with the family as a unit were underway, involving a variety of disciplines in various locations. Nathan Ackerman, Robert Gomberg, Murray Bowen, and Frances Beatman in the East; Don Jackson, Virginia Satir, Jay Haley, and Gregory Bateson on the West Coast; and the Family Service Association of America and the Committee on Family Treatment and Diagnosis in the Midwest— to name a few—were all involved in the early efforts to develop theory and a body of practice knowledge for treating families.

Many social workers in public agencies probably moved into working with families as a unit in a more or less indirect way. Our own experience in working with families began in the 1950s, in what was referred to as *multiple client interviewing*. For this new mode of problem solving, there was then only limited knowledge of process and outcome. Many things about it were unclear, but like a number of other social workers, we were eager to explore this new dimension of practice. These interviews usually involved two members of the nuclear family, most often parents seen together. New information not previously furnished by the individual when seen alone became available, and differences in the ways the members perceived the same problem situation were revealed.

These results were exciting, but it was soon evident that something different was needed if we were to engage the family as a unit effectively. It became clear that there was much more involved in these problem situations than what had been traditionally viewed as an individual problem within the context of a family. It seemed appropriate, if we were to seek more than individual change, to pay attention to the way people were experiencing each other in their various encounters. This was the beginning of a new way of thinking about problem configurations and ways of intervening with those involved in a family conflict. The client was no longer an individual with symptoms, but a family with a problem.

FROM INDIVIDUAL TO FAMILY INTERVENTION

The movement away from the traditional one-to-one treatment of family members and toward treatment of the family as a unit which has been described above is reflected in the individual experience of therapists and social workers. Many social workers who treat families begin their careers by working with individuals in the traditional manner, and they find some adjustments are necessary in moving from work with an individual to work with a family. The social worker working with families cannot be totally concerned about what one person is doing but must think in terms of two or more people interacting and influencing each other. It is necessary to acquire a different perspective of problem formation and solution in intervening with the family as a unit.

The transition from work with individual clients to work with families is not usually made in a smooth and orderly manner. The social worker most often tries to adapt, in a precise way, the knowledge and skill acquired in work with individuals to work with families. For example, it is not uncommon for a social worker engaging in family treatment for the first time to approach the problem by interviewing individuals in the presence of other family members. The worker carries on a dialogue with one member at a time and gives full attention to each transaction. There is likely to be overemphasis on changing the behavior of an individual family member, instead of focusing on changing the way members relate to each other. As a result the family may be unable to participate as a unit, and the opportunity to assess family interaction is greatly impaired.

We are not suggesting that attention should never be focused on the individual in family treatment. It may indeed be necessary at times to focus on an individual in certain situations, as when the family should listen to a member who is seldom heard or give support to a family member who needs help in gaining or maintaining a sense of individuation.

To illustrate the change in therapeutic considerations between the traditional one-to-one approach and the family treatment perspective, consider an adolescent client who is truant and has difficulty in school. In the traditional approach, therapeutic efforts would likely focus on the client's fears, feelings of inadequacy, and so on. The objective would be to help the client develop insight into the cause of the problem, which would pave the way for a change in behavior. The involvement of parents and siblings would most likely be peripheral. The parents might be asked to provide some information about the problem; contacts with them would likely be separate from those with the child, and neither they nor other children would be given more than minimum responsibility for the problem.

Conceptualization of the problem is quite different in the family treatment method. The family member whose behavior is in question is thought of as the symptom bearer of a family problem. Among the objectives of the social worker are to shift attention from the symptom bearer to the family and to involve other members in working toward necessary changes. Seeing family members together is useful because it provides an opportunity to observe various family patterns as members interact around the problem, and this reveals a more complete picture of the problem. The therapist who sees only one family member gets only that person's view of the problem, which represents the way it is experienced from the unique position held in the family by that individual.

Take the case of a child in treatment who reveals a reluctance to play with other children in the neighborhood. The mother responds to the child's remarks by saying she realizes this isn't good, but the playgrounds are unsafe and she is fearful that the child might get hurt if allowed outside to play. The mother's comment gives the social worker and the child a different idea about the problem. The child experiences a conflicting message with regard to the inappropriateness of staying in the house and the danger of going outside to play. And the worker now has a notion about the mother's role in the child's behavior. If they had not been seen together, the manner in which the mother impacts on the child's behavior may never have been connected in this way.

To understand the way people interact and perform as members of a family, it is necessary to be aware of conceptualizations about the family as a functioning unit. For example, some notion of family structure and the processes in which it engages as it maintains its existence is necessary. In this chapter we will present some of the essential concepts utilized in family treatment. These concepts are drawn largely from the structural and the communicative-interactive approaches to the treatment of families, but they also include contributions from clinicians and theoreticians who do not necessarily adhere to these methods. They lay the groundwork for a theoretical framework for understanding the dynamics of the family as a complex interactive system which will be developed further in Chapters 2 and 3.

THE STRUCTURAL APPROACH

The framework of structural family treatment as set forth by Salvador Minuchin consists of a body of theory and technique which places the individual in a social context. When the structure of the family is changed the positions of family members are altered accordingly, and as a result each individual experiences change (Minuchin, 1974, p. 2). The behavior of its members is regulated by transactional patterns established through repeated operations that reinforce a preferred way of relating. The psychosocial growth of family members is enhanced during this developmental process by the family's adaptation to changed circumstances as a way of maintaining continuity.

Among the basic underpinnings of this approach is the belief that the family is a system which functions through the support of subsystems. A hierarchical relationship involves the parental subsystem, with its executive functions, and the sibling subsystem, which is nurtured and guided by the parental subsystem. The existence of family boundaries which define the family and distinguish it from other families is also recognized.

In the course of developing and maintaining itself, a family passes through clearly identifiable life cycles in which systemic aspects of many family processes can be observed. A family of procreation comes into being when a man and woman join for the purpose of sharing their heritage and passing it on to their offspring. These two people compose what is known in the language of family treatment as the *spouse subsystem.*

The Spouse Subsystem

Minuchin (1974, p. 56) speaks of complementarity and accommodation as the primary ingredients of a successful spouse subsystem. This means that each spouse should develop patterns of behavior that lend support to effective functioning of the other. In carrying this out, a kind of joining and cooperating takes place. Yet the ability to be and act separately is also essential to effective functioning of the spouse subsystem. Therefore the spouses must seek a balance between being close and supportive, and maintaining the individuality necessary for independent action.

Thus the spouse subsystem, like all subsystems, is characterized by a boundary within a boundary structure. The inner boundary maintains the individuality of the participants, while the outer boundary defines the subsystem and protects it from the intrusion of outside forces. The outer boundary which surrounds the spouse subsystem differentiates it from other family systems and provides a turf over which these two participants are the rulers. When the boundary is appropriately in place, the spouse subsystem is clearly separated from the participants' families of origin, and it controls extended family interference. At the same time, the individual boundaries provide each spouse a turf over which he or she can rule within the subsystem boundary, as exemplified by the ability of each to act without complete support and validation of the other. A spouse with an individual boundary can identify a self and take responsibility for individual action.

When children are born into the family, the spouse subsystem boundary also protects against the children's intrusion into the husband and wife domain. This does not mean the spouse subsystem is isolated from other systems. However, it symbolizes the right of the spouse subsystem to engage in its own internal processes without interference from outside its boundary.

In spite of the boundary's objective of safeguarding the integrity of the system, boundary violations do occur. Take the case of a newly married couple who moves in with in-laws. The in-laws may insist on maintaining a parent-child relationship by invading the psychosocial space of the newlyweds, which is a serious threat to the boundary around this subsystem. If the newlyweds accept the in-laws' wishes to direct their lives, these two subsystems become diffuse, and the identity of two separate systems does not exist. And in the case of such encroachment, it is not uncommon to find a coalition existing between two principals who are of different generations. For example, the wife and her mother may enter into a coalition against the husband of the newly married couple. This is a generational boundary violation which reflects the lack of a clear boundary between the wife and her mother. It also contributes to dysfunctioning in both systems. While the mother is involved with the daughter against the daughter's husband, she is also likely to be neglecting the relationship with her own husband.

The Parental Subsystem

Up to the time of the first child the marital pair is viewed as a spouse subsystem, with the members reflecting primary concern for their roles as husband and wife. When the first child is born three new subsystems come into being which must be recognized in considering family functioning. The new family units are the parental subsystem, composed of mother and father; the sibling subsystem, which at this time is the only child; and the parent-child subsystem, which concerns interactions of a parent and the child.

The parental subsystem is largely child focused and has executive responsibility for the entire family system. In order to perform effectively, parents must be flexible and maintain a delicate balance between exercising control and promoting independence. Unlike the spouse subsystem, which is protected from the intrusion of children, the parental subsystem operates differently where children are concerned. The boundary of the parental subsystem permits free movement of children back and forth across the perimeters of the system. This new role of parent carries with it responsibility for the rearing of children. One of the first things parents must do is give up some of what they previously shared exclusively when occupying only the role of spouse.

In systems theory, a change in one part of the system requires change in other parts. With the birth of the first child, parents experience a demand for change in the family system; the addition of a third member automatically sets the change process in motion. The birth of the child has its first impact on the relationship between husband and wife. The previous balance they enjoyed in their relationship is disrupted, as a new boundary must be established around themselves and the child. The inclusion of the child means each parent must make room for an additional relationship. Because the child must be nurtured, the parents must restructure their own need-meeting activities to allow for meeting the physical and emotional needs of the child.

Sometimes changing to include a child is difficult for new parents. Before the birth of the child they are primarily concerned with their own and each other's needs and expectations, in an intimate and personal relationship. When they become parents there is likely to be less time for enjoying each other. Leisure time may have to be spent differently, or recreational activities may be sharply curtailed in the interest of child care. If parents are unable to make these adjustments by redefining the manner in which they interact within their own life space, in such a way as to include the nurturing of the child, functioning as a family is likely to be problematic.

These role adjustments must be repeated with each additional child, and the older children also become involved in the sharing and need-meeting process as it relates to each new member. For example, the birth of the new baby who joins an existing sibling subsystem affects the next oldest child, who must give up the role of "baby" in the family and relinquish some of the closeness previously shared with the mother. The mother must extend her nurturing role to include the new member, and by so doing she alters her relationship with the other children. Physical accommodations must also be made for the new baby which may affect the other children's play

9

activities, sleeping arrangements, and so on. Sometimes these changes will impact negatively on the older children, who may react with such behavior as withdrawing, thumb sucking, or bed-wetting. Such behavior is usually temporary if parents are able to demonstrate caring for the older children.

The role of parents can become more difficult as the children grow and seek increased individuality. This places great demand on the control and permission functions of the parental subsystem. Maintaining a balance between these functions in a manner that supports autonomy, while exercising the necessary control at appropriate points in the developmental process, can be a difficult task for parents. The difficulty is enhanced by our changing society in which values are continuously tested and disagreements are evidenced in many areas.

We believe conflict is inherent in the parenting role, and this should be kept in mind when working with families, especially around problems involving adolescents. Minuchin (1974) suggests, "Parents cannot protect and guide without at the same time controlling and restricting. Children cannot grow and become individuated without rejecting and attacking" (p. 58). This presents a difficult problem for parents and children and a challenging situation for social workers intervening with families unable to cope with these interlocking conflicts.

The Sibling Subsystem

In order to grow and develop individuality children need their own turf where experimentation can take place without interference from adults. This makes the sibling subsystem a very important part of the family organization. It is in this subgroup that children learn how to relate to each other, including how to share, disagree, make friends, bargain, and protect themselves from the down position of a complementary relationship.

This experience serves as a shield of protection for the child in encounters with other systems. The first use of this experience may be seen as the child interacts with the parents and learns to adjust to a relationship of unequal power. Although the young child does not master the skill of negotiation and compromise from the sibling subgroup experience, alternative behaviors in personal encounters are likely to be learned and will be further tested with elders in the future. In this way the child establishes and broadens patterns of relating.

This is not to imply that the child learns only within the confines of the

10

sibling subsystem experience. Much is also learned from interacting with parents and later with extrafamilial systems. However, experiences in this subsystem remain among the most important for the child, as they provide one of the earliest opportunities to test behavior and to learn from trial and error. And this type of learning is essential for the child's growth and development.

Like other subsystems, the sibling subsystem has a boundary which protects the system from intrusion by adults. Nevertheless, the boundary is permeable. This allows parents to move back and forth across it but gives children the right to privacy without parental interference when the need arises. For example, children need the opportunity to have their own special interests, try out their own thinking in specific areas, and offer their own kind of support to each other in times of stress, without direct guidance from parents. Some adjustment becomes necessary in this system as a result of the growth and development of children. With this growth and age differential come different interests, privileges, and responsibilities. At this point the subsystem is usually divided into two groups, along the lines of teenagers and subteenagers. Such a division ensures more effective functioning of the system, while at the same time it protects the integrity of the system as it relates to the life cycle of participants.

If a permeable boundary exists around the family, children should be able to interact freely with extrafamilial systems involving age-appropriate activities. The children will make inputs from these experiences into the family system, and if the substance of these inputs seriously threatens the way the family wishes to operate, the boundary around the family may become inappropriately rigid. For example, consider the teenage daughter who shares with her parents the desire to spend a weekend camping with her boyfriend, as others among her peer group are doing. The parents are very much opposed to such association between boys and girls and disapprove not only the weekend camping but also the daughter's association with the peer group. This reflects increasing rigidity in the family boundary and may well interfere with the daughter's separation from the family.

The Parent-Child Subsystem

In the parent-child subsystem, parent(s) and child or parent(s) and children interact as a functional unit within a boundary. It is different from

11

the three subsystems previously discussed in that at least one of the persons composing it is of a different generation. While a subsystem composed of different generations can become dysfunctional, this is not an automatic outcome. For example, mothers and young children are usually closely involved in an interactional process which forms a subsystem of two different generations, but as long as the boundary around this system is not inappropriately rigid and permits crossing by other family members, it is not likely to become pathological. If, on the other hand, mother and child should become aligned in such a way as to exclude the father from entering the system, it would then be dysfunctional.

Minuchin (1974) suggests that the clarity of boundaries surrounding a subsystem is more important than who makes up the system. Take the case of a single-parent family; the mother is employed and depends on the oldest child to help with the care of younger children. This places them in a boundary together with shared responsibility. However, this boundary will remain functional as long as the limits of authority and responsibility placed with the child are clearly defined. In other words, if the mother tells the child that overseeing the behavior of younger children is to be done only in the mother's absence, and when at home she will be in charge of the family, the system can function smoothly.

Difficulty will develop when the lines of authority are not clear and the child becomes locked in a rigid boundary with the mother. In this case the individual boundaries around mother and child become diffused, and the child's authority will not be limited by the mother's presence. The child then becomes a "parental-child" and may act indiscriminately as an extension of the mother where the younger children are concerned. This denies the other children free access to the mother and may result in problem behavior for these children.

SEPARATENESS AND CONNECTEDNESS

The importance of the ability of family members to act both in concert with others and individually is implied by a number of authors who have discussed family functioning. Among the various approaches to family treatment, Minuchin (1974), with the structural approach; Kempler (1973), with the Gestalt approach; and Satir (1967), with the communicative-interactive approach, to name a few, all emphasize the significance of separateness and connectedness in family relationships. Others, including

Hess and Handel (1967), Friedman (1971), Bowen (1966), and Boszor-menyi-Nagy (1973), have also contributed significantly to the understanding of this process. Our view as presented here takes into consideration some of the conceptualizations of these authors.

Human relationships are characterized by a process of being together and being apart from one another. Two strong emotional forces are at work in this process: the need for emotional closeness, which brings people together; and the desire for individuality and autonomy, which moves the individual away from the control of others.

The family is characterized by a connectedness between members and also a separateness of members from one another. Hess and Handel (1967) recognize this duality in their reference to the situation of the newborn infant. Although coming from the parents, the infant is physically a separate individual and must remain so. Returning to the womb is impossible, and the child's psychobiological individuality will exist despite experience with the socialization process. Hess and Handel likewise see the parents as maintaining their psychobiological individuality regardless of their emotional closeness. This type of separateness is always present.

The infant also exemplifies connectedness among family members. The newborn must depend on parents for nurturance in order to survive and therefore cannot sever this connection. And if the parents are to fulfill the infant's needs they must come together and accommodate to each other in the parenting role.

The other side of being separate and connected involves emotional issues. Friedman (1971, p. 171) sees fusion and differentiation behavior among family members as essential elements in their coming together and being able to separate. He defines fusion behavior as an adaptation of speech and actions designed to establish a system of feeling and responses that is in keeping with the family's preferred pattern of behavior. He sees differentiation behavior as the opposite of fusion behavior, in that the individual develops speech and actions that will disengage his own feelings and responses from a pattern of automatic compliance with what is preferred by others. This means the individual seeks freedom from control by others, freedom to be different from others, and freedom to be apart from others.

The ways in which family members want to be together and the ways they want to be apart is reflected in the family's patterns of behavior. Some families develop around an excessive need for emotional closeness, while

13

other families place great emphasis on separateness as shown in autonomy of behavior. If the need for closeness is too great, fusion within family relationships is likely to result. And when fusion is attained family members will not be able to express themselves in a manner other than what is preferred by the family. If the drive for individuality and self-determination exceeds all other interest, the ability of family members to be close and supportive in relationships with one another is lessened. Extremes in either case contribute to family dysfunction.

The pattern of relating within a family is not the result of an accidental process. It is influenced by the patterns established in the parents' families of origin. If the parents were never given permission to separate from their own families of origin, they will experience difficulty in establishing separate ego boundaries between themselves. The new parents will then transmit this need for togetherness to their children, who will also have difficulty separating from them. The implicit obligation in this type of family is to remain devoted to the families of origin. Individuation is not encouraged among family members, and the avenues through which this might take place are frequently blocked.

This blocking behavior is often subtle. It can be seen in the family that permits members to transcend its boundaries but systematically rejects all feedback from such encounters. A typical example is the adolescent who is allowed to interact with systems outside the family but is denied the opportunity to use this experience for personal growth. Families accomplish this denial in various ways. Sometimes they discourage differentiation indirectly by disqualifying the child's attempts at new behavior or expressing fear that great danger is associated with his or her wish to be different at such a tender age. In this way the avenue to differentiation is blocked, and the family goal of maintaining the devotion of its members is supported.

The experience of separateness in relationship is not entirely a physical phenomenon. Boszormenyi-Nagy and Sparks (1973) suggest that actual physical separation is not necessary for one to attain the individuation implied in being separate from the other. Instead, the ability to be separate is realized through the formation of a psychic boundary. With this boundary established, one is not always a product of and dependent upon the family but becomes a separate entity by reason of psychic emancipation. This type of boundary formation is reflected in the work of

14

Laqueur, Labrut, and Morong (1971), who report that as the child develops, primary objects of attachment are gradually replaced. This occurs when the child learns to transfer energies from these primary objects to a widening circle of outside figures, interests, and tasks. As this is accepted by other family members and they assist the child in this growth process, a psychic boundary is formed which facilitates the achievement of a sense of belonging and a sense of being separate.

We believe that one of the most important developments within the family, as it passes through its life cycle, is the determination of what it will do about sameness and difference in family relations. Most families are able to establish a workable balance in how its members will come together and support each other and how they will be different and able to be apart from each other. The need for professional help is likely to be influenced by the extent to which this balance is successfully established.

THE COMMUNICATIVE-INTERACTIVE APPROACH

The communicative-interactive approach to the study and treatment of the family developed largely from the work of the Palo Alto Medical Research Foundation Project. The focus of this project was on treating families of schizophrenic patients. Among those who were connected with it and contributed to the basic concepts of the communicative-interactive approach were Gregory Bateson, Jay Haley, Don Jackson, and Virginia Satir. It is accepted in this approach to family treatment that all behavior has communication value and conveys several messages on different levels. The family is seen as a living system that maintains a relationship with the environment through communication which involves the sending and receiving of messages and a feedback process. As a result, family relationships are products of communication. Family members establish rules that regulate the ways they relate to each other and to the outside world. Once these rules are established, the family seeks to maintain the status quo. In other words, the family is viewed as a rule-governed, complex, interactive system, with communication patterns playing a primary role in family functioning.

Satir (1967) refers to communication as all verbal and nonverbal behavior within a social context. This is supported by Watzlawick, Beavin, and Jackson (1967), who maintain that all behavior is communication. This speaks to the complexity of the process of communication; we can readily imagine a simultaneous sending and receiving of messages by gesture, manner of dress, tone of voice, facial expression, body posture, and so on.

In order to understand dysfunction in the family, the communication process operating within family relationships must also be understood. It is important to realize that the way a family communicates, member to member and member to the outside world, reflects the way the family perceives itself and how it will function. The way members of a family communicate with each other shapes the view they have of themselves and the others. This in turn influences the way members report themselves to others, including those outside the family. For example, if the family perceives a member's behavior as good and in keeping with the way it views itself, and it repeatedly communicates satisfaction with this behavior, the response will impact on the individual. This member's perception of self will likely be one of value, and this perception will be manifested in transactions with others. If, however, family feedback to a member is constantly negative, the reverse will most likely happen.

If the family decides it is best to rely on its own internal processes for validation of its functioning, and it increases interaction between members, the freedom to communicate across family boundaries will be restricted. This encourages more communication within the family and more dependence upon one another. If the family is successful in establishing this pattern of behavior, communications from family members will reflect a sameness, and family functioning will likely be characterized by enmeshment.

We support the suggestion of Satir and Watzlawick et al. that all behavior in an interactional situation has communication value. This means we believe the existence of one person in the presence of another sets the stage for communication and, at the same time, assures that the process will take place. This obviously makes possible the act of verbal exchange, which is the most widely understood form of communication. However, both persons may choose to remain silent, and communication will still take place. Messages are conveyed by silence and inactivity as well as by language and activity. The silence of a person who refrains from talking in the presence of another conveys a message to the other, who in turn responds to this silence. Communication has taken place. For example, if the message sent by silence is interpreted as a desire not to engage with the receiver, who respects the wish by also remaining silent, the communication cycle has been completed. The message has been sent, received, and interpreted, and the receiver has responded by the conscious decision to remain silent. And if these two people remain in an interactional situation, despite their silence, they will continue the communication process, with each being aware of the other and through body language, if nothing more, conveying messages one to the other. In other words, as implied by Watzlawick et al., one cannot refrain from communicating when in the presence of another.

The content and relationship of messages as presented by Bateson (1958), Jackson (1959), Watzlawick & Beavin (1977), and Sluzki and Beavin (1977) provide additional material for social workers in understanding human communication. These authors suggest that every communication carries many levels of information. One of these levels is concerned with the relationship in which the communication occurs; people in communication with each other are constantly attempting to define their positions in this relationship.

Jackson (1959) describes two types of relationships, and the positions of the participants in these relationships, complementary and symmetrical. In the complementary relationship the communication involves two people of unequal status, while the symmetrical relationship brings together two people of equal status. The behavior of each participant identifies his or her status in the relationship. For example:

In a complementary relationship—the two people are of unequal status in the sense that one appears to be in a superior position, meaning he initiates action and the other appears to follow that action. Thus, two individuals fit together or complement each other. . . . The most obvious and basic complementary relationship would be a mother and infant. A symmetrical relationship is one between two people who behave as if they have equal status. Each person exhibits the right to initiate action, criticize the other, offer advice, and so on . . . . The most obvious symmetrical relationship is a pre-adolescent peer relationship. (Jackson, 1959, pp. 126-27)

Double-Binding Communications

Bateson, Jackson, Haley, and Weakland (1956) have suggested the existence of a paradox in human communication which is represented by the double-bind phenomenon observed in the families of schizophrenic patients. The exchange of communication in these families was characterized by the sending of incongruent messages, usually within the boundary of a complementary relationship between mother and son. The incongruency of the double message is reflected in its request that the receiver obey and disobey the message simultaneously. This, of course, cannot be done, and if this type of communication is repeatedly used paradoxical behavior results.

To further illustrate double-binding communication, take the case of an adolescent who wishes to spend the night with a friend. In talking this over with his mother she remarks after much discussion, "You know I want you to go and be with your friend; don't worry that I'll be here alone in this big house." This message tells the youngster to go, but at the same time it calls his loyalty to his mother into question and speaks to her fright in being alone, which also says "don't go."

Incongruent messages may become double binding in certain relationships when a necessary set of conditions is present. The following conditions are set forth as the essential ingredients of double-bind communications by Watzlawick et al. (1967, p. 212):

1. Two or more persons involved in an intense relationship that has a high degree of survival value for one or more of the participants.
2. In this context, messages are given which assert opposing commands, i.e., the assertions are always mutually exclusive which means neither assertion can be obeyed without disobeying the other.
3. The recipient of the message is prevented from commenting on it or walking away from it.

Consider the case of the mother-child relationship. Here the relationship is likely to be intense and to have survival value for the child, who needs nourishment from the parent. This places the child in the position of being unable to comment on the opposing commands of the mother successfully or to walk away from them. As a result, the child is often exposed to the double-bind effect.

Double-bind communication is not peculiar to pathologic families. It may be observed to greater or lesser extent in a wide variety of families, most of which do not require professional intervention. The issue of family pathology may be determined by whether or not the double-binding transaction is repeated sufficiently to become an established pattern in family communication. When this has occurred and the self-perpetuating force of the pathological system takes over, family dysfunctioning results.

It should also be kept in mind that the double-bind process is not a unidirectional phenomenon. The paradoxical behavior that results from the double-binding message in turn double binds the sender of the message, thus creating and perpetuating pathologic communication (Watzlawick et al., 1967, p. 214).

Metacommunication

Metacommunication is an important part of the communication pattern observed in human interaction. Satir (1967) defines metacommunication as the sending of a message about a message, both of which are sent at the same time. The message conveys to the receiver how the sender wishes it to be received and how the receiver should react to it. Metacommunication also comments on the nature of the relationship between the persons involved, indicating the way the sender perceives the receiver and the attitude the sender has towards the message and towards self. The content of the message, tone of voice, facial expression, body posture, and so on serve to further shape and define what is verbalized by the sender. This adds to the complexity of the communication process and forces the receiver of metacommunicative messages to assess not only the content but the content within the context of the message.

For example, consider an interchange between husband and wife in which the husband comments, "The children really keep you busy." The literal content of the message is that the children are claiming the wife's attention in such a way that she spends a good deal of time responding. However, this seemingly simple statement may carry a number of messages on a metacommunicative level. First, the context within which the message is sent will help the receiver define it. If it occurs in a relaxed conversation after dinner and in a tone of voice that recognizes the wife's many responsibilities it may convey the message, "I value you and I appreciate your accomplishments as a wife and mother." Here the sender's attitude toward the message, the receiver, and himself is one of friendliness. On the other hand, if the same comment is made in a sarcastic manner as the husband restlessly awaits his wife's preparation of dinner, it may well carry the message, "I want you to give greater priority to preparing meals on time." The sender's attitude in this case would likely be, "I am not friendly, you are not treating me in a friendly manner, and the message is a warning to be heeded."

19

Metacommunication can also be sent on a verbal level. Satir (1967, pp. 76-77) suggests that this occurs when the sender verbally explains the message being sent. This too can occur at various levels of abstraction. For example,

1. It may involve labeling the kind of message sent and telling the receiver how the sender wishes it to be received—"It was a joke" (laugh at it).
2. The sender can verbalize the reason for sending the message by referring to a previous perception from the other—"You hit me. So I hit you back." "I thought you were tired and wanted my help."

The combination of verbal and nonverbal metacommunication creates for the receiver a complex situation from which to determine the meaning of messages received. Making this determination usually requires more attention to the context of the message and the nonverbal metacommunication than to the verbal aspects, as the latter is more explicit. Satir (1967) observes, in her discussion of human communication, "Whenever a person communicates he is also asking something of the receiver and trying to influence the receiver to give him what he wants" (p. 78). Since such requests are not always expressed verbally, those on the receiving end of messages must rely on metacommunication to understand what is asked of them and to determine how they will respond.

CONCEPTUAL TOOLS

Our understanding of the way the family functions as a system is aided by certain conceptual tools. These concepts, which are an integral part of the framework for study and treatment of the family, include homeostasis, triangulation, family rules, and the family myth.

Family Homeostasis

All systems have a self-regulatory mechanism through which a state of equilibrium is maintained. They seek to maintain a steady state, or a desired balance in their existence, through an error-activated feedback process. In regard to maintaining balance in human relationships, Haley (1963) suggests that "when one person indicates a change in relation to another, the other will act upon the first so as to diminish and modify that change" (p. 189). In the case of the family, homeostasis implies that the family acts so as to achieve a balance in relationships. This means that all parts of the system function in such a way as to make change unnecessary for realization of family goals.

Most families maintain a balance in relationships through wholesome growth-producing transactions. This implies that permeable boundaries facilitate feedback, and the feedback process promotes adjustments to life-cycle developments which maintain the desired balance. However, family homeostasis may be achieved in a variety of ways. For example, in the 1950s several psychotherapists, including Bateson (1959), found in their study of schizophrenic patients and their families that in some families there was a vested interest in the patient's illness; when the patient began to improve, family members exerted pressure to maintain the illness. In other situations when the patient got well, someone else in the family became symptomatic. This behavior suggests the need for a symptom bearer in the family in order to maintain the established pattern of relationships.

In such cases, the family, in its effort to maintain a homeostatic state, may not always serve the best interests of all its members. Therefore, the worker should keep in mind that in maintaining its emotional balance, the family may try to prevent unwanted change in the system by encouraging role performance that is destructive for the role occupant. Yet, much of the behavior that maintains the status quo within the family is accepted by its members as a legitimate part of the family's operation. This prompted Satir (1967) to suggest that someone outside of the family is most often the first to identify such behavior as deviant and to send out the call for help. For example, the school is often the first to call attention to the deviant behavior exhibited by the child. The family fails to recognize this behavior as deviant because it serves the function of maintaining equilibrium within the family.

To further illustrate the homeostatic process, consider the case of parents who fight in the presence of a child and frequently threaten to separate. The child fears loss of the parents and reacts to prevent this loss by displaying behavior that claims the parents' attention. When the parents focus their attention on the child, they must discontinue their fighting. The threat of loss for the child subsides, and the family remains intact. As this transaction is repeated it becomes a pattern of behavior in the family; the parents fight and the child acts out to keep them together.

21

Family Triangulation

A number of theorists have contributed to the development of the concept of triangulation in family relations. The work of Bowen (1966), Haley (1967), and Minuchin (1974) is particularly impressive.

Bowen (1966) suggests that the formation of a unit of three as a way of relating is a process common to all emotional systems. Knowledge of this process is essential to understanding the family as it struggles to maintain itself as a viable system. The triangle, as most commonly perceived, involves three persons (e.g., mother, father, child) or two persons and an issue (e.g., wife, husband, alcohol). The two-person system, Bowen says, has difficulty maintaining its stability under the pressure of anxiety and tension. When this system experiences intolerable frustration it triangulates a third person or an issue in the hope of reducing the level of tension. The social worker engaged in family treatment is also a likely object of triangulation, especially when dealing with a two-person system. In a triangled situation the third operative—person or issue—becomes the object of attention for at least one of the original two, and sometimes both engage in a struggle for the advantages offered by the third component of the triangle.

The concept of triangles in human relationships is most often applied as a way of describing the relations of a unit of three. However, more than three persons, or a combination of persons and issues, may be involved, as demonstrated in the family where two or more children alternate as the triangulated family member. In other families more than one child may be brought into the relationship struggle between parents at the same time. As an example, consider the mother whose actions convey to her son and daughter that their father is not interested in the welfare of the family. This encourages them to join with her to ensure survival for the three. It creates a situation in which three have come together against a fourth, and at least four people are actively involved in the triangulation process.

Haley (1967) speaks of the existence of a perverse triangle within the pattern of family relating. This triangle is potentially pathological and so can lead to conflict and possible dissolution of the system. In describing the perverse triangle, Haley suggests that one member is of a different generation (e.g., parent and child). These two people of different generations form a coalition against the peer of one of the members (e.g., mother and son against the father) but deny the presence of the coalition, in spite of behavior that confirms its existence. If the coalition continues and the denial of its existence is repeatedly offered, this pattern of relating is established and a pathological situation exists.

The concept of the triangle in human relationships provides the social worker with a way of viewing the patterns of relating within the family. To illustrate the working of this concept as it is frequently observed in family treatment, a case example from our experience is the H family:

Mr. and Mrs. H were both 31 years of age. He was a successful executive and she was a housewife and mother. They were married at 21 when both were in their last year of college. Their first and only child was a son, D, who was born one year after the marriage. D had just celebrated his ninth birthday when the family came for treatment.

The parents were very articulate, and Mr. H's skills in public relations and sales, areas in which he had been quite successful, were readily observed in the early sessions. He explained the family's route to therapy as a mutual decision, coming after D's increasing show of dependent behavior. In school he was demanding more attention, and the teachers thought he was showing signs of insecurity. At home his behavior was somewhat confusing to the parents, as he demanded more attention, yet at times he withdrew from their efforts to engage with him.

It was learned during the course of treatment that the beginning of this behavior followed closely what Mrs. H described as "rather serious" misunderstandings between her and Mr. H. For the past five years Mr. H had advanced steadily with his company and about one year ago was promoted to a position of increased responsibility. This position required travel and a good deal of entertaining, which forced curtailment of many activities the family had previously enjoyed. Mrs. H was feeling left out of her husband's life, and as both she and the job demanded more and more of Mr. H's time, anxiety and tension developed. In commenting on this Mrs. H stated "the job seemed to be winning" and they had more than once discussed divorce. As a result of the increasing anxiety Mrs. H experienced, she began to do more things with her son, shared her loneliness with him and in various ways conveyed abandonment by Mr. H and their need to be together. This led to a coalition between mother and son, as the son was triangulated by the mother to help in dealing with her relationship with her husband. Nevertheless, this was an uneasy coalition, as D was very fond of his father. When the father also bid for D's attention, D withdrew out of fear of hurting one of his parents. The burden this placed on D was too great to be contained within the family relationship and spilled over into his relationships within the school system.

The family triangle does not necessarily involve the same third person or object throughout the triangulation process, and usually a number of alternatives are available to complete it. In the H case, for example, Mrs. H might also have chosen to attach herself to her parents to help in dealing with her husband or attempted a coalition with the therapist for the same purpose.

It should also be noted that triangulation is not always an indication of pathology in the family. For example, the husband or wife may develop an interest in an outside activity such as volunteer work as a way of spreading out the tension that usually develops in intense intimate relating. It is not likely that bringing this third component into the relationship will become problematic, as long as it does not replace the other principal participant in the relationship. By redirecting some of the energy that otherwise goes into the buildup of tension, both the husband and wife are better able to carry out normal functions.

In summary, triangulation is a predictable way in which human systems handle problems in relating as they seek to relieve the buildup of tension. While it can under certain circumstances contribute to family dysfunctioning, it can also be an alternative which leaves the participants in an intimate relationship somewhat more free to function effectively.

Family Rules

Family rules are essentially relationship agreements which influence family behavior. Some rules are explicit and established along the lines of specific roles and expectations of family members. With these rules what is desired is likely to be discussed, which opens the rules to the possibility of negotiation and change. The most powerful family rules, however, are those that are implicit, having been established over time by repeated family transactions. For example, consider the case of a family in which the father is involved in an extramarital love affair. This affair has generated repeated experiences through which family members have come to realize that the extramarital relationship exists. The parents never openly talk about the relationship themselves or entertain discussion of it by the children. As this scenario is repeated it becomes an established rule that the family will not talk about father's affair.

The strength of this rule lies in the fact that without discussion, relevant information about the experience is not processed. When this does not occur, the family is less likely to take actions to alter the status quo. The self-perpetuating mechanisms within the family system take over and reinforce the implicit rule which continues unchanged among family members.

Families also have different ways of enforcing rules in treatment. For example, if the worker seems to be getting too close to a family secret in an interchange with one family member, someone else may enter the discussion with a different idea which changes the flow of information. In another situation, especially where children are involved, a child may suddenly display some form of disruptive behavior. This claims the attention of the group, taking the focus away from the possible revelation of the secret as awareness turns to this new and unexpected activity.

Some families also have rules governing communication around valued areas of family life such as sexual behavior and family illness. Whatever the governing mechanism, when it interferes with the effective course of treatment preventive measures should be taken.

The Family Myth

The family myth essentially consists of family members' shared beliefs and expectations of each other and their relationships (Ferreira, 1977). It is characterized by unquestioned sharing of beliefs and expectations by all family members, which results in automatic agreement on the myth without further thought by any member. Ferreira gives this example:

> The wife in a family of 16 years' duration did not drive an automobile, nor did she care to learn. It was necessary for the husband to drive her everywhere she wished to go, which he did at whatever personal sacrifice it required. The wife explained her position by saying she was not "mechanically inclined." The husband immediately agreed with his wife and corroborated her statement by adding that she often let things fall from her hands around the house, and had always been that way. He further reported that she also did not trust cabdrivers, while the wife nodded her approval. (p. 51)

The husband so completely shared the belief that his wife was not mechanically inclined and needed his assistance that he not only agreed with her statement but supported the belief by offering an example of her awkwardness. He obviously had no thought of questioning her position.

It is also important to keep in mind that in spite of the irrationality often apparent in the existence of a family myth, it is perceived by family

25

members as an emotionally indispensable and necessary part of their reality. As such, it not only determines the behavior of all family members but also reveals something about family relationships. It implies the existence of reciprocal roles in the family, which is to say, if the myth is around something someone in the family cannot do, it implies that it can be done by someone else in the family. For example, the wife cannot drive a car, but the husband can.

Watzlawick et al. (1967) describe the myths in family relating evident in the play "Who's Afraid of Virginia Wolf?" Much of the discussion between the characters in this drama, Martha and George, centers around the existence of an imaginary son. Although the son does not exist, both Martha and George believe him to be real and repeatedly express agreement on matters pertaining to him. Watzlawick et al. agree with Ferreira that the family myth serves a homeostatic function and is frequently called into action at times of high tension which threatens to disrupt family relationships. The myth prevents change in relationships, as do all balancing mechanisms, enabling the family to continue functioning in its customary manner.

SUMMARY

In this chapter we have introduced the idea of family treatment and discussed theory and concepts relative to family functioning. Some of the differences, advantages, and difficulties social workers might encounter in moving from treating an individual to treating the family as a unit are pointed out. A family developmental system is introduced, with emphasis on the structure of the family and various systemic aspects of family organization and functioning. The significance of the struggle for separateness and connectedness among family members is defined, and the process of communication as it relates to family interaction is described. Homeostasis, triangulation, family rules, and family myths are discussed as conceptual tools.

This chapter formulates the foundation of a framework for the study and treatment of the family as a complex and dynamic system. Chapters 2 and 3 will continue the development of this framework by discussing some of the problems that affect family functioning and the task of engaging the family in treatment.

REFERENCES

Bateson, G. *Naven*. 2nd ed. Stanford, Cal.: Stanford University Press, 1958.

Bateson, G. "Cultural Problems Posed by a Study of Schizophrenic Process." In A. Auerback (ed.), *Schizophrenia: An Integrated Approach*. New York: Roland Press, 1959.

Bateson, G., Jackson, D. D., Haley, J., and Weakland, J. H. "Towards a Theory of Schizophrenia." *Behavioral Science*, 1:251–64, 1956.

Boszormenyi-Nagy, I., and Sparks, G. *Invisible Loyalties: Reciprocity in Intergenerational Family Therapy*. Hagerstown, Md.: Harper & Row, 1973.

Bowen, M. "The Use of Family Theory in Clinical Practice." *Comprehensive Psychiatry*, 7:345–74, 1966.

Ferreira, A. J. "Family Myths." In P. Watzlawick and J. H. Weakland (eds.), *The Interactional View*. New York: W. W. Norton & Co., 1977.

Friedman, E. H. "Ethnic Identity as Extended Family in Jewish-Christian Marriage." In J. O. Bradt and C. J. Moynihan (eds.), *Systems Therapy*. Washington, D.C.: Bradt & Moynihan, 1971.

Haley, J. *Strategies of Psychotherapy*. New York: Grune & Stratton, 1963.

Haley, J. "Towards a Theory of Pathological Systems." In G. Zuk and I. Boszormenyi-Nagy (eds.), *Family Therapy and Disturbed Families*. Palo Alto, Cal.: Science & Behavior Books, 1967.

Haley, J. "A Review of the Family Therapy Field." In J. Haley (ed.), *Changing Families*. New York: Grune & Stratton, 1971.

Hess, R. D., and Handel, G. "The Family as a Psychosocial Organization." In G. Handel (ed.), *The Psychosocial Interior of the Family*. Chicago: Aldine Publishing Co., 1967.

Jackson, D. D. "Family Interaction, Family Homeostasis, and Some Implications for Conjoint Family Psychotherapy." In H. H. Messerman (ed.), *Individual and Family Dynamics*. New York: Grune & Stratton, 1959.

Kempler, W. *Principles of Gestalt Family Therapy*. Oslo, Norway: A-s Joh. Nordahls Trykkeri, 1973.

Laqueur, H. P., Labrut, H. A., and Morong, E. "Multiple Family Therapy: Further Developments." In J. Haley (ed.), *Changing Families*. New York: Grune & Stratton, 1971.

Minuchin, S. *Families and Family Therapy*. Cambridge, Mass.: Harvard University Press, 1974.

Satir, V. *Conjoint Family Therapy*. Rev. ed. Palo Alto, Cal.: Science and Behavior Books, 1967.

Sluzki, C. E., and Beavin, J. "Symmetry and Complementarity: An Operational Definition and a Typology of Dyads." In P. Watzlawick and J. H. Weakland (eds.), *The New Interactional View*. New York: W. W. Norton & Co., 1977.

Watzlawick, P., and Beavin, J. "Some Formal Aspects of Communication." In P. Watzlawick and J. H. Weakland (eds.), *The New Interactional View*. New York: W. W. Norton & Co., 1977.

Watzlawick, P., Beavin, J. H., and Jackson, D. D. *Pragmatics of Human Communication*. New York: W. W. Norton & Co., 1967.

CHAPTER **2**

The Impact of Problems on Family Systems and the Nature of Required Changes

The overview of the family system presented in Chapter 1 should help social workers to understand many of the processes operative inside the system and provide a partial basis on which to organize helping activities. Further, they must be aware of the myriad events and changes which can act upon the family to stabilize or upset its homeostatic balance. These events and their effects must be understood before the plan of action most likely to help a particular family can be formulated.

The presenting problem itself can have disruptive effects. This chapter notes how certain problems affect family organization and interaction and indicates the kinds of changes within the family that are necessary if the problems are to be solved.

THE INTERRELATEDNESS OF FAMILY PROBLEMS AND FAMILY PROBLEM SOLVING

Social workers encounter families in trouble when these families' usual means of problem solving have been of no avail. Several factors may prevent problem solving. The first and most obvious is unavailability of resources, either the family's own or community resources. Even though individual coping, interpersonal relationships, and role performance within the family are adequate, they can be adversely affected by a continuing lack of resources. Lack of medical care, for example, may lead to loss of vital roles in the family or in the external world. Or lack of economic means may deprive the family of needed medical care, day care, or other social services.

The need for services and resources is well established, and their lack is obvious. The task of the social worker when resources are lacking is to serve as a broker or advocate to connect the family with resources which will enable it to maintain itself and its members. Little change in family relationships or process is needed in these circumstances. The activity of the worker in encouraging flagging spirits and in making needed connections may be all that is needed.

When resources are known and available but the family does not mobilize itself to make use of them, the problem lies in the way in which the family responds to presenting problems. The means families ordinarily utilize to solve their problems may hamper rather than facilitate the resolution of a difficulty. In some instances these mechanisms may actually have created the problem. For example, family members may be discouraged from venturing into new positions or maintaining vital roles in the outside world, or at least not supported in their efforts by other members. They may not be able to alter their roles or behaviors due to role assignments within the family system. Thus they are locked by the family into performances that do not serve them well. The family needs to alter its organization and process to motivate or free its members to make use of available resources.

While faulty mechanisms may have caused previous difficulties for the family, their operation may have attracted little notice, or, if noticed, efforts to change them may not have succeeded. When a new problem arises, new mechanisms are required. The task for the family is to change in such a way that its members can make use of resources or engage in other behaviors to solve the problem. The solution of the family problem and the alteration of family interaction patterns thus proceed concurrently. If the family can achieve a constructive solution to a current difficulty, its means for solving other problems are also likely to be enhanced.

Awareness of the interrelatedness of problems and methods of problem solving is important. The families most frequently encountered in social work practice do not approach an agency or social worker asking for family treatment or improvement in family relationships. They ask for resolution of a specific difficulty they are facing. The family treatment plan we suggest accepts the family request at face value. The worker proceeds to help the family with its goal of resolving the difficulty, recognizing that an effort on the part of the family which is different from its past attempts is needed. This attention to the current difficulty provides a focus for both worker and family.[1]

Thus a current family problem may be seen as a critical phase in the family's development. Unsuccessful coping with the difficulty leaves the family with an additional source of strain, whereas successful coping may put it in a better position to cope with other problems in the future. The problem has injected a new element into the life of the family with which it is required to deal. Whether or not it may be technically labeled a crisis, the resolution of the difficulty is seen as critical to the continued growth and development of individual family members and to the workings of the family as a social organization.

This view of family problems and their resolution through family change efforts can influence the social worker's approach in various circumstances. In the case of a child who needs to leave the family for work, or school, or to form a new relationship and who is afraid to do so, for example, workers have often considered the child to be conflictfully involved in the parents' marital difficulty and have emphasized the need to work on this problem. The marital problem is presented by the worker as the focus for treatment, although the family's request was to change the child's behavior. In our approach the worker would identify the specific parental disagreement about how to help the child and ask the parents to find a solution to that problem rather than to their marital conflict in general. Reaching agreement on what to do about the child may help resolve the marital conflict or enable the parents to see the need to focus on it.

Another example is the failure of a handicapped individual to utilize a rehabilitation program. The worker may observe that family bickering and tension have left the handicapped individual angered, discouraged, and preoccupied by family problems, and this interferes with his ability to make use of the program. In our approach the worker would not identify the family tension per se as the problem to be solved but would seek to engage the family in making it possible for the handicapped member to make use of

---

[1] One way this dual focus is incorporated in the initial stage of contact is illustrated in Chapter 3 under the heading "Step 3: Working toward Problem Consensus."

the rehabilitation resource. Achieving that goal would of necessity alter family roles and relationships. We would expect that family tension might be reduced by the solution of this particular difficulty and that other family members might also be freed for growth and the achievement of their own goals. When the system changes, individuals can change.

These examples suggest that in this approach to problem solution the worker emphasis is on the achievement of definite goals rather than the delineation of family problems—more on what is wanted than on what is wrong. As problems impact on family organization and functioning, members seek new mechanisms and renegotiate their roles according to the type of problems with which they are coping.

A CLASSIFICATION OF FAMILY PROBLEMS

The problems of families that come to the attention of social workers are many and varied. Some of them can be viewed as arising out of the natural course of family events—out of the fact that families are made up of individuals who change and are of differing ages, sexes, interests, and temperaments. Others arise out of life events in the family's engagement with the external world, appearing to be imposed on the family.

Hill (1958) has classified the general categories of problems which arise in families under stress. We have adapted this list, as shown in Figure 1, to include problems that are due to both internal and external and normal as well as unusual family changes or events. While the list is not exhaustive, it does cover a large variety of family circumstances known to social workers. The occurrence of any of these events or changes does not necessarily result in a referral for help or a voluntary appeal from the family. Some families may adjust to the problem without external support. The concern is not whether the problem is definable as a crisis, but with the fact that the family appears in need of help.

There are five principal types of family difficulties which may be brought on by stressful changes or events. Classified by nature of the difficulty, they are: (1) accession, (2) dismemberment or loss, (3) demoralization, (4) demoralization plus accession or loss, and (5) changes of status.

These problems have consequences which affect individual adjustment, the family's group response to the outside world, and the family's own group adjustment, through changes in role relationships, tasks, and communication efforts. The ways in which these consequences are felt in various types of family problems are explored in the sections to follow.

31

FIGURE 1

A Suggested Classification of Crises in Families

By Source of Trouble
Extrafamily events such as catastrophes
Intrafamily events

By Nature of the Difficulty
1. Accession
   Marriage or remarriage
   Pregnancy (wanted or unwanted) and parenthood
   Deserter or runaway returns
   Stepparent addition
   War reunions
   Foster child addition or adoption or foster adult addition
   Restoration to health (e.g., terminated alcoholism)
2. Dismemberment or loss
   Death of a family member
   Hospitalization (illness or disability)
   War or employment separation
   Child leaving home
   Wife starting employment
3. Demoralization
   Nonsupport or other income loss or job loss
   Infidelity
   Alcoholism or addiction
   Delinquency
4. Demoralization plus loss or accession
   Illegitimate pregnancy
   Runaway or desertion
   Divorce
   Imprisonment
   Suicide or homicide
   Hospitalization for mental illness
5. Changes of status
   Sudden shift to poverty or wealth
   Move to new housing or/and neighborhood
   Change in status of women
   Maturation due to growth (e.g., adolescence, aging, changes due to therapy, or other sources of individual change)

Each event has consequences for:
   Individual adjustment, both psychologically and behaviorally
   Family group adjustment, role relationships, tasks, and communication
   Family group relationship to the outside world

Drawn largely from R. Hill, "Generic Features of Families under Stress," *Social Casework* 39:139–49, 1958.

FAMILY ACCESSIONS AND ROLE CHANGES

The addition of a family member requires both the redefinition of existing roles and a definition of the role of the new member. If the incoming member is a child, infant or older, natural or foster, new or returning, the role definition for parent or parents will be enlarged or altered. When both parents are present in the home, the new role definition for Parent A should have the concurrence or consent of Parent B, and vice versa. Similarly, the roles and responsibilities of the added child member need a definition, varied according to the age and need of the child, which has the concurrence not only of the adult members, but of other children in the family. These role definitions are necessary if the enlarged system is to operate in a way which is gratifying to all members and which avoids conflict resulting from incongruent role conceptions.

If the added member will occupy a parental role, a similar process is needed. A returning adult member may expect to move into the role as it was previously occupied. This is not likely to occur automatically without some readjustment on the part of the family members already in the system, since their role expectations will have been shifted to account for the fact that the reentering member had not been participant in the ongoing activities of the family. The difficulty of reentry will vary according to the status of the individual. Jackson (1956) has detailed the difficulty alcoholics have in reentering the family system upon recovery from alcoholism, largely due to the fact that their participation, status, and esteem within the family had ebbed to an extremely low level. On the other hand, McCubbin, Dahl, Lester, Benson, and Robertson (1976) report that prisoner-of-war families which had maintained the expectancy of return and a clear definition of a husband-father role were likely to facilitate reintegration of the serviceman.

Reconstituted families are another example of the accession of family members. When two partial families are joined it is not strictly a matter of adding one person to a family but rather of adding two families together. The two adults in the family are working out their role relationship as spouses and as parents. Simultaneously, the children are comparing the role taking of the new adults with that of the now-separated parent. They are reflecting on their own positions vis-à-vis the new parent and their new siblings. In difficult stuations, the two families may not become a family but remain as two sets of individuals within the same household. The degree to

33

which they achieve solidarity or remain distant will be a function of the parents' ability to join constructively with each other and with each other's children (Duberman, 1975). More attention will be paid to the tasks of merging and joining such family groups in Chapter 10, on divorce and family reconstitution.

Another complexity in relation to accession of members arises in foster care situations. The child and the family have the task of connecting to each other while simultaneously being prepared for separation. In addition, each party to the new arrangement is likely to be dealing with separations from prior relationships, the child from his or her family or origin, the parents from a previous foster child. All participants now have to gain an image of themselves and of each of the new others in relation to themselves. Meanwhile, the images of prior relationships continue to be real and to guide behavior, however appropriate or inappropriate those images may be to the new set of relationships. Thus both child and foster parents face a considerable adjustment task, one in which they often have little or no assistance. Their efforts meet with varying degrees of success.

There are two additional points in relation to the shifts in patterning of role relationships (both of which will be elaborated on later). One is that changes in role relationships occur within and across the different family subsystems. They affect both the hierarchical, intergenerational relationships of parents and children and the relationships in the separate parental and child subsystems. The second point has to do with the communication processes by which these role relationships are altered. If the family has effective communication capability, these changes in family structure can be achieved in spite of tension and turmoil. If effective communication capability is lacking, new role relationships may not be clearly defined and may remain problematic.

In the individual, changing roles require both an internal, psychological change and a change in overt behavior.[2] As a part of role definition, images and feelings about self and others guide individual behavior. They develop in the interaction between family members as the result of members'

---

[2] Rapoport and Rapoport (1964) discuss both intrapersonal and interpersonal adaptations as essential to successful coping in the honeymoon phase of family growth. This is put forth as a model for adaptation in any kind of family crisis, and these adaptations are seen as essential to individual mental health as well as family functioning.

attempts to regulate one another's behavior. They are, therefore, both consequence and cause of the overt behavior between members.

MEMBERSHIP LOSSES OR SEPARATIONS AND ROLE CHANGES

Similar considerations apply in the case of losses to family membership. Even temporary losses like extended hospitalization or business trips require readjustment of the expectancies of all members. In general, there is the expectation that remaining members will compensate in some way for the gaps left by the missing member. At the same time, however, the degree of role rearrangement required upon loss or departure of a family member depends upon the position and status of the departing member. Fathers, for example, may expect older children to assume household responsibilities during mothers' illnesses. Wives, upon loss of husbands to extended illness or occupational duties, may rely upon children to assume parenting or even spouse roles. Children will look to the remaining parent to carry both parental roles. The departure of a child will have a different effect. The normal departure of a child would ordinarily not achieve problem status in a family, though it may if that child has assumed significant family responsibility. Rosenberg (1975) describes a case in which a daughter's separation from the family for college became problematic because of her role as a peacemaker between her parents.

None of these readjustments comes easily. Remaining family members may lack skills required in adding to their roles, or they may lack the willingness to undertake new responsibilities. Further, the readjustments may entail blurring of generational boundaries or previously adhered-to sex role definitions. Since there is an element of loss in the various types of separation, a grief reaction on the part of the remaining individuals may also be expected.

Family members may handle their individual reactions to each of these types of readjustment to loss or separations with varying degrees of speed or success. Compounding the individual variations in response is the fact that the readiness of one person to respond constructively may not concur in time with the readiness of others, so that not all members are at the same place at the same time in their readiness to adapt.

Some of the adaptive difficulties following loss or separation of a family member are illustrated in greater detail in the following case material

(Deykin, Weissman, & Klerman, 1971). While the loss to the family is due to the psychological withdrawal of a depressive mother, rather than physical absence, many of the problems are the same. Such psychological withdrawal may in itself be seen as a function of family operations, but it also affects the response of the family system.

Even before hospitalization, many families have to deal with the discrepancy between the patient's former functioning and her depressed state. Some relatives are unprepared to cope with role reversals and may themselves become discouraged when their emotional needs are unfulfilled. While this reaction can be seen in any relatives, it is most evident in the patient's spouse. Many husbands develop symptoms similar to those of the patient's, especially somatization. In such marriages, it appeared that both the patient and spouse were vying for the position of the "sick" person. . . .

A spouse who has had to assume many household responsibilities may feel overwhelmed and resentful. Concentrated attention to the patient without any exploration or acknowledgement of the husband's position tends to entrench the spouse's feelings of burden and to diminish his ability to cope with these responsibilities. A simple acknowledgement of the spouse's difficulties may suffice to support him over his trying period. Occasionally, the caseworker has to initiate intensive work which may include helping the spouse to modify his existing living patterns.

The interruption of the characteristic interpersonal family balance, whether it be between spouse and patient or between the patient and other relatives, may have repercussion on all other family relationships. (Deykin, et al., 1971, p. 277)

The family's response to the depressive behavior also may serve to exacerbate the anger, despair, and hopelessness already inherent in the patient. The conflict between patient and spouse may reflect an effort to alter, or restore, a previously existent complementarity. Relief from depression might result if greater symmetry could be achieved.

DEMORALIZATION AND ROLE CHANGES

Role and task adjustments are necessary in relation to demoralizing problems in much the same way they are with additions and losses to membership. Here, however, the basis for role reassignment may arise as much from the needs and feelings of family members about the demoralizing behavior as from the actual need for change in the performance of responsibilities and tasks. Role adjustments as a consequence of additions or losses are also accompanied by a great deal of feeling, but they are likely to be more intense if the presenting problem is a demoralizer.

An example is a family dealing with alcoholism. Where failure to fill expected family roles is involved, the behavior of the alcoholic necessitates compensatory behavior on the part of other family members. But these adjustments may be minor in comparison to the intensity of emotions aroused and the need of family members to find ways of coping with their own feelings and the reactions of others. Another case example (Hajal, 1977) describes the efforts of a 10-year-old girl to take over her father's role after his suicide, based on her identification with him. Her effort placed her in direct conflict with her mother's attempts to deal with her own feelings and her efforts to compensate for her loss of her spouse and the children's loss of their father. The need to address both the intrapersonal and interpersonal aspects of a problem is evident in this case.

When there is added intensity of feeling because of presenting problems in the demoralizer category, several factors are involved. One is the threat that the problem poses to the family's physical survival, as in the case of loss of support or the imprisonment of one of the adults. Additionally, the problem may represent deviations from the family's own value system, or society's. Infidelity or adolescent unwed pregnancy are examples. The problems are violations of the rules by which some family members thought the family was governed. Rejection of the rules may be experienced as a rejection of the family or of persons who made the rule. Or the problem may be seen as a threat to the image or esteem of the family or of individual members in the community.

For these and other reasons, feelings of threat, blame, anxiety, and anger arise when demoralizing problems are encountered. The family should have at its disposal a means to deal with the intense feelings and resolve the conflicts that arise.

FAMILY RESPONSE TO CHANGED CONDITIONS

Factors Influencing Family Response

All types of family problems have a clear impact on family organization and process. The degree to which family members are capable of accommodating themselves to the adjustments required by additions, losses or the occurrence of other problem events, however, depends on a number of factors. These include: (1) the value placed on the family group in contrast to the priority given to individual goals, (2) the members' ability to communicate and negotiate, and (3) the family's authority and leadership structure.

Members vary in their commitment to the family. Some may see themselves as peripheral and prefer the pursuit of their own goals. Some may feel their own needs will be met by continuing family participation. Others may support or participate in family operations to the neglect of their own interests. These priorities may vary among individuals in the same family. They also vary among families. Where the family has seen the outside world as alien and hostile, as minority families often have had to, mutual support and "family first" may be emphasized, to the detriment of individual pursuits, though putting the family first need not be detrimental to individual growth. Josselyn (1953) reports on the importance for the development of individual identity of a widowed parent's effort to "keep the family together"—an effort in which the value of the family group was primary.

Families in which both individual and family group goals are important should be able to maintain some flexibility in movement to allow for the resolution of particular difficulties. Lacking this flexibility, they will have difficulty when problems arise.

The second factor affecting family members' response to a particular problem is their ability to communicate about the changed circumstances and to negotiate about possible responses. In closed family systems, communications may not allow for the assimilation of new information and ideas and may dictate the "one right way" to think about or do things. Differing points of view may be poorly tolerated, even though the occurrence of the problem calls for new ideas and new solutions. Tallman (1970) says:

> What seems necessary is a structure which allows for the expression of a diversity of conflicting views, all of which are subject to evaluation and criticism. At the same time, the integrity of the individual must be protected. A structure which allows for creative problem solving, therefore, should maintain open channels of communication within an evaluative framework which provides for a critical examination of the ideas presented. (p. 95)

The value system must provide for the freedom to communicate differences and to evaluate the ideas presented by others, in order to solve the problems presented to it. Members need freedom both to negotiate and to promote change in response to the problem. They also need effective mechanisms for negotiation. Some communications, such as denial, blaming, or withdrawal, are not particularly useful to a family in coping with the tasks at hand and solving the issues presented by a particular problem. Other strategies, such as efforts to understand each others' feelings, values, and goals, may be more useful but may not be available in the family, especially under present circumstances. Additional difficulties may arise if some members verbalize feelings and others wish to withdraw, or if some continue to blame while others seek reconciliation. Individuals respond on the basis of their own needs in the situation. Whether these conflicts are resolved depends on how the family has handled differences in the past, and whether they can permit worker suggestions or directions to influence them to develop new responses.

Lacking effective modes of communication, family members may lose their investment in the system and their willingness to contribute to solution of its difficulties. They may attack the system, or fall silent or otherwise withdraw from it. Their potential inputs are lost to the system, as is the system's value to them. The relative value placed on family as over against the individual and the degree of freedom to communicate derive from the family value system, which is largely determined by the adult members.

The third factor which affects the family's problem-solving capability is the element of authority and leadership. Generational boundaries may be defined in various ways. In some families the pattern is of strong parental leadership and control; in others, children participate more actively in decision making. These patterns are derived from the way parents value and define adult and child roles, based on their own prior life experience. Strong parental leadership or control may have caused the problem. It also may exacerbate the problem, stand in the way of its solution, or contribute to its resolution. Similarly, depending on the ages of involved family members, *weak* parental participation and leadership may have caused the problem, may exacerbate it, or may stand in the way of solution.

The abdication of a family role by one of the adult members, or his or her involvement in a demoralizing event, may well limit his or her capacity to provide leadership in the solution of problems. This allows the movement of other members, children in particular, into leadership or parental roles.

Another aspect of family leadership is that adults may see a problem as a threat to their leadership or authority within the family. Parental leadership which allows for the inputs of child members, however, can contribute significantly to problem resolution.

Stages in Family Response to Problems

Numerous studies of individual adaptation have delineated phases of responsiveness to crisis. These phases have been noted in response to death (Kubler-Ross, 1970), to the birth of a defective child (Wright, 1976; Wolfensberger, 1967), and to catastrophes (Grossman, 1973). The phases appear to be remarkably similar, no matter what the presenting crisis: denial, then disorganization and anger, then reorganization, recovery, or coping at some level—better, worse, or the same.

Some studies, notably Jackson (1956), have suggested that families as well as individuals go through phases of responsiveness to family problems. These seem similar to the phases of individual responsiveness, but the implications for family relationships and organization at each phase have not been clearly delineated. While we have not identified such phases of response to family problems (nor are we aware that others have), awareness of the individual responses in the family context is extremely useful.

We have noted that individual family members respond at differing paces to problem presentation. The denial of one which encounters the anger of another, for example, brings added stress to the family system. The Hajal (1977) case study referred to earlier illustrates this point. The mother's increasing readiness to acknowledge anger at her husband's suicide was persistently countered by the daughter's continuing efforts at denial. The pressure of each on the other to adopt her own point of view resulted in intense conflict between them, interfering with individual growth and performance and with the overall functioning of the remaining family group.

Similar phased responses are noted in Chapter 9, on family adaptation to chronic illness. Whether there are phases of family responsiveness to other family problems cannot be stated with certainty. That stages exist for individuals has been clearly demonstrated, as has the impact of individual stages on other members of the family. Phases of group response to family problems would appear to be a fruitful area for investigation.

SUMMARY

This chapter has given major attention to the renegotiation of roles as families experience the impact of increases or decreases in family membership, changes in family members or conditions, and demoralizing events. A family's ability to survive such changes requires a great deal of flexibility in role definitions and role behavior. Rigid adherence to previously existent role definitions stands in the way of problem solution.[3]

We have also described adaptability in role performance as a function of the members' conviction that the family is of value to them and of their consequent willingness to commit themselves to participate in problem solution. Problem solution is further seen as contingent upon family communication capacity. Changing role requirements necessitate a capacity for open negotiation among family members. Family values which provide this freedom and modes of communication which lead to problem solving are both needed. Finally, the family's ability to respond to changed conditions depends on the effectiveness and quality of family leadership. The degree of control and direction provided by the adult members of the family should maintain generational boundaries and enable all members to continue age- and sex-appropriate roles.

The way in which the family accomplishes needed role changes in response to changed family conditions, or fails to accomplish them, demonstrates the interrelatedness of family problems and family problem solving. If needed problem-solving mechanisms are available, family problems can frequently be solved. If they are not available, these mechanisms can be created or improved. This is accomplished in the course of work on the presenting problem, so that solving the problem and changing the family become simultaneous activities. The problems of poverty families addressed in Chapter 4 are a clear case in point.

The introduction of the constructs of this chapter elaborates the discussion on the nature of family systems begun in Chapter 1. Their application and use will become more specific and clear in relation to the particular family problems outlined in the chapters of Part II.

---

[3] Spiegel's (1968) discussion of the resolution of role conflict within the family usefully elaborates what we have in mind here. He suggests that "role induction" is a less useful strategy in the long run than "role modification." The former method is used by self to induce others to take the role as the self would define it. The latter method results in changed behavior on the part of both, or all, participants.

REFERENCES

Deykin, E., Weissman, M., & Klerman, G. "Treatment of Depressed Women." *British Journal of Social Work,* 1:277–91, 1971.

Duberman, L. *The Re-Constituted Family.* Chicago: Nelson-Hall Co., 1975.

Grossman, L. "Train Crash: Social Work and Disaster Services." *Social Work* 18:35–45, 1973.

Hajal, F. "Post-Suicide Grief Work in Family Therapy." *Journal of Marriage and Family Counseling,* 3(2):35–42, 1977.

Hill, R. "Generic Features of Families under Stress." *Social Casework,* 39:139–49, 1958.

Jackson, J. K. "Adjustment of the Family to Alcoholism." *Marriage and Family Living,* 18:361–69, 1956.

Josselyn, I. "The Family as a Psychological Unit." *Social Casework,* 34:336–43, 1953.

Kubler-Ross, E. *On Death and Dying.* New York: Macmillan Co., 1970.

McCubbin, H., Dahl, B., Lester, G., Benson, D., & Robertson, M. "Coping Repertoires of Families Adapting to Prolonged War-Induced Separations." *Journal of Marriage and the Family,* 38(3):461–71, 1976.

Rapoport, R., and Rapoport, R. "New Light on the Honeymoon." *Human Relations,* 17:33–56, 1964.

Rosenberg, B. "Planned Short-Term Treatment in Developmental Crises." *Social Casework,* 56:195–204, 1975.

Spiegel, J. "The Resolution of Role Conflict within the Family." In N. Bell and E. Vogel (eds.), *A Modern Introduction to the Family.* New York: Free Press, 1968.

Tallman, I. "The Family as a Small Problem Solving Group." *Journal of Marriage and the Family,* 32:94–104, 1970.

Wolfensberger, W. "Counseling Parents of the Retarded." In A. Baumeister (ed.), *Mental Retardation.* Chicago: Aldine Publishing Co., 1967.

Wright, L. S. "Chronic Grief: The Anguish of Being an Exceptional Parent." *The Exceptional Child,* 23:106-9, 1976.

CHAPTER 3

The Social Worker's Approach to Family Treatment

The theoretical framework for family treatment from a systems viewpoint is operationalized when it is put into practice by the social worker or practitioner. In making plans for intervention in a family problem situation, the worker must assess the way the family is organized and functions. The underlying issues of family structure and dynamics must be understood before decisions regarding change strategies can be made.

Given the assumption that the family as a group needs to find the means to solve the problem at hand, rather than simply having solutions promulgated by the social worker, one goal of the initial contacts between the worker and the family is to gain the participation of needed family members in the problem-solving process. In achieving this goal the worker must be clear about who the needed family members are and how they can be involved in the process.

TREATMENT FOR THE FAMILY OR FAMILY GROUP TREATMENT

There are three separate but interrelated issues to be addressed in assuring the participation of needed family members. The first is whether

43

treatment for the family and family group treatment mean the same thing. The second raises the question of whether family treatment is appropriate or needed for all problems, or whether there are certain situations where it is contraindicated. The third has to do with the age and family status of persons to be involved.

Conjoint interviews are treatment sessions which include two or more family members. Family treatment and conjoint interviewing are sometimes thought of synonymously. In our view, they should not be. Family problem solving *may* make use of conjoint family sessions. They are highly valuable, for reasons that will be detailed shortly, but their exclusive use in problem solving is not required. Individual sessions with various family members, sessions with pairs or triads of family members, and sessions with the entire family all may be productive in altering roles, communication processes, and problem-solving capability. This view, consistent with systems theory, holds that when one member of the family system begins to change, other parts of the family system must also change. A change produced in one person upsets family equilibrium, requiring adaptation (or incurring resistance) on the part of other members of the system. In this vein, Haley (1971) notes that family therapists "realized that traditional individual therapy was actually *one* way to intervene in a family, whether the therapist thought of it that way or not. It was the intrusion of an outsider into a family even if the therapist considered himself to be dealing only with one person's fantasies" (p. 3).

What distinguishes this view from traditional individual therapy is the consciousness of the worker about the consequences that work with the individual may have for that person's behavior in the family and for the family system. When the worker holds a family systems rather than an intrapsychic view of the problem, treatment is more likely to be undertaken with family consequences in mind. The worker can anticipate these consequences, and the client can be prepared in the treatment relationship to anticipate them and to cope with family reactions. Or the client can consciously set new family processes in motion.

There has been considerable discussion in the family therapy literature as to the appropriateness of conjoint family treatment for various presenting problems. Scherz (1962), for example, suggests family treatment for character disorders, but not for adolescent separation problems. Cookerly's (1974) data suggest the usefulness of conjoint sessions for marital problems when the couple is staying together, but not when they intend to separate. Much of the difficulty in such discussion results from the equation of family treatment with conjoint family interviews.

Our position is that all treatment involves the family, but it need not all be family group treatment. In deciding whether conjoint family sessions are the best vehicle for promoting change in a family problem situation, other means of involving the family should also be considered.

Family members can be involved in treatment constellations other than conjoint sessions. Work on family problems can take place in parent groups, groups for husbands or wives when the identified problem person is one of the family adults, multiple-family groups, or multiple-couples groups, for example. (These are discussed in subsequent chapters.) The individual learning and change that are begun in these groups are carried back to the family. When the identified problem patient is a child, it has not been unusual for treatment to be offered primarily or only to the child's parents. Treatment has been offered less often to another adult when the person manifesting the problem is an adult. An exception is Murray Bowen (1971), who sometimes works with another family adult who manifests more capacity for change, with the expectation that this will change the family system. Even with a severe demoralizing problem such as alcoholism, however, some reports indicate that treatment of family members other than the identified problem person has resulted in change, both for the family and for the individual (Cohen & Krause, 1971; McDowell, 1972).

CONJOINT FAMILY SESSIONS

Almost all problem solving in family situations can benefit from family participation. We can think of no category of problems that cannot benefit from family problem-solving efforts. Our theory suggests that no family member is untouched by problems occurring in the family group. Each member is affected by the occurrence of the problem and has some reaction to it. It may alter the person's image of self or of others or of the family group. It may change his feelings about self and others. It may alter his willingness to participate in family life. These reactions become manifest and enter into family interaction and relationships. Or the family member may be a participant in the creation of the problem, or in its perpetuation.

In all instances, with all problems, family participation is needed and useful *at some time* during the life of the case. The purpose of such participation is to help the family members deal with their feelings about the changes occurring in the family group and to enable them to cope with these changes constructively, or to involve them in the creation of change. In this we differ slightly from Perlman (1961), who suggests that only those whose participation is necessary to the solution of the problem should be involved. Our purpose is to see that needed family members are served in some way, while helping them to redefine their roles and positions in the family to promote their own growth and that of the family. This is the critical issue, not the particular mix of conjoint, or individual, or group participation.

Small children may not contribute to the thinking-through process, though this is not impossible in some instances. Their behavior in some sessions, however, can reveal emotional currents or relationship sequences that might not otherwise be noticed. The participation of older children may be revealing, if not crucial, even if they appear at first glance to be detached or may even be living elsewhere. Divorced members have sometimes been involved, even when the fact of divorce would suggest their omission (Leader, 1973). Involved members of the extended family also can be helpful participants. The definition of family is flexible enough to include relevant persons in the family network (Speck & Attneave, 1971), whether they are related by blood, marriage, presence in the home, or social relation to family members.

The emphasis is on the potential contribution of the family member to problem solution, as well as on the gain the family member may experience by participation. Family members often interpret the worker's efforts to involve them in treatment as blaming them for the problem. That is never the intent. While it may often be true that certain members have helped create the problem, there is no advantage to the establishment of blame or causation, and no efforts are expended in this direction. However, if causation is defined as an interactional sequence, it may usefully be understood. All members participate in that process, but this is not the same as ascribing blame.

On all of these issues we approach the position of M–type family therapists as delineated in the 1970 report by the Committee on the Family. In their view, family members may be involved in therapy both individually and in groups. Z–type therapists, in contrast, would meet with the family only as a group, eschewing separate individual interviews. For example, John Bell (1963), a Z–type therapist, says:

46

I am absolutely firm about my unwillingness to meet with a part of the family privately. I make it a rule that all relations between me and the family members must be in the group and known to all of them. Being alerted to the deviousness of their efforts to break this rule, I am prepared to affirm and reaffirm my position without apology as the need may arise. This is immeasurably reassuring to the group and protects its solidarity.

We agree with Bell that the worker's relationships to all members in the group must be known to all. Continuing secrets and alliances with any member of the family must be avoided. However, family members may be assisted in separate individual or group sessions to explore particularly painful and sensitive issues, and they can be helped to find ways to bring them up and work them through with the significant other family members. In some instances destructive emotions may be drained and constructive ways of relating identified. There is no doubt that individual family members may seek a devious alliance with the worker, but the worker's awareness of this possibility avoids the permanent creation of such an alliance. It does not seem neccessary, in avoiding alliances, to insist on conjoint sessions at all times.

A–type therapists, unlike those who hold Bell's position or ours, maintain a primary focus on the individual. If they see family members, such sessions generally are separate from sessions with the identified patient.

Advantages of Conjoint Sessions

There are advantages to conjoint sessions, some of which we mention here. Others will be discussed in subsequent chapters. One advantage is that they enhance the worker's diagnostic understanding of the family's operations. Given the worker's theoretical position that the family operates as a system, certain observations about the nature of relationships may be more likely in conjoint sessions. We concur with Sherman (1965) that interactional processes "are very involved and not immediately apparent under the best of conditions. . . . They are more likely to be detected when . . . the family members are observed and experienced when physically assembled together" (p. 44). Workers in conjoint sessions may be able to observe interactional sequences, often repetitive ones, between family members of which the members themselves are unaware and which they do not observe and would not be able to report. In conjoint sessions they

47

can see more readily how interactional processes facilitate or disrupt the problem-solving task of the family.

Some workers (e.g., Moynihan, 1974) advocate the use of home visits as a means of observing whole-family interaction, as well as a way of engaging family members in the treatment process. The participation of family members other than the identified problem person minimizes individual isolation (Binder, 1971), provides support (Gallant, Rich, Bey, & Terranova, 1970), and permits continued communication (Preston, 1960). Conjoint sessions also provide a greater degree of objectivity to workers who too readily or continuously get ensnared into side-taking, and they minimize the frequent distortion of information which takes place in individual interviews. A similar advantage accrues to family members who may be distrustful of both therapist and other family members. Exchanges that take place in the presence of all can reduce the fears of suspicious members that alliances and plans are being made without them.

Conjoint sessions are maximally useful where problematic communication interferes with problem solving. A variety of communication problems occur. Communication sequences are filled with frequent interruptions, changes of topic, and simultaneous talking (Minuchin, 1967). They may manifest incongruencies between the verbal message and the accompanying body language or confusion between the content and command aspects of the message (Satir, 1967; Watzlawick, Beavin, & Jackson, 1967). Wynne (1971) refers to these processes as "bizarre, disjointed, fragmented," reflective of "collective cognitive chaos and erratic distancing." Conjoint sessions allow not only for observation of such sequences, which likely would not otherwise be observable and reported by family members, but also for efforts to interrupt and change them as they occur.

Another communication failure is the lack of sharing of perceptions and information. Family members often hold differing and distorted images of themselves and of each other. Family events are often perceived differently by different members, and often these images and perceptions have not been shared. Conjoint sessions hold the possibility for sharing positive images and feelings along with negative ones, and members may find support along with the opposition they frequently experience. The exchange of perceptions of events can lead to new definitions and to changes in interpersonal behavior. With the worker's assistance, conjoint sessions can help reticent members express themselves to others when they have not been able to do so on their own. These sessions can also

48

enable members to confront differences which have been denied or deemed unresolvable.

The net effect of such disordered communication processes is serious interference with the family's problem-solving ability. When problems are presented and responded to by distraction, opposition, silence, and distancing, they are never solved. Individual and family goals are not achieved. Tasks are not completed. The use of conjoint sessions enables the family to focus on the problem and to pursue meaningful verbal exchanges until the issues can be effectively addressed, to the satisfaction of all members.

Disadvantages of Conjoint Sessions

There are, nevertheless, some situations in which conjoint sessions are less useful, if not contraindicated. If certain requisites are not present, family members will not participate or may sabotage the sessions. One such requisite is investment in or identification with the family group. Members who value the family's togetherness, cohesiveness, and unity are more likely to participate. In many families this sense of togetherness may have been lost in the tensions created by present or past problems, though it may be recoverable.

The conviction that achievement of personal goals is possible in the family situation is also necessary to the success of conjoint sessions. Family and individual goals are not necessarily incompatible, though they may be in some families, or some members may experience them in that way. The worker's efforts to help the family redefine the problem may help members see that individual and family goals can both be achieved. In the absence of such problem redefinition, family members will refuse to participate, be indifferent, or persist in expressions of hostility and blame. Inability to desist from blaming contraindicates the continuation of conjoint sessions, though the worker will not know, until conjoint sessions have been tried, whether this is the case.

In some situations the involvement of all family members in treatment may not necessarily be contraindicated, but it may be unnecessary. All members of the family may not be involved in the problem as it is defined at a particular point in time. In different phases of contact, issues between spouses, between a parent and a child, or between siblings may have priority. The way the issue is defined determines who should be involved at any given time.

49

Family members must be able to agree on the definition of the problem on which they should work. Often family members point to another member as the problem. They are unable to see that family member as reacting to their own behavior, sometimes denying that their own behavior even affects the other. When family members can agree that the behavior affects all of them, that they don't get along very well with one another, they may become willing to address the common problem affecting them all. Some members may be more centrally affected and more willing to participate than others. The participation of all members in conjoint sessions may be necessary to pinpoint or provide a focus on problems, but their continued participation may not be required.

In summary, there seem to be no presenting problems for which conjoint sessions could not be utilized at some time. The dangers of causing the identified problem person to decompensate, or act out, or the likelihood of general family disruption do not appear to be great. In some instances the continued or sole use of conjoint sessions may be unproductive and therefore contraindicated. Rosenblatt (1975), in his analysis of the Bunkers in "All in the Family," describes the type of family that is not likely to be responsive to conjoint treatment sessions (nor perhaps to any other means of intervention in the family):

We knew from the outset that the four main characters would always be impervious to change, that in their particular comedy of humors Edith would shuttle between Bewilderment and Right Instinct, and the children would play Young Generation forever, permanently settled into lip-service liberalism and the latest freedom vernacular, their every reaction more predictable than Archie assaults. On the surface, Archie's humor seems more variable. At times he appears as Hate, Stubbornness, Selfishness or Cowardice, but all of these group under the presiding humor of Death itself, which governs every form of immovability, in Archie and in his kin. . . . The Bunkers . . . do not learn from past mistakes. They repeat old jokes and epithets. None seems to have much of a memory for former events which might guide their present decisions. . . . By blocking out the past, of course, they block out the future. (p. 31). (Reprinted by permission of *The New Republic*, © 1975, The New Republic Inc.)

Scherz (1962) and Wynne (1971) seem to concur that families which persist, in spite of the worker's efforts, in such fixed role-taking and inability to respond to the inputs of those about them would not be likely candidates for conjoint family sessions.

ENGAGING THE FAMILY IN TREATMENT

The social worker's desire to include a number of family members in the diagnostic process, if not in treatment, influences the procedures used for the first contact. Certain actions at this time are facilitative and may be undertaken for the purpose of engaging needed members in the problem-solving process.

The process of engaging a family in treatment is both similar to and different from beginning individual or other group treatment. Perlman (1957) appropriately notes that an applicant for service in a social work agency is not yet a client, and the task of the worker in the initial phase of contact is "to engage this client with his problem and his will to do something about it in a working relationship with this agency, its intentions and special means of helpfulness" (p. 113). The person who initiates agency contact may be certain only about the need for help but not about the kind of help needed, or may have a specific kind of help in mind which is different from what the agency and the worker have to offer. Negotiation is needed to clarify how expectations of the applicant are or are not congruent with those of the worker or the agency. In case of the family there are, additionally, differences between family members about what is needed and sought. There are differing reactions to what is made available by the worker and the agency. Before family members willingly engage themselves in a treatment process, negotiations among themselves and with the worker as to the purposes, goals, means of treatment, and the nature of their participation are needed to establish a basis for treatment work.

Perlman (1968) conceptualizes the task of the worker as that of enabling family members to undertake the role of a client. Strean (1974) notes that clients are simultaneously attempting to place workers in a role that reciprocates with their idea of their own role in the treatment process. This is immensely complicated in family work because each family member is attempting to place the worker in a role particularly advantageous to self, a position that may not be at all desirable to another family member. The worker is immediately sought as an ally by various individuals or coalitions of individuals in the family.

Elements of Resistance to Treatment

There are numerous obstacles in the path of engaging family members in treatment. One is the view held by family representatives that one of the

51

members is the problem—not the family as a whole. It is a difficult obstacle to remove if the family has been encouraged in this view by the referring person. Whether such referral sources are inside one's own agency, in the case of a multidisciplinary agency, or representatives of other agencies, family-oriented workers should educate referring workers to a family systems view of presenting problems. Such a view will put them in a better position to help families accept referrals. The worker also needs to take steps to gain acceptance of the need for family participation by the family member who is the contact initiator.

A second kind of obstacle to family participation in treatment is the view held by many referred families that no problem exists. They contact the family-oriented worker under compulsion from a school, a probation officer, or an employer. They profess no awareness of the reasons for referral, or they see only that others are creating problems for them. They do not know why the school sent them, or why the employer is upset with them. The individual identified as the problem may be willing to keep a proffered appointment to comply with the referring person, but only for that reason. He sees no need for the family to be involved. Or the family may agree to have the identified person come, but sees no need for their participation. The worker, however, may readily sense the need for treatment of the problem and sees the benefits of involvement of the family in treatment.

Families obviously have the right to refuse treatment and to take whatever consequences may come with their refusal. Our concern is to enable the family to establish and maintain contact with helping persons long enough for them to know what it is they are refusing, and what the potential gain for them individually and collectively might be. They may or may not be aware of the consequences of refusal for their relationships with referral sources or other community systems.

Work with a family may begin under coercive circumstances. In some situations the agency or the workers may have the authority to force family members into treatment. Such use of authority may be useful in opening up other possibilities for the family or in considering the consequences of no effort to change. Procedures used by the worker in the initial phases of contact may enable the family to move from participation under a sense of coercion to voluntary participation, with an expectancy of personal and family gain. (Other aspects of the use of authority are touched on in Chapters 4 and 6.)

Because so many families known to social workers are of this type, we will devote considerable space to an explication of procedures that help in moving the family into the role of client. The procedures are directed not only at such scapegoating or denying families; they are useful with all types of families. The method described is the process of engagement by means of conjoint interviews. Other beginnings may be made with families, but the conjoint session has special value in the assessment of family functioning, and special usefulness in enabling all family members to see their parts in the family problem-solving process.

The Family Encounters the Worker

The therapeutic situation itself evokes certain responses by virtue of the fact that another person is added to the system. Family members calculate how to adjust their responses to account for the new person in their midst. Each family member has his or her own preferences about what to do and what is needed to cope with the problem. Since the conflicts about possible actions have not been resolved within the family process, there is a natural tendency to seek the support of the worker for one's own position, along with depreciation of the views of others.

These efforts are understandable both in relation to the need of each member to preserve individual integrity and esteem and in relation to the level of caring and trust among family members. There is the expectation that others will not appreciate one's own needs and therefore will not take them into account. There is the expectation that other members will take advantage of expressions of weakness and error. Efforts to blame and demand change in others are a defense arising out of this view of others. The exercise of these approaches among family members is accompanied by efforts, observable in the family group interview, to enlist the support of other family members.

As these efforts become manifest to the worker, they are also interpretable as efforts to seek the worker as an ally, to strengthen one's own position vis-à-vis other family members. This is revealed with dramatic clarity in some situations when, in separate interviews, individual members are able to be less defensive and accept more responsibility for family problems than they can in conjoint sessions.

The worker, in response, attempts to establish a caring, understanding relationship with the family members and to value the contributions of each

53

of them. These attempts serve to resist the family pressures to take sides. Family members are forced to take this resistance into account. Failure to take individual responsibility for action is gradually, more or less directly, confronted. Family members may resist the worker's resistance to their usual routines by intensifying their previous efforts; new responses may be found and learned to take the place of the anger and blame.

Thus, while the behaviors that family members display during their contact with the worker are manifestations of familiar family routines, they are not fully interpretable in this light. They also should be understood as responsive to the worker's entry into the family system. It is important for the worker to become a part of the family system, while at the same time not becoming entangled in its usual routines. The family must be helped to accept the worker's entry into the system and to be responsive to the worker's inputs demanding change.

The Worker's Role with the Family

It has been said of family work that the social worker is in charge of the treatment, but the family members are in charge of their lives. The worker's task in treatment, especially in beginning treatment, is to provide the family with a structure that enables problem solving to take place. The worker actively takes charge of the procedures at this beginning stage. He or she has certain steps in mind for the session and asks the family to cooperate. Though the family may appear to have the initiative in the interview, this may be because the worker has asked the members to struggle with a problem in order to see how they go about solving problems. If problem solving does not succeed, the worker interrupts, either to facilitate or move on to other tasks. (While it is conceivable that a family's interaction may not be interruptable, the worker does have means of gaining the family's attention and cooperation.) The degree to which the worker is able to establish control over the process in the session is a measure of the worker's skill. It is also a measure of the family's ability to gain from participation in treatment, and it thus provides diagnostic information about the family's workability and flexibility.

The diagnostic and treatment efforts should help the family members take charge of their lives. In the sessions the worker requires them to talk about their concerns to the worker and to each other. While it is expected that talking can create new understanding and awareness and can generate

54

ideas about what to do, awareness and understanding are only part of the help available. The worker's requirement that family members engage in different kinds of action in the conjoint sessions vis-à-vis each other sets up new ways of relating that are more productive in problem solving than were their old ways. We expect the family to see the usefulness of the new patterns, learn them, and appropriate them for regular use. But family members are free to accept and make use of, or reject, what they learn in the sessions about themselves, each other, and their interactions with each other.

The worker obviously is concerned about how they run their lives and may at times offer specific suggestions or directions about what to do. In some institutional settings the worker may even be in a position to tell the family members how to manage their lives outside the sessions and may have some expectation that they will follow the suggestions. It may even be useful to propose courses of action in order to solve a problem or prevent the occurrence of one. The worker's principal task, however, is to structure treatment sessions so that constructive decision making about life issues is possible for the family. While it is important to solve a problem, the worker's goal is not necessarily to solve it for the family, but to make it possible for them to solve it. The beginning phase addresses both aspects. The decision about what to do is the family's.

OPENING PROCEDURES

Steps or phases in the process of engaging the family in treatment have been identified by both Haley (1976) and Solomon (1977). While there are differences between their approaches, both have elements that we utilize and have incorporated in our formulation of a procedure to be followed by the social worker in initiating contact for family treatment.[1] As we have noted, these stages are similar to but more complex than the engagement and contracting efforts required in individual treatment.

Most family treatment begins through contact with one family member. The worker takes a position at first contact that the family needs to be involved. Starting with one person and waiting until later to insist on family

---

[1]For very contrasting ways of beginning treatment, see Satir (1967) and Bowen (1971). Though their treatment methods differ greatly, they both suggest that treatment begins by gaining a historical perspective on the family problem.

participation results in lost time and requires a second start. In the initial contact, whether in person or on the telephone, the worker seeks to learn who the family members are. There is enough exploration of the problem to give the worker some sense of agency appropriateness and family relatedness. But the exploration is brief, for two reasons. The problem cannot be adequately understood from one person's reporting, and the image of an alliance between the initiator and the worker needs to be particularly avoided in this phase.

Attention therefore shifts rather quickly to the need to engage both the initiator of the contact and other family members in the treatment process. The caller is asked to join an initial session and to bring other family members along. The value of the information they can provide and of the suggestions they might offer is emphasized. Family members are frequently responsive to this emphasis on the importance of their contributions to problem solving. If they are not responsive, the worker's efforts must focus on the resistance, rather than on the problem presented by the family. If the problem presenter in the initial contact seems resistant, the resistance should be explored. If the problem presenter attributes resistance to other family members, their anticipated reasons and the presenter's intended means for handling their responses can be explored.

If the presenter's means for handling the resistance of other familly members seem inadequate, alternative responses may be suggested. The suggestions are, in effect, new inputs into the family system. If the suggestions are adopted, both the behavior of the initial problem presenter and family processes are thereby altered. Treatment of the family has begun. If the resistance is not strong, family members may recognize that each family member's view of the problem is important if it is to be fully understood, and they may respond to the request that all family members participate at least in the initial exploratory session.[2]

Stage 1: Relieving Initial Anxiety

Once the social worker has succeeded in arranging an in-person meeting with the needed family members, his or her first task in the initial session is

---

[2]The first example in Chapter II illustrates the use of this approach in an in-person walk-in interview.

to relate to each family member's feelings about having to be there. Family members may have arrived at the appointment with different understandings of what is to take place and what is expected of them. They may be fearful of revealing secrets or expect undesirable changes to be demanded. They may fear blame, punishment, removal from the home, or shock treatment. They may expect helpers to take sides against them.

The worker's overall objective (as in individual treatment) is to establish a safe, nonthreatening relationship with all persons present. The worker inquires about conversations the family members may have had with each other about the appointment, how it has been explained to them, and how they felt about what they had been told prior to coming. This procedure has both communicative and metacommunicative value. On the communicative level it elicits information regarding their anxieties about meeting the worker, airing family problems, asking for help, and revealing themselves to other family members. It provides data about the way family members view both the relationship with the worker and relationships within the family. Family members may have communicated little or much about coming. Clear communication may have gone to some members but not to others. They may feel free to speak in the session or wait for cues from others. The procedure's metacommunicative value to the family is that it regards each person's view as important and permits it to be heard and valued. The individuality and separateness of family members is emphasized, while their value to the problem-solving effort is affirmed. The procedure allows for each family member to be heard by other family members. If family members do not spontaneously comment, the worker may ask them if they are aware of each other's point of view or solicit comments on what has been said.

Stage 2: Eliciting Problem Definitions

After the family members' anxieties about the interview have been reduced, the social worker can proceed to elicit from each one a statement about the problem or problems that have brought the family to the session. There will likely be differences in statements of the problem. For some families this may be the first time that different views have been expressed and heard. The worker's presence may create a tolerance for these differences that was not present in the family's own efforts to deal with the problem. The extent of the members' ability to wait for one another's expressions will offer the worker some beginning cues as to the family's ability to listen and to learn. If they are able to convey appreciation for having heard something from others that they have not heard before, the worker will have an even greater sense of their treatability.

This is not often the case, however. Frequently family members single out one of their number as "the problem." The worker gets the clear impression that the identified problem person is blamed and isolated and finds little support in the family. The worker may sense little tolerance for the position that the views of each family member are important where the identified problem person is concerned. Such rigidity offers little to support the view that the family can change in order to solve the problem. At this stage the worker primarily is listening and thinking. Only limited efforts are directed at expanding expressions of feelings or changing feelings or problem definition. The important goal at this time is to hear from everyone.

Family members will not always sit patiently to hear what other members have to say. They experience difficulty in remaining in an observer status. There are likely to be interruptions and, if the first speaker does not stop, simultaneous talking. In this event the worker does need to become active to avoid repetition in the session of what the family ordinarily experiences at home. The stage is set for problem solving by disallowing interruptions. At the same time each participant is assured that his or her point of view will be heard. Strenuous efforts by the worker may be needed along these lines in some families. Minuchin, Montalvo, Guerney, Rosman, and Schumer (1967) found it necessary in their experience with severely disorganized families to remove some family members to a position behind a one-way glass when persistent interruptions revealed their inability to listen to others. Even at this beginning stage, the worker's efforts to regulate the conversation may afford the family an experience that they have not had before, and this may make them feel that the worker and treatment have something to offer them.

There may also be a reaction to the interviewing situation which is quite the opposite of interruptions and simultaneous talking. Some family members may be extremely reticent to say anything, much less express an opinion, point of view, or difference. The worker will be aware of halting speech, looking down, and looking to other family members for cues, or avoiding involvement. Such reticence can be as much of an obstacle to problem solving as is overactivity. The worker may attempt to draw the individual out during this initial phase of the interview by asking for elaboration or may comment on how the situation makes for difficulty in talking, thereby offering encouragement. It may be useful to ask whether other family members can enable the reticent person to speak. These efforts to gain the reticent member's participation become particularly important in the case of the family member whose contributions have not been valued by others. In response to the worker's attitude, other family members may begin to respond differently to the reticent member. The reticent behavior gives diagnostic information about patterns of power, deference, and decision making in the family.

While a prime purpose in this initial contact is achievement of diagnostic understanding, the efforts to elicit information from all members represent a change for family members. For many families this is a requirement that they respond differently to each other. Insofar as they can respond to and benefit from this requirement, treatment has begun for them.

Up to this point in the initial contact procedure, the role we have defined for the worker requires an exploratory, investigative stance. It minimizes commentary on family operations but does require the worker to regulate relations between the worker and family members and among family members as they participate in the interview. The worker values each member's contribution and is thereby supportive of each, but he or she also sets expectations for participation. The pairing of support and participation becomes particularly evident in the next stage of the session, in which there is an effort to define the family problem.

Stage 3: Working toward Problem Consensus

Social workers often see the problem differently than the family does, but they still need to start with the family's definition of the problem. The worker sees the problem presented by the family as an evidence of family malfunction and thus as a symptom of the problem, while the family sees it as the problem. In the procedure we have outlined, the worker's efforts are directed to both definitions at the same time.[3] The following example will illustrate what we mean.

The problem is presented by parents who are concerned with altering the behavior of a child. In such a case the worker can operate on the premise, likely to be shared by the parents, that the parents have both the prerogative and the responsibility to regulate the behavior of the child. The worker wants to support them in this and to help them with it. A dual purpose is suggested: The first need is to correct the child's behavior, and the second need is to build the parents' capacity to correct the presenting problem and others that may occur. The family's problem-solving mechanisms have not been working successfully in relation to the presenting problem. Since the family is not asking for help with their problem-solving routines, but only for help in correcting this problem, the effort to change problem-solving routines must be focused on these routines as they apply to the presenting problem.

This should lead the worker to inquire what kinds of efforts have been made by the parents to correct the problem, in order to understand what has not worked and the reasons for the lack of success. Throughout the discussion the parents can be credited for their continuing involvement with their child as a manifestation of their concern for the child's welfare. They can also be credited for not giving up on their child and for their wish to be successful as parents in enabling their child to perform well and to succeed in life. The worker's accreditation of the parent's concern and caring may be something the child has not heard before through all the parents' commands, controls, accusations, blame, and punishment. Such new awareness may make it possible for the child to manifest a wish to have a good relationship with the parents, even if there is not always a wish to please them. Both the parents' and the child's feelings about what has been happening may be aired.

---

[3] Several recent publications discuss work with difficult-to-involve families which emphasize a similar point of view. Chilman (1966) emphasizes this dual approach with very poor families. Larson and Gilbertson (1977) accept parental definitions that the child is the problem but train the parents in a new child management approach, thus changing their child management behavior (see also Larson & Talley, 1977). Oxley (1977) describes a residential program for latency-age boys in which parents are required to participate as a condition of acceptance of the boys in the residential program. For some parents this assured only their bodily presence, but many became less resistive and, during a follow-up study, indicated they had benefited from treatment. Both programs required family participation in problem solving, while accepting initially the family's definition of where change needed to occur.

Along with this accreditation of good intentions and recognition of continuing involvement and concern, it becomes obvious that the techniques and strategies utilized by the parents have not been successful in regulating behavior, as evidenced in the discussion of what has been tried. Having supported the parents' wish to succeed with their child, the worker may now be in a position to suggest that new strategies are needed. If the parents can accept this, a basis for work with the parents has been established.

Of course, the effort of the worker to establish an alliance with the parents may produce a negative reaction in the child. A positive relationship with all family members must focus on the child as well as the parents. The worker will relate both to the child's feelings about being present and to her or his definition of the problem. While feelings of anger and blame are likely to be expressed, the worker may also hear the child's wish for approval and understanding from the parents and the desire for a positive relationship with them. If, by the worker's focus on the positive wish instead of the blame, the parents are able to hear something new from their child, a change in family feeling may be begun. At a minimum, the child may experience enough of the worker's support and concern to enable him to consent to the helping relationship.

In this situation the parents and the identified problem child may be the central actors, but the worker also solicits views of the problem from other members of the family. The worker conveys an interest in what each has to say as a member of the family, valuing their presence and their contributions. Their responses may emphasize support for or blame of parents or their sibling. The worker attempts to understand how they have related themselves to the problem or how they have been affected by it—by becoming involved in trying to solve it or by withdrawal—and how they see themselves relating to it now.

Acceptance of the problem focus defined by the family at the outset appears necessary to the family's willingness to participate in treatment. At the same time, the requirement that the family participate emphasizes the family role in finding a solution to the problem. Without the latter requirement we would expect no change in family organization and a continuation of the problem or problematic behavior. Oxley (1977) noted that during the treatment of some nonvoluntary families, members other than the identified patient began to focus on their own problems as their comfort in treatment and their self-esteem increased. We see this as a healthy shift from the initial problem focus, an increase in the sense of individuality and separateness of the members, which is necessary to a positive sense of togetherness and solidarity.

In the procedure we have described, the worker is supportive of all family members, even those in apparent opposition to each other. The means the worker uses to provide the support are based on recognition of the need of family members for positive relationships. Communications which drive them apart are relabeled as caring, concern for the well-being of others, and a wish for connectedness. We do not see this relabeling as deception or trickery. It is an effort to identify positive aspects of family relationships. The family members' continuing engagement with one another is seen as an expression of their meaning and importance to one another, however negatively such feelings have been verbalized. Expressions of hostility and blame are common in many families and seem easier. Expressions of caring and concern, paradoxically, seem more threatening. They entail a risk of rejection which negative feelings do not. Satir (1967) suggests that low self-esteem lies behind the hesitance to risk the expression of positive feeling. Worker efforts to relabel and thereby promote a positive relationship with the worker and among family members may not have an immediately successful effect. They bear repetition, however; along with other efforts, they will have a cumulative, positive effect.

Stage 4: Focus on Interactional Mechanisms

The fourth stage in the social worker's efforts to engage the family furthers the worker's diagnostic effort. The worker will have gained in understanding how the family works to cope with its problems from the previous stages. The effort at this stage is more specifically directed at understanding the family's ways of dealing with the presenting problem. This stage can be approached in several ways.

Members' Response to Worker's Questions. One approach is for the worker to inquire of family members how they have responded to the problem, how it has affected them, and what they have tried to do about it. Some members will have been more affected, others less so. Less-affected members may have remained uninvolved and may show little feeling or reaction. Others, more involved, may have attempted to remain aloof but now are willing to manifest their reactions and suggestions. Still others may blame, depreciate, or get angry or aggressive. Some may have attempted to talk it over, without productive results. Patterns of involvement and withdrawal, of support and opposition are evident in these differing responses. The worker may comment on the responses to emphasize that each family member does have some connection to the problem, even if he or she has tried to ignore it. This base of connectedness to the problem is the primary incentive for participation in problem solution.

The worker-imposed requirement that each family member hear what the others have to say allows for new information—other members' ideas about a solution—to be shared for the benefit of all. Members who may have already heard other members' ideas for solution can become more conscious of differing ideas about what to do and the reactions of others to their own ideas. They can consider what seems to have helped or hindered solutions and recognize the need for negotiation of these differences. The worker specifically draws such reactions and differences to their attention and asks what the family does in the face of differences about how to cope with the problem. Awareness of the difficulty in dealing with differences may ultimately be the basis of agreement to participate in treatment. The wish to do something about how they get along with each other may serve as a common problem definition, a rallying point.

In such a talking approach to problem solving, the worker elicits a response from all present family members, requiring others to listen while one member talks and assuring that each one's turn to talk will come. In some families this regulation of communication may require considerable effort on the part of the worker.

Family Discussion. An alternative approach is to ask the family members to talk with one another about how to solve the problem, while the worker observes what happens when they do. Though the worker may assume that there will be a replay of family operations similar to their usual ones at home, this assumption should be validated. Frequently family members will confirm that this is the usual routine and express discontent with the process. Often they will report restraint in their behavior due to the presence of the worker, thus confirming the systems theory assumption that the entry of a new member alters the operation of the system. That may be a positive sign about the treatability of the family, but it is not to be assumed that the restraint will necessarily continue in subsequent sessions.

Whether or not family members have been restrained in this procedure, the worker will have acquired some knowledge of the family's mechanisms for problem solving and an awareness of operations that frustrate its problem-solving work. The most observable difficulties are in communications. Communications may be unclear; topics may be changed without resolution, statements interrupted, blame affixed, support offered. Statements may be addressed to nobody in particular, and some individuals may attempt to speak for others. Third parties may enter into disputes as peacemakers or allies of one or another member. Various aspects of family relationships, such as levels of respect and caring for others, become evident in this flow of communications. Family solidarity and cohesiveness may be manifest or demonstrably lacking. Each family member also gains a sense, from how others respond to him, of whether he is affirmed, supported, and accepted, and by his own response he conveys to others whether he is affirming and accepting of them, or rejecting and critical.

Communications represent strategies for negotiation and problem solving which have in the past been learned and reaffirmed, and now are apparently in continual use. It is possible that what the worker observes at this point is the simple result of faulty negotiations procedures, and what is needed is that the family learns new negotiation procedures. The family can begin to learn these from the worker's efforts, beginning with the initial interview, to regulate the conversation.

It may be evident to the worker that family members do not feel very good about each other at this point; negative feelings may be intense, and difficult relationship problems, going beyond communication difficulties, may be present. Faulty communication mechanisms clearly can create relationship problems. It may not be at all clear at this point whether changing communication patterns can solve the relationship issues. Traces of goodwill and the ability to recall positive feelings are important in the willingness of family members to continue both in treatment and in relationships with one another.

Two-Party Discussing. A third alternative approach for Stage 4 is also diagnostic in effect but has a clearer treatment component. The worker may select a specific issue which has been referred to in the discussion and ask an involved pair of family members to work on it. They are asked to talk to each other to try to solve the problem. Other family members are asked to observe. The worker is in a position to observe what happens between the two parties involved and what the behavior of other family members is.

Both participants usually direct their efforts at getting the other person to see their own point of view. They may both become wider ranging in their arguments, increasingly insistent and intense, or one of them may become insistent and the other may withdraw. Both may turn to the worker or to other members of the family for support when their frustration at gaining the understanding of the other reaches a certain level. The worker may respond to this sense of frustration and hopelessness at being unable to work out their difficulties by helping each participant to become more aware of her or his own feelings of anger and despair and those of others. Noting the strategy that each participant has used in relating to the other and the other's response, the worker may inquire whether they see this description of their interaction as accurate and ask for their estimate of the effectiveness of their actions. In the midst of this awareness of anger and despair, the worker needs to know whether there is also a wish and a hope for change. Some clients may find the possibility of change so inconceivable that they dare not hope for it. The worker's attentiveness to these feelings can enhance the awareness of all family members and may be useful in prompting members to reach for the help offered by the worker. In such a case, the worker's expressions of hopefulness, if warranted, may be useful (Perlman, 1957, p. 186).

The worker may suggest a brief attempt to continue negotiations between the two participants, with guidance from the worker. Such efforts at guided communication are demonstrations of the treatment procedures and may help the family see that alternate ways of coping hold some hope of correcting the problem it is experiencing. The worker regulates the conversation by requiring (1) that the two participants not interrupt each other, (2) that the other person respond relevantly rather than with a topic change to another issue or a different experience, and (3) that the speakers talk about their own feelings and needs, rather than talking about the other person and what the speaker thinks the other one should be doing.[4]

The emphasis is on the immediate experience in the interview rather than on past events, though past events may be the starting point of the

---

[4] See Kempler (1973), Satir (1967), and Gordon (1970) for development of the use of statements about self rather than other.

discussion. Thus, A might be talking about feeling understood, or hurt, or lonely, or unsupported by B, not only in relation to an earlier event but in the present discussion of the event. B might respond empathetically or in anger, but B would be in a better position to respond empathetically than if A's comments had been focused on the things that B had done and shouldn't have done or on what B should have done. The intent is to make it possible for family members to feel that their views and feelings have been heard, an experience they have often not had in their own efforts at problem solving.

Whether the effort succeeds at this point or not, it serves as a demonstration of the kind of work that would take place during treatment. If it does not fully succeed, the worker is clearer about the amount and kinds of effort needed to help. Behind the ineffective negotiation procedures lie the varied needs of the individuals and the reasons that each has for not being able to accept the other's view. They may reflect an effort to maintain integrity and individuality or a struggle for control and power. Such difficult relationship issues will need to be addressed in the treatment.

While the worker is observing how two family members work on a specific family issue, simultaneous observation of the behaviors of other family members is possible. Other family members may not be able to remain in the observer role; they may become distractors, allies, or peacemakers or otherwise inject themselves into the negotiations. The reasons for such behavior are many and varied. Children may feel threatened by a too tense exchange between parents and act to draw attention away from the argument and onto themselves. A sibling may identify with the feeling of another child generated in the interaction with a parent. A parent may feel strongly abut the behavior of the other parent in relation to a child.

However well intended, these behaviors have negative side effects. They inject another relationship into an issue that could, and frequently should have been, resolved by two persons. In effect, the issue is left unresolved rather than resolved. The original disputants are more divided than they were before. The third person becomes occupied in the intervening role and is not free to pursue his or her usual separate activities.

The worker may respond in several ways. The worker may choose to ignore these behaviors at this time, being alert to whether their occurrence is a regular pattern of behavior. The worker may move to block the activity of the third party, indicating that others' observations will be asked for later. Or the worker may comment on the sequence of behaviors among the three family members, inviting discussion of the sequence (not of the problem) by all three. Feelings and reactions of each of the participants to the immediate events then become the focus of the discussion. The worker ascertains whether the family members are aware of the sequence and whether they see it as helpful or not.

Stage 5: Reaching a Treatment Contract

The final stage of the social worker's efforts to engage the family in treatment is achievement of an understanding with the family members about what they want to have changed and what they want from treatment. The emphasis shifts from what is wrong to how the family wants things to be, and how the worker can help them get there. The need to define goals and establish working contracts between social workers and clients about their ongoing work together is well recognized. Again, the process is similar to but more complex than that required in individual treatment.

The prior stages of the engagement effort have been preparation for the family to approach this one, but considerable work remains to be done. The discrepancies in problem statement now must be resolved into a problem definition to which family members can subscribe as one that they are willing to work on. The shift from what is wrong to how they want things to be moves away from complaining to positive, goal-oriented activity. It is not an easy shift to make. The definition of the kind of help needed from the worker is difficult to achieve, since the family has only the present experience with the worker to go by and consequently knows little about what the worker and agency have to offer. Agreement on the problem definition and how the worker will help are both needed.

In resolving the many issues that arise in contracting with a family about the problems and the goals of treatment, another type of worker activity is required. While previous stages have been worker-directed and structured, they have minimized analytical comment and feedback to the family about the way the worker sees the family working (or not working) together. Worker activity has focused on the process of the family session. In this stage the worker participates with his or her own observations and restatements and focuses on key aspects of the problem.

67

The worker's effort is directed at achieving a problem definition that is in harmony with the family's needs and wishes. The worker may see a variety of family problems that the family members themselves do not see. He may be aware, for example, that a marital problem exists, and that it interferes with the solution of the problem that the family has presented. The worker may make the connection, but the family may not be able to see this as the problem to be solved. If the presenting problem was a child's behavior, the focus at this stage is not on how the parents can get their marriage together, but on how they *together* can cope with the child's problem. The parents may be able to accept the need to join together to help the child, but they may not see the need to work on the marriage in general. While they may subsequently come to see that work on the marriage is needed in order to help their child, the starting point in treatment is with the problem they see and are willing to try to solve.

The worker's emphasis on what the family would like to accomplish in treatment requires the worker to seek responses from family members about what each wants and is willing to do about the problem. A number of difficulties will be encountered in these responses. One is that goals will be stated in terms of the need for someone else to stop doing something or to be different. Unfortunately, such statements make the definition of the family goal difficult if not impossible. They are statements about expectations of others rather than expectations of self. They concern behavior to be eliminated but not behavior that is to replace what is now occurring. They do not convey an image of what desirable family life would be like. All family members are not likely to find such definitions acceptable. The work of the previous stages of the initial contact should have helped to take the edge off some of these tendencies to blame or scapegoat, but it will not have eliminated them. More work is needed to arrive at acceptable definitions.

Another difficulty is that responses from family members may be in global terms. Either the specifics of change do not become clear, or the proposed changes in the family seem so extensive as to appear unattainable. Demands on others and global expectations reflect the continuing difficulty family members have in defining problems or in communicating their needs in a way that others in the family can accept and agree to. If they had other ways of addressing the tasks that the worker now puts to them, they probably would not need treatment. Specific help is needed.

One means the worker has of helping with these difficulties is the ability to restate or reformulate the problem. The worker may use knowledge of the members and of the group acquired earlier in the session. Knowledge about how members see themselves connected to the problem and about their wish to continue as a group may be used to convert negative statements into positive ones, global statements into more specific objectives. "I want him to stop arguing" or "We are always fighting" may be reformulated to "I wish that we could talk things over." General unhappiness and dissatisfaction may be converted to a wish for family members to "show more appreciation" or to "get along better." In rare instances members may comment about specific things they themselves can do to improve and may show signs of willingness to do them. The worker may offer formulations that express expectations and goals for the family rather than for individuals, or reformulate statements about problems to make them specific rather than global. The general adjustment problem of a family member may be specified in terms such as "planning how things will be when Sally returns home from the hospital," or "what we can do so grandmother won't be so unhappy." Agreement from members to work to solve these problems and achieve these goals is then sought.

Along with the effort to restate goals, the worker draws attention away from individual behavior to focus on the interactive process between members. For example, she or he may offer observations about family interactions which help to clarify for the family the nature of their difficulties. The worker may comment that when members disagree they become more forceful in their arguments, and the resistance of each stiffens. Nothing changes, and they may therefore wish to consider other means of resolving disagreement. This would be followed by a question about what they wish to do about it. Or the worker may note that when the parents, or any pair of family members, were working on a disagreement, they were distracted by a third member of the family, leaving their disagreement unresolved. This may be proposed as something that could be changed. This attention to the interactive process and the effort to define the problem as one of interpersonal relationships rather than as a problem of the individual serves to reduce defensive behavior and minimize guilt. It should help to free members from resistance to participation in family problem solving.

The worker at this stage also needs to learn what kind of help the family had expected and to define what kind of help he or she has to offer. The worker's means of helping will, in part, have been demonstrated by his behavior in the interview prior to this point, but these means may be very different from what the family wants. There may be a range of expectations of the worker, from removing a member from the home for placement elsewhere; to "straightening out" a member; to getting a member to go to school, or to work, or to a doctor; to refereeing the family arguments; to helping the family find a way to get along or to talk things over. The worker may judge the requests as desirable or undesirable directions in which to move, as needed or unneeded, as possible or impossible to fulfill, given the range of his skills or the availability of services in his own or other agencies. A request for placement may be accepted and recommended, or it may be countered with a recommendation of family counseling and an offer of worker involvement in that way. However the family and the service requests are evaluated, the worker's thinking and judgment about both must be conveyed to the family for discussion and decision. The worker needs also to convey his own and his agency's capacity to respond to the requests.

The family's response to the worker's evaluations, suggestions, and offers of help provide further data on which to base judgments about family potential for change and responsiveness to helping efforts. The new information and direction serve to upset the family's usual interchanges. The new inputs may be resisted, in order to maintain the usual balance, or they may be assimilated, in order to promote change.

Whether the family can begin to change or even accept the possibility of change depends on a number of factors, some of which have already been noted. The family's value of family togetherness is one such factor. Even though disaffection and discouragement about the family's situation may be great, there may still be hope that things could be different. Some members, however, may have already lost hope completely, and they cannot be interested in participation in the family. A second factor has to do with the willingness of members to risk. A member's willingness to respond positively to a worker reformulation that says, in effect, "I want you, care about you, wish to be with you" implies a willingness to risk the possibility that other members may not share those desires. Behind this willingness must lie a strong need and perhaps some confidence that other members do care and share the same wishes. Worker sensitivity can sometimes enable a member to claim ownership of such sentiments when this might not under other circumstances be possible.

70

Another factor affecting members' consent to participate and willingness to change is the fear that the individual will be lost in pursuing the goals of the group, that he or she will be unhappily bound to the family and never be free to leave or to grow as an individual. All of the procedures described are intended to convey the worker's support for both individuality and connectedness, and not just for a connectedness that keeps the individual inappropriately bound to the family. If, as a consequence of worker activity, the family indicates a willingness to continue in treatment, it is a sign of their capacity to accept outside contributions to their problem solving, and perhaps also of the worker's skill in conveying helpfulness and trustworthiness.

We have described in some detail a procedure for assessment and engagement of the family at the time of initial contact. The process need not always be lengthy, however. With some families it will be simple and short; with others it may take several hours. If a clear family and worker agreement does not result, the contact may have to be carried over into second sessions. Workers may eliminate some stages and still achieve clarity, begin work on a problem, or arrive at a contract with greater efficiency.

SUMMARY

Our concern in this chapter has been to further the understanding of the nature of treatment and the social worker's role in it. Treatment that promotes change in any family member or any set of interactions may be considered family treatment, since it will upset family balance. Conjoint family interviews may be used in treatment but are not synonymous with treatment. A variety of modes of involving family members is possible. Criteria for worker decisions about whom to involve and how to involve them have been suggested.

The worker's task in the initial stages of contact with family members is twofold. The first task is to come to an understanding of the nature of the problem presented by the family and of the nature of the family's difficulty in solving the problem. This assessment effort is concurrent with the worker's second task of engaging family members in the treatment effort. Engagement is complex because different family members may disagree

71

both on definition of the problem and solutions to it, and they may also differ in their willingness to participate in working at solutions. The section on engaging the family has delineated worker activity pertinent to both of these tasks.

While the section on beginning treatment has focused on procedures, we have also considered some of the ways in which the worker's knowledge about family systems is utilized in assessment and in the worker's contract with the family for further treatment. In our family treatment approach, the worker conceptualizes the presenting problem as a problem of the family system, as one that the family needs to come to terms with rather than a problem of an individual within the family. In this frame of reference, the worker proceeds in a way to help the family also think of the problem that way. The worker's intent is not to fault the family for the existence of the problem but to indicate that the existence of the problem requires the family to respond and to cope in some way. The worker conveys a willingness to help and to use her or his skills in finding ways of coping, offering hope that constructive solutions can be found which may motivate the family's problem-solving efforts.

REFERENCES

Bell, J. E. "A Theoretical Position for Family Group Therapy." *Family Process*, 2:1–14, 1963.

Binder, S. Zu neueren therapeutischen Ansaetzen bei Alcoholkranken [New Therapeutic Approaches to Alcoholics]. *Psychotherapie und Medzinishes Psychologie*, 21:239–47, 1971.

Bowen, M. "Family Therapy and Family Group Therapy." In H. Kaplan and B. Sadock (eds.), *Group Psychotherapy*. Baltimore: Williams and Wilkins Co., 1971.

Chilman, C. "Social Work Practice with Very Poor Families." *Welfare in Review*, 4:13–21, 1966.

Cohen, P. C., and Krause, M. S. *Casework with the Wives of Alcoholics*. New York: Family Service Association of America, 1971.

Committee on the Family. "Premises about Family Therapy." In *The Field of Family Therapy*. New York: Group for the Advancement of Psychiatry, 1970.

Cookerly, J. R. "The Reduction of Psychopathology as Measured by the MMPI Clinical Scales in Three Forms of Marriage Counseling." *Journal of Marriage and the Family*, 36:332–36, 1974.

Gallant, D. M., Rich, A., Bey, E., and Terranova, L. "Group Psychotherapy with Married Couples: A Successful Technique in New Orleans Alcoholism Clinic Patients." *Journal of the Louisiana Medical Society*, 122:41–44, 1970.

Gordon, T. *Parent Effectiveness Training*. New York: Peter H. Wyden/ Publisher, 1970.

Haley, J. "A Review of the Family Therapy Field." In J. Haley (ed.), *Changing Families*. New York: Grune & Stratton, 1971.

Haley, J. *Problem Solving Therapy*. San Francisco: Jossey-Bass, Inc., Publishers, 1976.

Kempler, W. *Gestalt Family Therapy*. Hollywood, Cal.: Kempler Institute, 1973.

Larson, C., and Gilbertson, D. "Reducing Family Resistance to Therapy through a Child Management Approach." *Social Casework*, 58:621–24, 1977.

Larson, C., and Talley, L. "Family Resistance to Therapy: A Model for Services and Therapist's Roles." *Child Welfare*, 56:121–26, 1977.

Leader, A. L. "Family Therapy for Divorced Fathers and Others Out of Home." *Social Casework*, 54:13–19, 1973.

McDowell, F. K. "The Pastor's Natural Ally against Alcoholism." *Journal of Pastoral Care*, 26:26–32, 1972.

Minuchin, S., Montalvo, B., Guerney, B., Rosman, B., and Schuner, F. *Families of the Slums*. New York: Basic Books, 1967.

Moynihan, S. K. "Home Visits for Family Treatment." *Social Casework*, 55:612–17, 1974.

Oxley, G. "Involuntary Clients' Responses to a Treatment Experience." *Social Casework*, 58:607–14, 1977.

Perlman, H. H. *Social Casework*. Chicago: University of Chicago Press, 1957.

Perlman, H. H. "Family Diagnosis in Cases of Illness and Disability." In Monograph VI, *Family Centered Social Work in Illness and Disability: A Preventive Approach*. New York: National Association of Social Workers, 1961.

Perlman, H. H. *Persona*. Chicago: University of Chicago Press, 1968.

Preston, F. B. "Combined Individual, Joint and Group Therapy in the Treatment of Alcoholism." *Mental Hygiene*, 44:522–28, 1960.

Rosenblatt, R. "All in the Family." *The New Republic*, 172:36–37, 1975.

Satir, V. *Conjoint Family Therapy*. Palo Alto, Cal.: Science and Behavior Books, 1967.

Scherz, F. "Multiple Client Interviewing." *Social Casework*, 43:120–5, 1962.

Sherman, S. N. "Practice Implications of Psychodynamic and Group Theory in Family Interviewing." In *The Group Approach to Treatment of Family Health Problems*. New York: National Association of Social Workers, 1965.

Solomon, M. A. "The Staging of Family Therapy: An Approach to Developing the Therapeutic Alliance." *Journal of Marriage and Family Counseling*, 3:59–66, 1977.

Speck, R. V., and Attneave, C. L. "Social Network Intervention." In J. Haley (ed.), *Changing Families*. New York: Grune and Stratton, 1971.

Strean, H. "Role Theory." In F. J. Turner (ed.), *Social Work Treatment*. New York: Free Press, 1974.

Watzlawick, P., Beavin, J., & Jackson, D. *Pragmatics of Human Communication*. New York: W. W. Norton & Co., 1967.

Wright, L. S. "Chronic Grief: The Anguish of Being an Exceptional Parent." *The Exceptional Child*, 23:106-9, 1976.

Wynne, L. "Some Guidelines for Exploratory Conjoint Family Therapy." In J. Haley (ed.), *Changing Families*. New York: Grune & Stratton, 1971.

Part II

Intervention Strategies

Part II consists of seven chapters focused on intervening with families to change dysfunctional patterns of interaction. In this part the theory and concepts presented in Part I are operationalized in work with specific populations. The populations we have chosen to discuss by no means form a definitive group, and their inclusion does not imply their prevalence or our preference with regard to other populations seen in family treatment. They simply represent a sampling of the kinds of families and family problems that social workers encounter in contemporary practice. The choice resulted from our own practice experiences, discussions with practitioners in social work agencies, and information provided by students in field work placements. We readily acknowledge that there are many other populations involved in treatment, and we hope to contribute to the discussion of these populations in the future, along with other educators and clinical practitioners.

We have called on the specialized experience of several other educators and practitioners for Chapters 7, 9, and 10. Chapter 7 represents a joint effort of one of the authors, Oliver C. Harris, with Pallassana R. Balpogal. Chapter 9 was written by Judith Fine and Chapter 10 by John Goldmeier.

The first chapter in this part, Chapter 4, addresses the problems of

74

poverty families and the techniques for treating this population in contemporary society. The impact of external systems in shaping the structure and functioning of these families and the role of the social worker as advocate and broker in meeting family needs are emphasized. The uniqueness of this type of family in relation to communication, rules, and expectations is highlighted. Procedures for intervening with the problem poverty family are discussed, with emphasis on the value of home visits, working with extended family members, and maintaining a suitable climate for effective intervention.

Chapter 5 focuses on the shifting roles of adult children and their aging parents. The difficulties encountered when adult children must take a major role in decision making relative to the welfare of their parents are brought clearly into view. We take a look at existing attitudes toward the older members of society and the process of aging as conceptualized in theory. The significance of earlier parent-child relationships and life-styles of the parents is discussed, and problems encountered in engaging a family composed of adult children and their parents are explored. The impact of role reversal, spouse-parent relationships, and adult sibling relationships and how to deal with them in treatment are also examined.

Chapter 6 is concerned with the treatment of families involved in cases of child abuse. We offer an understanding of the abusing parent and discuss the necessity of meeting the unmet needs of parents who abuse their children. Establishing a relationship between worker and parents that is free of blame for the abuse is emphasized, as well as the necessity of involving the child in treatment. Suggestions are made for working with the parents and the abused child separately in the early phase of treatment.

Chapter 7 discusses intervention with the black middle-class family, an area about which very little has been written. We expand on the framework presented in Part I to examine what is unique about black middle-class family structure and how the family carries out its functions. Recognition is given to the importance of the history of the black family as it has affected the roles of husband and wife, their pattern of relating, socialization of the children, and so on. This chapter provides an understanding of this growing population and suggests the tools to be used for successful intervention.

Chapter 8, a reprint of an article in *Social Work* by the principal author, Curtis Janzen, is devoted to the treatment of families in which alcohol abuse is a major source of disruption. Issues of control and interpersonal payoffs are presented as an important part of family dynamics. Major emphasis is placed on the use of a systems approach to treatment, which calls for the involvement of spouse, children, and extended family to promote necessary change.

Chapter 9 explores how the various aspects of family functioning are affected by the impact of family treatment in a medical care setting. Family power structure, perception of reality, affect, individuation, separation and loss, and adaptation at transitional phases of illness are discussed in relation to different family classifications. The social worker's role in intervening with each family is emphasized in this chapter, which gives an in-depth view of family treatment in a medical hospital.

Chapter 10 deals with the breakup and reconstitution of the family. The influence of changing concepts in family life is discussed in relation to separation, divorce, and remarriage. Intervention strategy and various types of interference in problem solving are explored. Phase-specific problems and techniques for helping the family at each phase are also defined. This chapter addresses an increasingly apparent problem in present-day families. It calls for an expansion of existing concepts and techniques normally used in family treatment to facilitate effective intervention with the family undergoing change through separation, divorce, and remarriage.

CHAPTER **4**

Family Treatment for Problem Poverty Families

INTRODUCTION

In the large body of literature on families in poverty, the terminology in reference to the family's needs and problems is often different from the terminology describing general family treatment. The difference does not appear to be accidental but rather to represent variant ways of conceptualizing the family. Our emphasis with poverty-level families is on the family as a group, which represents a primary difference from other approaches to poverty families. Those who treat malfunctioning poverty-level families, and the families themselves, may benefit alike from this effort to bring together knowledge and insights from family practice and work with poverty-level families.

Our approach to the problem poverty family views the family as an organized system of internal subsystems which is engaged in varying ways and degrees with external systems. Events inside the family system are seen as affecting the nature of transactions with the outside world; conversely, events in other systems are seen as influences on internal family relationships and events. The behavior of external systems is viewed

Note: We are extremely grateful to Leonard Press, Associate Professor, School of Social Work and Community Planning, University of Maryland at Baltimore, for his review and constructive suggestions of this chapter.

77

as particularly important in the internal operations of poverty families. Further, we pay primary attention to the ways in which family members engage each other in seeking to have their needs met, to gain cooperation, establish order, negotiate differences, or otherwise regulate family activity. While knowledge of early life deprivation or training is relevant to understanding behavior, as in traditional casework, more attention is paid to the way that current problems evoke, and current patterns reenforce, nonproductive modes of relating and problem solving. Individual behavior is viewed in the context of family and external system events.

The problems poverty families face have all been noted in the literature on problem families.[1] They include problems in marital relationships, including those of single parenthood; in parenting; in household management; in role performance at school or on jobs or in other aspects of community life; in family isolation from relatives, friends, community organizations, and other support systems; and in lack of health, material means, or education and skills. The focus of this chapter is on the way in which the poverty-level family is a participant in the development of these problems of functioning, and on how it can promote or be assisted in promoting their resolution.

POVERTY FAMILIES AS PROBLEM FAMILIES

Problem poverty families have variously been labeled "disorganized," "multiproblem," "hard-to-reach," and "hopeless." The labels prompt images of the kinds of parents and children that inhabit the families, of the kinds of relationships they have with one another, of the ways they cope with family life in general and their own specific problems, and of the ways they engage with the outside world. Though these labels may in a sense be accurate, they are in another sense more appropriate to the ways social workers and other practitioners have thought about and responded to them. As Wiltse (1958) has noted, the sense of hopelessness resides in the social worker as well as in the family. "Disorganized" is an appropriate label only in the sense that social agencies and helpers have not understood the kind of organization that occurs in families and have lacked the concepts

---

[1]The literature is replete with descriptions of poverty families. Wiltse (1958), Geismar and Ayres (1959), King (1967), Bandler (1967), and Hallowitz (1975) are particularly vivid or detailed.

necessary for understanding. "Hard-to-reach" follows at least in part from inadequate conceptualizations and a related lack of skills and techniques.

The conceptualizations of problem poverty families offered here will provide new understanding (and perhaps new labels) that should help social workers feel less hopeless about them and more able to find ways to enable their responsiveness and growth. Given the present deficits in services to poor families, we also hope that agencies will gain new understanding and become more willing to commit needed resources and services to the effort.

Families in poverty do not all fit the images. Many poverty-level families function well in spite of great adversity; marital relationships, child rearing, and performance in the outside world proceed satisfactorily and with success. It is important to know that such families exist, and it would be extremely useful to know the factors that account for their survival and success. Such knowledge would enable workers to deal more effectively with the problem-ridden families about whom we are concerned here, and enable the family members to succeed as families and individuals.[2] Thus, we will be discussing a subgroup of poverty-level families—those that do not function well and therefore come to the attention of social workers in social agencies.

Nevertheless, there is a relationship between poverty and the problems of these families. Chilman (1975) sees poverty as clearly causal of family problems, particularly where the family has lived in poverty for a generation or longer. The problems of the family may become the central handicap in its ability to extricate itself from poverty or its other problems.

These poverty conditions contribute to such attitudes and behaviors as fatalism, alienation, distrust between family members, separate male and female worlds, little communication between mates and between parents and children, and punitive and authoritarian methods of child-rearing. Attitudes and behaviors of

---

[2]Ideas about why problem families do not function well have for the most part been developed out of clinical work with these families. Such work could, by inference, give rise to descriptions of healthy families, but few attempts have been made to lay these out systematically, especially in regard to poverty families. Studies designed to understand well-functioning families in general are few in number. Some efforts have been made to compare families which function well with those that do not. The work of Lewis, Beavers, Gossett, and Phillips (1976) is a particularly good example of such an effort. They compare family processes in physically healthy and nonhealthy families. H. McAdoo (1977) and J. McAdoo (1977) are studying successful black families in an effort to account for their difference from the stereotype of lower-class black families.

these kinds growing out of long term, severe poverty, tend to further the problems of poor families, adversely affecting family relationships and developmental outcomes for both parents and children—especially the latter. (Chilman, 1975, pp. 58-59)

The problems of family functioning in poverty-level families will not be resolved without some change in the family's poverty status. However, the reverse also appears to be true—some changes in family functioning must occur if the family is to be extricated from poverty status and from the perpetuation of individual and family problems. Adequate external system supports, such as the worker orientations and agency commitments described below, are essential to motivate change in poverty families and to forestall the repetition of present patterns in succeeding generations. Extrication from the poverty status rests not only with the family but also with a change in the perspectives of the external systems which affect it. We are concerned with facilitating change at both levels.

EXTERNAL SYSTEM/FAMILY SYSTEM OPERATIONS

We see the poverty problem family as a bounded system, subject to inputs from external systems. The limitations of material means are, initially, limitations in the support provided by external systems for the family. The economic system has not made available opportunities for employment and income production to meet the family's needs. Where these are lacking, the social system, because of public attitudes and consequent public policy, has not provided adequate alternate means of support for the family, either in income or services. Limited resources and restrictive agency policies are the measure of society's attitudes. These limited inputs from external systems diminish the family's ability to maintain itself materially. They also affect the status and role assignments of family members, particularly those of the family breadwinner.

Further, negative attitudes and sometimes outright hostility toward the poverty family may be manifested by the public, by agencies, and by workers. Middle-class values lead to expectations of certain responses from the family and to disparagement and rejection when the family does not manifest these responses. The feedback to the family depreciates the family's image of itself and of its individual members. When the family is lacking in self-enhancing feedback from the outside world, the esteem of family members for each other suffers. Self-esteem, useful as a source of strength and motivation, is diminished, and the burden of promoting it is left totally to the already overburdened family.

Another negative impact external systems have on the poverty family is the existence of policies which divide families rather than bring them together. In some states policies are still in effect which provide support for mother and children when father is not there, but do not support them when he is present but unable to provide financial support. This serves to divide the family and inhibit family strength and growth. Kaslow (1972) has drawn attention to the way such policies work against the strengthening and integration of the family and the family therapist's effort to promote these results.

Other agency policies also serve to divide and fragment the family. Examples are service to the health or mental health needs of some family members, but not of others, or attentiveness only to the physical or mental health of a family member, without attention to the family circumstances that affect health.

Agencies which require the family to conform to agency policy operate as though the family is an extension of the agency, subject to its bidding. Instead of providing support to the family's own problem-solving efforts, the policies of agencies and the actions of workers often serve to inhibit the capacity for independent thought and action. In conceptual terms, the family loses its boundaries as a separate system and becomes incorporated as part of the agency system, thus increasing rather than decreasing its dependency. Families known to more than one agency as Hoffman and Long (1969) suggest, may find themselves faced with contradictory requests which may result in breakdown of family structure or family boundaries.

Family interaction with other, less official or public systems may operate similarly. The extended family, the siblings or parents of the adult family members, sometimes provides little or no support. In poverty families these persons often are psychologically or materially not in a position to be supportive and are themselves in need of support. When a relationship exists, extended family members often see the members of the poverty family as people to be controlled, or directed, or drawn upon for their own support. Consequently, the inputs to the family system from the extended family leave it diminished in capacity for independent operation.

Extended family members, however, can be helpful in providing supports, sometimes financially and materially, sometimes in services such as child care or homemaking during illness. Stack (1974) has noted the particular means of helpfulness of kin and kinlike networks. When such relationships are tenuous, family members can sometimes be helped to strengthen them, to their own gain.

Often problem poverty families are simply lacking in their connection with the outside world. Friendships are meager or nonexistent. Encounters with institutions such as churches, schools, and health services are dreaded and avoided. The potential for connectedness, interest, and self-affirmation is not available.

In these and other ways, external systems can affect the processes operative within the family and leave its members alienated, depreciated, distrustful, and hostile toward the outside world. They are thus more intensively dependent on one another for affirmation and rewards and are subject to heightened interpersonal tension. Fewer exchanges with external systems mean that family members often lack awareness of the standards and expectations of the outside world (King, 1967). There is a lack of knowledge of what may be available to them or how to make use of what is available. Agencies sometimes even operate to make such information inaccessible to family members. Therefore, problem poverty families often lack the repertoire of appropriate knowledge and behaviors available to them. The family system has in effect been closed off to inputs from the outside world which could be potentially helpful in solving the family's problems. Because of deficits of information and skills, contacts with social institutions often end in failure and disappointment. In Chilman's (1975) view, such family limitation may be a function of the duration of poverty status over extended periods of time, especially when it continues into a second generation.

Thus, a negative interaction occurs between the poverty family and external systems. Over time, relationships deteriorate unless processes are set in motion which alter the behaviors of either the family or external systems, or both. The failure to achieve the desired positive connections must be attributed to the stance of the outside world *and* to the family's limitations. New behaviors initiated by the family or by the external systems affect the interaction between them and offer hope of improvement in the family and in its relationship with the outside world. If new information and resources are made available, the family has to be able to respond to make effective use of them. It may need assistance in learning to respond to the altered situation, since its responses have been tailored for the external systems as they had been behaving. Treatment, therefore, must contain a substantial element of advocacy to change external systems. In other instances, the limitations in the family's knowledge and coping skills should be the focus of treatment.

Since there is a reciprocal influence between the family system and the systems external to it, transactions within the family system, between family members, will be affected by the transactions with outside systems. Similarly, changes within the family will alter the transactions with the outside world. Present patterns of transaction may have developed and persisted over time, but they represent adaptation to current circumstances. A systems viewpoint emphasizes the need to understand what is occurring in the present as each system responds to inputs from the other. This is true whether the family is responding to the requirements of external systems or to the appearance of new problems. Further, to the extent that present behavior is determined by past experience, it is determined by learning rather than by psychological conflict. That is, people cope in present transactions because they have learned to cope that way and have not learned other ways which might now be more useful to them (Cade, 1975; McKinney, 1970). This emphasis on here-and-now transactions, which is reflective of family treatment in general, is especially useful in helping families who have immediate material needs as well as problems of individual and interpersonal functioning. The emphasis is on what is to be done rather than why the family is in a particular situation. As a focus of treatment, teaching and asking the family to try out new behaviors takes priority over understanding and insight into past causes as a means for promoting behavioral change.[3]

INTERNAL FAMILY SYSTEM OPERATIONS

The nature of the problem poverty family's boundaries, rules, communications, and identity follows from the nature of the family's relationships to external systems. The negative nature of the relationships

---

[3]Research by Reid and Shyne (1969, pp. 82-93) shows that even though psychoanalytic theory suggests a focus on the development of insight into causes of behavior, caseworkers have nevertheless focused more on current interactions of the client with the family or other systems.

with external systems for these families has been defined; there is little in them to offer either adult or child a sense of positive meaning or affirmation. As breadwinners or as clients of an income maintenance program, adults feel depreciated and find no status; children receive minimal affirmation or recognition for their efforts in school. Consequently, for gratification of their personal needs, each member turns to other family members. The need to seek all gratifications within the family places undue stress on internal family operations. Unsatisfactory patterns develop and persist as long as the family's position in the community persists.

The internal operations of problem poverty families are viewed in relation to family structure, which incorporates generational boundaries and family rules, and to family communication processes. These elements are not totally separate from one another, though we do describe them separately. These aspects of family functioning relate to the family's integration, solidarity, and sense of identity, which in turn are important elements in its structure and process.

Boundaries

Family boundaries define the various subsystems in the family structure (see Chapter 1). The marital pair first forms a marital subsystem, which may become a parental subsystem. Family operations and strength depend in large measure on the ability of the adults to form a strong bond with each other. Satisfaction in their own relationship derives from that bond, as does the ability to support each other in child rearing. In problem poverty families, however, the relationships between the adults are characterized by distance, conflict, and transiency. They interact with each other primarily as parents, minimally as spouses.

While communicational and interactional problems (which we will describe shortly) are primary sources of the inability to form a strong marital bond,[4] the structural outcomes must also be considered. When relationships do not work partners may withdraw from them, psychologi-

---

[4] The parents' inability to provide love and affection for each other and for their children has been attributed to their individual need for love and affection, due to the deprivation they have experienced in their own growth and development (Bandler, 1967; Lance, 1969). While this is no doubt a factor, other factors enter in. Current material limitations reinforce the parents' sense of deprivation. Current communicational and interactional modes (which we describe subsequently) frustrate their efforts to obtain satisfaction from each other.

cally or physically or both, and the withdrawal may be temporary or permanent. Or they may engage in overt conflict, verbal or physical or both. In families with children a parent may withdraw from the parenting function as well as from the spouse role. Withdrawal from the parenting function represents the relinquishment of parental leadership. The role of the withdrawing spouse/parent may thus become more that of a child than of a parent. The usual generational lines are crossed.

When the failure of marital bonding results in conflict which cannot be contained within the bounds of marriage, a second form of generational boundary violation may occur. A parent may seek a member of the child generation as an ally, sometimes to gain support for self, sometimes as a means of attack against the spouse. If both parents have remained in the home or are significant for the child, the child is placed in an untenable position between them.

The child who responds to this boundary breakdown by moving to comfort or support one of the parents increases his or her isolation from the other parent. Thus he deprives himself of the support of the other parent and may thereby accentuate the conflict between the parents. He may seek to reconcile parental differences, a function which places him more in the parent generation, or he may actually take on parental functions. Or he may develop other emotional, physical, or behavioral symptoms because of this uncomfortable positioning. Cues from the parents will suggest to the child the ways in which he is needed.

The breakdown in parental leadership is manifest also in those instances in which children move into parenting roles with other children. Such movement may be prompted by the parent, and it gains parental approval. While it often results from parental conflict or default, it may in other instances often be necessary for a child to perform in the role of a parent, as for example when work, illness, or errands leave both parents unavailable. This becomes even more likely in single-parent families. An older child may take on a child-caring role with younger siblings during after-school hours, before the parents return home from work. Or they may be asked to undertake extra household tasks during an illness of one of the adults. Troubles may arise when parents have not provided sufficient direction.

An older girl was left in charge of several siblings who began fighting with each other. Having no instructions from the parents about what to do about this behavior, she separated them and did not allow them to play together until the parents returned home. The younger sibs complained to the parents who, in turn, chided the girl for her actions. No instructions were offered about what to do if the behavior recurred. The girl was left with negative feelings toward her siblings for causing her trouble and toward her parents for not supporting or directing her. The younger siblings were likewise left with angry feelings and a reduced need to be cooperative.

In these circumstances the parent failed to provide a clear unambiguous structure within which the parenting child and the other children could relate, leaving cause for disagreement and fighting. Where parental leadership is clear, all children will know their limits and responsibilities during a parent's absence.

The likelihood of a child's becoming a parental child seems greater in problem poverty families than in other families. The parents' poor position in the outside world, as we have suggested, leaves the parent with reduced need satisfaction, self-esteem, and status within the family. These factors combine to reduce parental assertiveness and leadership. Seeking affirmation and status, they may more readily seek a child as an ally or yield to the wishes of a child, especially when these needs are not met by a spouse who may have similar needs and may be unable to meet the other's needs. Furthermore, in single-parent families, which many of these families are, the tendency to rely on parental children increases.

Rules

Closely related to a lack of structure evidenced in generational boundaries and parental leadership is a lack of clear and consistent norms and rules for behavior. In problem poverty families, parental responsibilities in setting limits to behavior often are not fulfilled. What is a limit today may not be a limit tomorrow, or even ten minutes from now. A limit defined by one parent may not be held to by the other parent. Behavior is regulated by injunctions on a particular piece of behavior but with no further explanation about why it should be stopped, about circumstances under which it is permitted, or about what desirable behavior should be substituted. Children consequently have no consistent guides for behavior which they can internalize and thereby become self-regulating, either in the parent's presence or away from them. Parents are constantly required to regulate the activity of the children, leaving them totally enmeshed and

86

absorbed in child care and less free to meet their own needs. They feel overburdened and overwhelmed.

The parents' abdication from regulation or their total withdrawal from the family, either temporary or permanent, leaves relationships disrupted and reenforces the sense of inconsistency and instability. Parental behavior in this area is also attributable, at least in part, to the parents' limited status outside the family and their own and family members' reactions to that status. Where the parents have themselves been raised in similar families, these behaviors are learned in their families of origin.

Such interaction of course interferes with the growth and development of the children and the parents. The process does not allow for individuation and separation of family members but instead keeps them dependent upon and bound to one another. It is a kind of being "stuck" together that is very different from being able to see oneself as an individual, but an individual who takes satisfaction and enhances her or his identity out of belonging to the family. The "stuck togetherness" is similar to the situation of "enmeshment" described by Minuchin and associates (1967) and to the "undifferentiated" family situation described by Bowen (1971).

Similar, but less often described, is the lack of clear expectations and rules about marital behavior. Dissatisfaction with marital relations may result. Adults may think of themselves primarily as parents and devote little attention and effort to their roles as spouses. Frequently spouses are unsure of themselves as males or females. They become aware of their spouse's expectations primarily when they fail to meet them, not through transactions which result in explicit definitions of what is expected and desired. Complaints are frequent; the freedom to say what "I want, need, or would like" is lacking, as is the means for expression. As in parent-child relationships, it is easier for spouses to learn what is not wanted than to learn what is wanted. Role performance cannot be achieved with confidence. Since role expectations are not clearly defined, the interpersonal process leaves spouses feeling insecure and lacking in self-affirmation.

Communications

When clear and consistent rules for behavior are lacking, communications are likely to be dysfunctional to family stability and problem solving.

87

Communication is characterized by interruptions, simultaneous talking, topic changes, and unclear meanings. Members do not really listen to each other and frequently do not really expect to be heard. When others respond it is often to make a counter point of their own, rather than to respond to what has been said. Voices escalate in volume in an effort to be heard, and in the noise, affect rather than content is communicated. The verbal message is lost and is not responded to. Interaction reveals affect and feelings rather than information and ideas, and the interpersonal aspect of the message predominates over the content aspect. In some instances limitations of language ability affect the ability to achieve understanding and solution of a problem. The families are thereby impoverished in their attempts to generate information and solutions to problems.

These characteristics of communication in poverty families, as contrasted to other problem families, differ in intensity, not in kind. Intense need and seeking on the part of family members are implied. In such families, consequently, efforts at problem solving by means of verbal communication are unproductive. Nothing in the family changes as long as communications operate in this manner. Furthermore, the members' frustration with one another and their sense of isolation are increased. They get no sense of being listened to and really heard. They do not obtain understanding, self-affirmation, or nurture from the unresponsiveness or arguments of others.

The communications thus reflect family relationship and structure. The isolation or lack of support within the structure that one or more members may feel becomes evident through the lack of supportive communications and the volume of negative messages directed at them. Members feel isolated from other family members or fear that others are allied against them. For example, when a child communicates as though he or she were a parent, one of the parents may feel as if the other parent and the child are allied against him or her. Or parent communication may seem to derogate a spouse in favor of a child.

Thus the communicative effort at both the content and the relationship levels serves to perpetuate the unsatisfying relationships rather than to change them. A homeostasis is reached, and problem solving does not occur. Family structure is maintained in its disabling form. The family system is stable (morphostatic), but in a form that gradually leads to less effective functioning rather than more.

88

Identity, Integration, and Solidarity

A number of writers have attested to the importance of a sense of family identity in family coping and problem solving. In our view, this is both consequence and cause of the problems in family functioning.

Hess and Handel (1959), in their research on normal families, refer to the image members hold of the family as a group with a particular past and future. This group identity has meaning for the individual and is seen as important for individual growth and role taking within the family. The image may take various forms, such as "the people that I live with" or "the family that I belong to." Holland (1970) and Laing (1967) also identify images of the group and of the member's place in the group as significant for individual identity and role taking. The term "family" contains within it a sense of integration and solidarity, factors which Angell (1934) found to be significant for the family's ability to manage the stresses of the depression of the 1930s.

Wiltse (1958) takes the position that the concept of family identity is significant in problem poverty families. He defines it as "a mutual relation in that it connotes both a persistent sameness with a family (family character) and a persistent sharing of some kind of essential family character with other families like it" (p. 21). Rabinowitz (1969) observes that it is this sense of being a group which is lacking in poor, multiproblem families:

> Researchers participating in the Wiltwyck study were struck by how little these families seem to be recognized by their members as groups of people who belong together. Parents seem to disassociate themselves from each other and from their children. They seldom have conversations with each other or with a child. . . . Both enjoyment of family life and any positive valuing of family relationships are notably absent. . . . Although they maintain a family form they do not develop a family consciousness. (p. 180)

Having a sense of the family and of belonging to it is as important to individual functioning as is the sense of separateness of self. But it is difficult to develop a positive image of the family in the midst of the structural and communication deficits found in poverty families. The modes of coping with problems and of handling relationships have served to drive members apart rather than to promote a sense of unity and harmony. The family's material status also has its effect. It becomes easy, when material necessities and the means for acquiring them are lacking, to doubt, argue, and blame, and over time to come to feel alienated and apart from the group. The group, in turn, holds insufficient meaning or value for the individual, since it is not a source of nourishment or support. Members are not likely to be committed to preserving it or making an effort to improve it.

We have observed the opposite effects in certain cases, however. In some families the children are able to become upwardly mobile. Such families seem to be characterized by a family theme, defined by the parents, which conveys that though the external world is hostile, the family can succeed if everyone joins together. Goals of survival and achievement are emphasized. Parental leadership is strong, and rules are explicit and clearly enforced. Long-term family survival is given priority over immediate individual goals. Staying together and working together are essential to survival. Under these circumstances, individuals can achieve and advance despite poverty. The individual is enhanced through the *esprit de corps* of the family group. In some instances, however, the individual may experience a sense of rigidity and overcontrol and have difficulty achieving individuality or separateness from the group.

It usually is not possible to identify all the possible difficulties in any given problem poverty family. Social workers need generally to be aware of the stresses on the family, of the behaviors and responses of other systems toward the family, and of the way the family reacts to, copes with, or processes its experience with the outside world. They face the task of identifying the varying degrees to which the problem-solving effort needs to be directed toward external systems, and family structure or family process needs changing, and of deciding how their efforts should best be directed.

To some degree, the worker's effort should be directed toward both external systems and the family itself. Modes of intervention related to external systems, to changing family structure, and to changing the communication process are suggested in the following section. The choice of intervention, as always, depends on the worker's judgments about the family's needs and capacities. The primary emphasis is on working with the family as a group, but this does not mean that work with individuals is not possible or necessary. Our particular purpose, however, is to show how work with the family as a group is undertaken.

FAMILY PROBLEMS AND FAMILY PROBLEM SOLVING

All too often, social workers and other helpers have concluded that reality problems such as income, housing, and health care must be solved before obvious problems of individual and family coping can be addressed. Workers make heavy investments in obtaining needed services for families, and, in spite of considerable frustration, these often result in improvement for the family. But they become disappointed when the family does not then show improvement in its coping capacity, in parenting, in sibling relationships, in individual adaptation in the family or outside of it, or even in a willingness to try to wrestle with these problems. It seems, when work on one aspect of the family situation is delayed until work on the other is satisfactorily concluded, that the family is lost before work on the former begins. To avoid this dichotomy, it is necessary to focus simultaneously on the problems and realities posed by life and external systems for the family, and on the way in which the family manages its relationship with them.

Umbarger (1972) discusses this dual focus and concludes:

A family therapy approach oriented toward the ecological systems that form the context of behavior can attend *simultaneously* to the realities of poverty and to intrafamilial issues. The tactics necessary for assistance with poverty problems, such as home visits, school visits, agency visits, and work with the extended family, are the occasion for restructuring relations within the family unit. The management of poverty is part of the treatment procedure context, and not simply an effort to remove obstacles so that the "real treatment" might then begin. The therapist works at the interface between the family and non-familial systems, using typical poverty events—such as unemployment, legal troubles, unpaid rent, or housing difficulties—as the occasion for interventions into the affective, communicational, and structural aspects of family organization. Every new external emergency is an opportunity for restructuring the psychosocial interior of the family. (pp. 156-57, italics ours)

These emphases are congruent with our position about the interrelatedness of family problems and the family's problem-solving mechanisms (see Chapter 2). The solutions to the very real problems of employment, housing, health care, and school performance are achieved, at least in part, by focusing on the way in which the family works at the solutions. Interactions between family members which encourage or discourage, help or hinder, speed or slow progress are a concurrent focus for family work.

The orientation to families described by Umbarger (1972) and Cade (1975) is consistent with an emphasis that has long existed at some places in social work practice. Perlman (1957) writes that the social caseworker has the dual task of achieving solution to a problem and increasing the problem-solving capacity of the persons being served. She delineates how this is accomplished in work with individuals, though the work she describes with individuals is done on behalf of the family as well as of the individual. We will emphasize the means for developing the problem-solving capacity of the family group through efforts on behalf of the group as well as the individual.

CONJOINT FAMILY TREATMENT

The balance of this chapter is concerned with treatment. Some of our formulations for working with problem poverty families, along with strategies that have been described in the literature, are presented, and various ways of working with the family are noted. In the mix of techniques and methods, three themes give coherence to all of the worker activities: (1) the view of the family as a system in interaction with other systems, (2) the concurrent focus on solving problems and improving the family's problem-solving process, and (3) the conjoint effort of the members. The work reported was done in a variety of family and mental health services.

The treatment approach presented here envisions work with all members of the family, often in conjoint sessions of members with the social worker. The advantages of conjoint family work named in Chapter 3 apply to problem poverty families.

McKinney (1970) notes that work with the entire family serves to promote a sense of family cohesiveness and strength:

Family group casework, with its emphasis on transactions and communication within the family and with significant others, focuses immediate attention on the family as a unit. This point needs stressing because often the multi-deficit family is seen as an amorphous collection of individuals vying with each other for attention or for the immediate meeting of their own needs, often at the expense of others. This attention to the family as a constant, allows the worker to be flexible in giving importance, when indicated, to family members as individuals within the context of family, to parental functioning, and to parent-child and sibling relations.

Worker activity is guided by the premise that the family as a group can develop

92

more strength to cope with maturation and family roles and tasks by an emphasis on transactional processes within the family rather than by casework with individual family members. (p. 327)

Engaging all family members in the problem-solving task thus is useful in engendering in the family members a positive image of themselves as a unit. It conveys the idea that each may gain from common effort and work on problems that affect them all. The conjoint effort serves to stimulate motivation for participation in treatment and in family problem solving. Wiltse (1958) says that "By actively promoting family identity the social worker can exploit its force to give greater cohesiveness and direction to a family's development, and therefore the power of the family as the basic socializing agent in the life of its individual members is enhanced" (p. 21).

BEGINNING TREATMENT

As the "hard-to-reach" label often given problem poverty families attests, traditional approaches in family agencies, mental health services, and public social services have not been successful in meeting needs or gaining cooperation in treatment efforts. Social workers and their supervisors and consultants have frequently concluded that these families are unmotivated for help or change. Recently, some new ways of looking at the families have changed worker attitudes and have resulted in the development of special means for engaging them in the problem-solving effort. These means involve: (1) efforts to relate to the family's own special needs and concerns, including material ones, rather than those of the worker; (2) meeting the family at home rather than an office; (3) being available when not scheduled to be; and (4) engaging in activities with the family, as well as talking.

While these strategies have been utilized with a variety of families, their use with poverty families is especially necessary for successful engagement. In these aspects of beginning the treatment and continuing throughout the treatment effort, the worker acts to meet real needs, both material and psychological, while also working to develop trust, to teach and educate by instruction and demonstration, and to alter structure and interrupt dysfunctional interactive processes between family members. Such activity implies not only special efforts, orientation, and attitudes on the part of workers but also a special commitment of agency purpose and resources that is not always required in treatment of other families.

These efforts are similar in some ways to commonly accepted treatment practice with individuals. The similarities lie in the simultaneous emphasis on developing a positive relationship, defining the problems that the client wants solved, and finding ways to achieve a solution. The differences stem from the effort to involve all family members in the process and from the focus on transactions between family members.

Worker Orientation

Describing these families as hard to reach seems to be another way of saying that as family systems they have been closed to inputs from external systems. Family system boundaries are impermeable, and members are unreceptive to the expectations and help of others. Clearly, ways must be found to make them more responsive to the inputs of the outside world and more accessible to the help that is offered.

Two identifiable factors affecting success in engaging troubled poverty-level families in treatment are the conceptual stance and the attitudinal orientation of the helper. It is first necessary to conceptualize the problems as problems of the family rather than of an individual and to be able to identify what the family needs. Sager, Masters, Ronall, and Normand (1968) report that success in reaching low-income mental health center clientele increased when their staff members were trained to see the relevance of the family to the psychiatric problem and when they could acquire a different image of the needs of the family. It was noted that families expected immediate response and offers of clearly defined help. When the clinic changed its intake procedures to expect family participation at the outset, to eliminate the delays resulting from screening, history-taking interviews, and transfers to other workers, successful engagement of families increased.

The Sager group report indicates that the negative attitudes of workers can be reduced by training which places behavior in the context of the family system and improves their ability to see behavior as adaptive to the social situation. It is also evident that when the worker's negative attitudes are replaced by the ability to manifest respect and trustworthiness (Freeman, Hoffman, Smith, & Prunty, 1970), and to "tolerate the dependency" of the family (Lance, 1969), successful engagement with the

94

family can occur. Since negative attitudes on the part of external systems have a deleterious effect on the problem poverty family, changed orientations and responses are needed in agency systems as well as in workers to produce responsiveness and change in these families.

Problem poverty families often exhibit behaviors that test the worker's attitudes, interest, and concern. Previous experience with workers may enhance the family's doubts about the worker's interest, reliability, and concern. Families often report experiences of being unresponded to, rejected, and controlled by workers and agencies. Repeated and consistent responsiveness is needed to overcome the family's wariness and lack of trust. During the initial phase families distance themselves in various ways, such as absence at the time of scheduled appointments. Workers have responded by seeking clients at other locations if they were not home at the unexpected time. When they are home, families often leave the radio or television on at loud volume or have friends, neighbors, or relatives present. Such behavior may continue over many months, though it decreases over time as workers persevere and family members become convinced of the worker's interest and dependability.

Viewed as an interactive, intersystems process, this changed agency and worker orientation to seeking out and reaching out appears in numerous instances to have had the capacity to induce family cooperation and participation.

Home Visits, Activity, and Talk

There is persistent reference in the literature on family treatment to the value of home visits in acquiring a clear picture of how the family works (e.g., Moynihan, 1974). These visits benefit the worker's understanding; they also serve to make the family more accessible to worker input. Home visits seem more natural to problem poverty families and serve to avoid the negative connotation that some groups have about utilizing mental health services (Levine, 1964). They lend themselves more readily to approaches which are not so specifically suggestive of treatment but allow the worker to be seen as friend and member of the family, images which appear less threatening to the family's already low self-esteem. Home visits also utilize approaches that are oriented to activity and doing (to be described shortly), as well as to talking. They also enable the participation of more members of the family than referrals to separate services for the individual problems of family members would.

Workers have engaged in a variety of activities with family members. Art, crafts, games, fixing toys and furniture, repairing or making clothing, cleaning house, and setting hair have all been reported. In addition, workers have participated with families on outings and trips to agencies and clinics. These activities have been successful in promoting participation in treatment and change in family functioning.

Levine (1964) has found that activities quickly reveal the nature of family interaction. For example, when parents competed with children in games they had difficulty in playing according to the rules, as did the children. They were unable to provide consistent rules and structure. In fixing toys and furniture, parents lacked skills and confidence. The worker would undertake to enforce game rules and demonstrate how to fix, modeling these activities for the parents and encouraging them to take over.

Scheinfeld, Bowles, Tuck, and Gold (1970) also introduced games and toys, inviting all members to participate. Activity sometimes began with only one or more of the children participating, though the interest of others was gradually attracted. Parent participation was sought as a means of promoting parental interest in the child's growth and learning, although sibling participation also allowed workers to help with these relationships. They report particular difficulty in getting fathers involved in activities with the children, which they attribute to cultural conditioning which sees fathers as having a minimal role in the socializing of children. Most studies suggest that the father's role in the family is an important one, but this observation implies that participation does not have to be manifest in this particular way.

Bandler (1967) likewise reports that the worker's participation in low-income family-life activities—becoming a member of the family—was crucial to the family's involvement. In that project, the worker engaged initially in discussion with the family rather than in activities, in an effort to identify problems that were not too anxiety provoking and held some promise of solution. Workers "moved toward solution of the problem before identifying it." At later stages, after more trust of the worker had developed, more explicit efforts were made to identify problems and establish priorities for the problem-solving effort.

Like Bandler, Lance (1969) is also explicit about efforts to work with the parents. Both gave relatively less attention to engaging the children in the initial phases of contact, though they appear to do so at later stages. They, along with King (1967) and McKinney (1970), are very concerned to meet the material needs of the families, and they minimize the fear that meeting needs will result in insatiable demands. The needs are real, not just a manifestation of psychological dependency. Meeting needs is essential to the functioning of the family on the material level. It is also important psychologically in conveying a sense of being valued and cared about.

Even though the worker often enters these families initially due to referral because of the needs of the children rather than the needs of the parents, the meeting of children's needs takes into account the parents' rivalry with their children for attention and affection. Therefore, worker efforts in initial stages convey that the worker is there for the family, not only for the children. There is no necessity for a parent to feel that workers are concerned about the children "but not about me." The worker is in a position, in the conjoint sessions, to be responsive to the needs of all by being responsive to their communications and moving to meet needs as they are expressed. The worker's regulation of his relationship with the children, as with the parents, provides a structure which can offer relief and hope to the parents. As Levine (1964) and Scheinfeld et al. (1970) report, this has accomplished more by demonstration and modeling and less by telling or taking over. Parents are supported as adults and as parents by these means in the group.

There is a range in the responsiveness of poverty problem families to worker contact. Success is predicated on the family's willingness to continue contact with the worker, even though the members may be reluctant to allow the worker any power of influence in the family system. In other instances there may be total refusal of contact, except with authoritative pressure.

The authority to require family participation may be necessary in some instances. While the application of authority is a complex effort, we suggest its use in the initial phase primarily to require continuation of contact with the worker, rather than to require family members to engage in specific actions toward each other or with other systems. Where necessary, it can be valuable in allowing the worker time to establish credibility, trustworthiness, and interest so that the family can experience the worker as someone who can be useful to them. The inducement of specific behavior is better left to later contacts, when the family may be more ready to accept the worker's suggestions and try out new behavior.

97

Authoritative pressure and home visits may both be useful, but with some families they are not necessary for successful engagement. In the experience of Sager et al. (1968), some families were not only willing to continue but kept office appointments. Powell and Monoghan (1969) were successful in engaging families—mothers, identified child patients, and siblings of identified patients—by use of a multiple-family group which they saw as less threatening than work with one family at a time.

Assessment of the family's ability to cooperate is necessary to determine whether authoritative pressure, home visits, or office visits are initially most likely to result in family engagement or when shifts from one to the other technique may be needed.

In summary, initial contacts are characterized by the worker's efforts to become part of the family and thereby gain the trust of family members and their willingness to work on problems confronting them. Worker participation involves being available when needed, arranging to meet the family at home, encouraging the participation of as many members as possible, and being responsive to needs, problems, and process as they occur. The worker may participate through discussion or activity, or both. Activity covers a wide range, from games to tasks in the home to accompanying family members on visits to an agency, a clinic, or a school.

This emphasis on participation in the family is highly congruent with the activity orientation and the here-and-now emphasis of the family therapy field. The worker is placed in a position from which it is possible to alter the actions of family members by introducing information and behavior which the family itself does not generate, so as to achieve more favorable outcomes. Less emphasis is placed on insight and awareness than on trying new behavior and ways of relating. Worker participation makes support, information, suggestions, and other interventions possible when assessment indicates that they will be most meaningful. Proposing change in the midst of process offers opportunity for immediate tryout. The worker's intention is to provide nurturance and to demonstrate new coping skills which the parents may emulate and adopt as their own, activities which Wiltse (1958) has called "parenting the parents."

Problem Focus

In the initial phase, little time is devoted to making explicit the nature of the problem. The worker manifests interest and is responsive to the needs and concerns of the family as they are able to reveal them. Bandler (1967) has the worker making moves to meet needs without explicit joint definition of a problem. McKinney's (1970) examples indicate that problems or concerns identified by the children may be the basis for beginning work. In all instances, the response is to problems defined by the family rather than to concerns brought by the worker. Worker concerns may indeed be legitimate, but presentation of them at the outset is experienced by the family as yet another criticism from the hostile world rather than as a manifestation of caring about what the family cares about.

Some problems and concerns are revealed in the family's telling of them to the worker. Others are revealed in the interactions between members observed in the worker's participation with the family members in various activities. There are problems for the family to solve and problems in the problem-solving process to be corrected. Worker activity is directed to both.

Minuchin (1965) demonstrates one way in which work proceeds on both levels. In the early part of each session, specific concerns that have arisen are defined. Involved family members are asked to work on that concern while other members observe. The worker directs the interaction between family members in the problem-solving process. Within the overall definition of problems in family relationships, different problems may be addressed in each meeting with the family. These moves gradually make the definition of the problem to be solved more explicit. The problem to be solved becomes the problem in the family's problem-solving process. An example from our practice serves to illustrate what we mean:

A sequence began with the father's expressed concern about the inability of the high school graduate daughter to mobilize herself to find employment. Father was pushing mother to get the girl to "move." Her compliance would help with material needs and would serve as self-affirmation for him. Mother was defending the girl's inactivity, experiencing father's demands as an attack on her. Father became angry and discussion ended.

The worker focused attention on the parents' communication about the problem. Both agreed that the sequence was typical, and both were dissatisfied with the outcome. The worker agreed that the daughter's unemployment was a valid concern but promoted discussion between the parents so they could, as a parental subsystem, join together in helping their daughter. Both parents valued the opportunity for further discussion, particularly for the further expression of their respective points of view. Each of them felt the other had heard them in a new way. Mother could sense father's feelings of helplessness in helping the daughter. Father became aware that mother, beyond her defensiveness, shared his concern for the daughter's immobility. The interaction could now shift from "attack-defend" to "what can we do."

Thus the worker in the initial phase seeks to be responsive to family definitions of problems, without necessarily making them explicit. As the family's trust in the worker grows, the worker may take initiative in defining problems and even in ordering priorities among them. While work on the problems proceeds, the worker also attends to the problems in the family's problem-solving process which may increasingly become the focus treatment work.

INTERVENTIONS IN FAMILY COMMUNICATIONS

The interventions described in this section are directed to the family's problem-solving operations which have resulted in ineffective responses to internal or external problems. Some of them have been introduced in the discussion of initial engagement of the family, when they are indeed useful and often needed.

When family communication patterns are faulty, they do not result in decisions to change or undertake new action. Things are left hanging when attention is diverted, or there is overt disagreement and no way to resolve it. As the family persists in its unproductive ways, positive feelings shared among members dissipate. The worker's role in regulating the family's communications must therefore be an active one.

Satir (1967) suggests communication procedures which apply in treatment of problem poverty families, and Minuchin (1967) offers rules for the regulation of communication in treatment sessions. The worker's activity regarding communications in poverty families is not notably different in kind from that used in other families. The need to persist in regulation due to the family's intense persistence in familiar modes is increased, however.

The worker may attempt to state rules of communication at the outset, though this is not generally effective, or may simply attempt to regulate communications according to the rules. The particular topic or problem

100

under discussion may be money, school work, employment, going out, housekeeping, caring, or obedience. Any topic or presented problem serves the purpose. The worker's attention is directed to the way in which the family works on the problem.

The first rule for such communication disallows interruptions. The worker conveys an interest in what each member has to say, making clear that other members will have their chances to be heard. The worker may block interruptions in various ways. A verbal intervention may be used: "I want to hear what mother is saying. Then I will hear from you." Sometimes a hand motion directed to the interrupter and a body inclination toward the speaker will serve the same purpose. In other instances the worker may need to move himself between the speaker and interrupter to block the interruptions. Though the no-interruptions rule is useful when there is much simultaneous talking and interrupting, it is not absolute. Interruptions for purposes of seeking information or clarification have been found to be useful (Alexander & Parsons, 1973), and worker directives may permit or encourage such interruptions.

There are other forms of interruption. Two members discussing an issue may be interrupted by a third. The third person may be diverting attention to his own needs or may, in the midst of intense disagreement, take sides or assume a peacemaker role. While this is interruption of process rather than of speech, it leaves the situation unclear and lacking in resolution. The worker who becomes aware of the pattern therefore may draw attention to the process or block its reoccurrence. The worker may give recognition to the interrupter's anxiety and the reasons for it or may return to the original speakers to encourage them to work on the issues at hand.

The worker also seeks to have family members be specific about the person to whom a communication is addressed, and what it is that the person is being told. Thus, if a parent is complaining about the children that "they never" or "they always," the worker may determine which child is of particular concern and ask the parent to address that child about a specific behavior. Similarly, in response to a generalized complaint about a spouse, the worker might suggest talking to the spouse about a specific incident. One intent in this procedure is also to help family members talk to each other rather than to the worker. Talking to the worker rather than to the family member carries a message about the inability of family members to talk usefully with one another, and thus it represents an impasse in their communication. A second intent of this procedure is to begin the process of separating persons out as individuals. It makes clear that persons have separate identities and are not simply a part of the family mass.

The language deficit in problem poverty families may mean that members have difficulty putting into words what they feel or want. Workers can usefully put things into words for family members, being careful to check that this expresses what the individual wishes to convey to others. Rephrasings are often necessary to capture the meaning intended and to enable the person being addressed to understand. Failure in comprehending may be neither lack of clarity of expression nor lack of understanding, however. Rather, the hearer does not like what is being said. Once it is certain that the hearer is clear about what is being said, his or her disagreement or agreement with it may be pursued.

Many communications reflect a continuing tendency to express blame, anger, or hostility. Behind angry communications lies an unexpressed wish for relatedness and self-affirmation. Angry expression defeats the fulfillment of the wish and does not gain the end desired. For example: "You never take me anywhere" sounds like an accusation, which arouses defensiveness. The wish for companionship and relatedness is not revealed. If it were revealed it might serve to bring the sender and the receiver of the message together in a new way. Similarly, a parent's command to a child may be perceived as hostile or controlling but it may be due to concern about what may happen to a child in the present or the future. The child hears only the command and resists, but if the caring or concern can be identified and labeled, a new, more responsive relationship might develop. The worker may relabel or rephrase such negative communications to draw attention to the wish imbedded in them and to the self-defeating aspects of their continued use. This activity alters communication processes as well as the relationships among family members.

The injunction to address remarks to someone specific implies an expectation that the person addressed will respond relevantly. If the communication has been clear relevant responses are easier, and irrelevant ones are easier to detect. Topic changes are the most frequent form of irrelevant response. These often come in the form of countercomplaints or the raising of another issue that takes precedence in the eyes of the respondent. Though it may be a defensive maneuver, it has the overt effect of substituting a new issue for one already stated, which is then left unresolved. The worker may regulate the irrelevant responses in several ways. He may comment that the response did not seem to connect with the original comment. He may ask the speaker whether the response was what he wanted the other to comment on. Or he may ask the respondent to reply to a specific aspect of the previous remark.

These directives require family members to convey clear, explicit messages, and to listen. Since verbal expression and active listening are frequently not part of the family's repertoire, compliance with the worker's directives will not be easy, automatic, or prompt. The intense and immediate need of family members to be heard and recognized will promote the persistence of established patterns. However, if the need to be heard and recognized is to be gratified, it is important that the old patterns be interrupted. There may be extreme difficulty in interrupting them. Minuchin (1965) has removed some family members to another room behind one-way glass with another worker to make certain that their listening status is enforced. Most interviewing situations, either at home or in an office, do not allow for such separation unless there are co-workers for the family. In that case separate discussions may be possible, though separate listening or observation is not. Even then, space limitations may prevent the separation. In the most difficult situations, workers may have to schedule separate interviews for different family subsystems.

The worker's efforts to enable the exchange of information that is useful to problem solving also has the effect of reducing the negative affective component of the communications and enhancing positive messages. Over time, as issues are dealt with and members feel heard, the noise level is reduced, and the aggressive, hostile overtones become minimized. The atmosphere becomes more conducive to positive feeling about other members and about the family group.

In problem poverty families there is frequently a need to reduce the negative affective component of communication in relation to the informational or content aspect. In this regard they appear to contrast greatly with other families, in which the communication of feeling and information has been inhibited. However, feeling may also be inhibited in some members and in some families in the problem poverty category. In that event, worker activity seeks to draw out the member who is silent or who avoids expression of feeling in what she or he says. This effort enables that member to produce missing information or to express feeling for family reaction and processing.

The worker's regulation of the family process through these rules of communication blocks or alters existing processes within the family. The underlying assumption is that effective use of language to convey information and meaning is essential to problem solving. When meanings and exchange about the problems become clear, effective problem solving can take place.

The worker's regulation of the communication process during the interview also provides family members with a different experience with one another. New information can alter the images they have of one another and provide them with new understanding. The communication process the worker requires in the interview can be modeled by family members for use in day-to-day exchanges when the worker is not there. In addition to correction of the family problem-solving process, specific family problems such as school attendance, finances, health, or employment are also being solved.

INTERVENTIONS IN FAMILY STRUCTURE

Interventions in structure are designed to do several things. They serve to support the adults as parents who can provide the direction and structure needed by the children for adequate socialization and emotional growth. In this there is an implication that there will consequently be less need for the children to function as parents or for generational boundaries to become unclear and diffuse. Interventions in this area also seek to strengthen the marital relationship, if there is one, or to provide the single parent with some source of satisfaction of the need for growth and emotional support outside of the relationship to the children.

The first aspect of worker intervention in structure relates to family rules. Engagement with the family in activities or in interviews ensures the worker's presence during parent-child interactions, which reveal the inconsistencies about rules and expected behaviors. A worker engaged with a child in a game or activity can make his or her expectations of the child's behavior in the game clear and consistent. Parents may observe and use the worker as a model, or the worker may be able to discuss with parents what has happened, what the parents might have done if the worker had not been there, and whether the parents see the intervention as useful. Discussions can elicit what behaviors parents want from their children and can clarify whether the means the parents use are successful in obtaining those desired responses. Their wish to be good parents and to have children who know how to behave, to be responsible, and to succeed is identified and openly supported. Parental directives to a child, even when they sound hostile or attacking, may be redefined, for both parent and child, as an expression of parental concern. Parents may be more readily able to acknowledge such wishes and concerns as they feel the interest and support of the worker. If a parent, for example, responds with an angry "no," the worker may label this as the parent's concern to provide guidance for the child. This relabeling provides the child with new information about the parent's behavior and also increases parental awareness of the caring component of his or her own behavior.

The worker may also clarify whether the parental directive is just for the present situation or for other similar occasions also. If it is also for other occasions, the parent may be encouraged to provide explanation or further instruction. Rewards for compliance and consequences of noncompliance are discussed in advance. If the parent does delegate household or parenting tasks, the parent may be helped to be explicit about the exact duties, how much authority the child has over the other children, and what they are to do when other children do not cooperate. Such discussions assume that parents are operating out of a deficiency of knowledge and skills about parenting and can gain by awareness and specific direction (Wiltse, 1958; Levine, 1964; McKinney, 1970). They also, by implication, leave the parents in control of the structure provided for the child. The child can be gratified by parental attention. As his behavior becomes more consistent and tests the parent less and less, he can also be gratified at the fewer occasions for hostile outbursts. Parents can be relieved that the child has become clear about the rules for behavior and welcome the reduced need to regulate it.

Another aspect of worker intervention in structure relates to the role of the parental child. The delegation of responsibility to a parental child has served to provide the parent some needed support. It also puts the child in a special position with the parent. Both parent and child may therefore have difficulty in relinquishing the special relationship. The parental child needs to feel that other activities and relationships can be rewarding. The worker therefore acts to move the child back to a child's role and to connect him with his peers, as well as to connect the parent more explicitly to the adult generation.

In the sense that parents compete with their children for recognition and attention, they operate more as members of the child generation, less as an adult subsystem. The worker's attention, therefore, needs to be directed to enabling both parents to move back into the parent generation. They need to feel that becoming more active as parents can produce results and be gratifying. If needs for self-affirmation and affection have been met by the child, the worker moves to connect the parents with other sources of adult support.

Where both parents are present in the home, this means work on strengthening the marital relationship, in addition to strengthening parental functioning. Work on the relationship between the parents, similar to any such effort in marital counseling, can be productive. Work on communication processes, on clarification of roles and expectations, and on finding ways of gratifying and supporting each other is useful, as it is for any other couple. Achievement of some success as parents may also reduce the stress on the marriage. Successful involvements outside the home, such as a satisfying work situation, can also be useful in relieving the burden on the marriage for satisfaction of emotional needs, putting the partners in a better position to be responsive and giving to each other.

Where only one parent remains in the family, the worker similarly seeks to reduce the parent's dependence on the children for support, gratification, and self-affirmation. Relationships with other adults are encouraged, and if none exist, the worker may provide a bridge to new associations with peers or peer groups. Single-parent associations, therapy groups, or family life education programs may provide both support and guidance. Encouragement of the parent's participation with peers in recreational, educational, or community-directed activity has specific value of its own, but it also emphasizes to the parent his or her worthwhileness and provides needed separateness from the children.

WORK WITH THE EXTENDED FAMILY

While not an immediate part of the family system, extended family relationships are a problematic aspect of family experience and have a strong impact on family structure and functioning. Orcutt (1977) has drawn attention to the ways in which the problems of the extended family become the problems of the family. In problem poverty families, the need to help family members deal constructively with the problems of their kin may mean enabling them to connect with needed services. In Orcutt's example, the worker helped with the psychiatric hospitalization of a parent. When relieved of these burdens, the nuclear family began to cope more effectively.

In other instances, the problem is more one of conflicted relationships. The parent or parents have not separated and are overconnected to families of origin. They are still struggling with issues of control or being cared about and find themselves unable to maintain their separateness from parents or siblings. Material dependence may inhibit individuation and achievement of psychological independence. Their lack of material and psychological independence from the family of origin leaves them in conflict with spouses. Or, the struggle over separateness draws the children in, leaving the child distanced from a grandparenting relationship which might otherwise be gratifying. In other instances, a grandparent may compete against a natural parent for a child's favor. The social worker assists the parent in achieving individuality and separateness from his or her parents. In Orcutt's example, the achievement of psychiatric hospitalization likely required the resolution of ambivalence between the older two generations, and achievement of some capacity for separation of self and other. Work on these problems may be undertaken conjointly, as is the work within the nuclear family group, or in separate interviews.

Minuchin et al. (1967) comment on the "nonexistent grandmother" often found in problem poverty families. This role is taken by the mother in a three-generation family in which the middle generation is an adolescent daughter who has borne children and still lives in the same household with her parent or parents. She herself has not achieved sufficient emancipation and separation from her parent or parents. She is still dependent on them for guidance, direction, and control. She is both child and mother, and caretaking responsibilities for her child are ill-defined. Expectations and role definitions of grandmother/mother and mother/daughter are unclear. Treatment work needs to clarify these with much the same procedure used to make explicit any of the family's roles, rules, and expectations. Duties can be defined so that the grandchild is not neglected and so that a reduced amount of conflict occurs between mother and grandmother.

The "man in the house," another member in problem poverty families who often suffers from role ambiguity, may both be and not be a part of the family. The family therapist sees his presence as an important element in the family system and therefore includes him in the problem-solving process. This male figure often offers real support of both a material and a psychological nature. He may provide the affection and satisfaction needed by a mother so that she can lead the family or reduce her inappropriate leaning on her children in general or a parental child in particular. Kaslow (1972) notes that this person's presence gives rise to an issue for family treatment in public social services when his integration in the family may mean a reduction in the financial assistance provided it. This tenuous position may interfere with his effective integration.

Other factors also attest to his not being an integral part of the family. His position vis-à-vis children to whom he is not father is often ill-defined. The mother conveys contradictory messages about whether she does or does not want him to assume parenting responsibility, preventing him from disciplining the children, even if they are left in his care. The unclarity of his role creates conflicts for him and for the children. What to do becomes an issue of the work in treatment for her, for him, and for the children. This is accomplished by resolving ambivalence and by clarification of roles and rules of the relationships.

The definition of family for treatment purposes should include all those who are significantly related to the family, whether by blood, physical presence, or social contact. Activity among any of these persons in the network of relationships affects the functioning of the family for better or worse. Worker-induced change any place in the network may bring about significant improvement in the life of the family.

REDUCING FAMILY ISOLATION

Because the problem poverty family often lacks constructive contact with community institutions, it may not make use of the resources that are available. Children are not enrolled in day care centers or after-school free-time programs. Parents themselves do not utilize available enrichment or educational groups that could offer them psychological support as well as direct guidance and help for the family and thereby reduce the stress on the members and their relationships. Therefore it is an explicit goal of family work to establish connections to community institutions (Bandler, 1967; Scheinfeld et al., 1970). The bridging effort often requires the worker to accompany one or more family members to new locations to establish contacts with the workers providing those services or with members of other families who are participating. Since some family members may be more ready than others to participate, the worker must direct attention to the way some members undermine the efforts of others to relate to new services or individuals.

The family's increasing openness to these new relationships may be attributed to the trust they acquire in the worker. It is also, in part, a function of the restructuring of the relationships and communication processes. The family's utilization of these resources offers more natural support for the family and may reduce over time the amount of worker investment required.

REORIENTING EXTERNAL SYSTEMS

In the systems frame of reference only part of the family's isolation in the community and lack of positive relations in the community may be attributed to the family itself. We have suggested that the operations of external systems often work to the direct disadvantage of the family, through policies that divide the family or restrict the resources available to it. In addition, as Hoffman and Long (1969) suggest, agencies sometimes work at cross-purposes, further undermining the performance of individual members and the integrity of the family group.

Family members may learn, when they don't know how, to relate to external systems in ways that produce advantage for them. But direct worker intervention is often needed to help loosen interpretations of restrictive policies or to coordinate when policies of different agencies are at cross-purposes. The worker's interpretation to agencies of the functioning and needs of the family is one direct way of intervening. Case conferences with several agencies are often needed. Joint conferences between the family members and workers from several agencies may also be helpful. These are particularly significant when a given agency is acquainted with only part of the family and is unaware of or does not understand significant aspects of the family situation. The effort of the family worker is to orient all personnel involved with the family to the family as a whole.

Worker brokerage on behalf of the family brings full circle the range of interventions with poverty problem families. More complete discussions of this function have been undertaken elsewhere (Orcutt, 1973; Grosser, 1965). Though we have directed our attention primarily to work with the family itself, and to the need to participate with the family in engaging agencies, we do not thereby minimize the importance of the worker's roles of broker and advocate for the family.

109

NOTES ABOUT CO-WORKERS AND AGENCIES

The work with problem poverty families suggests a number of reasons for the involvement of more than one worker with a family. The first has to do with the need for the ready availability of workers. The family's sense of urgency as well as the immediateness of some needs often require quick responses, when a specific worker may not be available. A second worker involved with the family may be able to meet these needs or to help them cope with the issue.

A second reason for the involvement of more than one worker is for simultaneous work on family issues by subsets of family members (Mostwin, 1974). Subsets of family members may be separated to work simultaneously on the same issue, or to continue work on a separate issue by one subset of persons. Parents and children may be separated into subsets for work on a particular issue, or a parent and a child may become a subset, while other children are withdrawn to observe or work on different problems. These arrangements are more feasible if more than one worker is engaged with the family.

A third reason for using co-workers is that simultaneous work on the involvements and concerns of more than one member of the family as they affect the family may be necessary. The extent of worker activity required would sometimes exhaust the time, if not the energy, of a single worker. The multiple problems of problem poverty families require that some problems be given priority over others, but long delays in the work on any of them may not be possible. The involvement of a second worker may avoid the necessity of leaving work on a particular problem incomplete while another crisis is addressed.

Co-workers of different sexes are suggested, to offer models of the ways males and females can work together as well as the ways two adults can work together. While their work together can generally be expected to be harmonious, it may also demonstrate conflicts. Family awareness of these conflicts is not destructive if the workers can also demonstrate means for the resolution of disagreement.

The presence of a second worker can provide support for a family member when, in the midst of all that is going on, the other worker may not be as aware of the need. A male's support of the wife's position may offer something new to the husband. A female worker's support of the husband can have similar effects. Disagreements with persons of the same or opposite sex and efforts to resolve them may also provide a new experience for family members. Besides being advantageous for the family, a co-worker's presence may be an advantage to a worker who has become overidentified with a member of the family and has thereby lost the ability to be effective with the group. A co-worker can sometimes spot such pitfalls and help extricate the therapeutic effort from them.

The involvement of more than one worker with the family requires substantial agency, and thereby community, commitment to the family. Intervention with problem poverty families also requires agency commitments to change in attitudinal orientation, information supply needs, scheduling arrangements, and adequate provision of services and resources to help these families. Such commitment of personnel and services on behalf of the poor is largely lacking. Unless increased commitments are made, it will be difficult to know how much of the despair and conflict in individuals and families can thereby be lifted, and how much more direct work on the family's organization and process will be needed.

TREATMENT PROGRAM EFFECTIVENESS

The techniques and strategies described here have been tried and found useful in a variety of settings with problem poverty families. They have been shown to work where other types of efforts with similar families have produced minimal or no change. Our experience, and that of others we have referred to, does not suggest that this approach and these techniques always produce change. It only suggests that the conceptual orientation and techniques may in some instances be more effective than other strategies.

There is no systematic research on the application of these techniques to problem poverty families. Such research would require before-and-after measures of family performance and would match the change against change in families which had not experienced treatment. While some of the efforts reported have attempted before-and-after measures and could assert with confidence that change took place, it is possible that the change might also have occurred without treatment, since no control families are reported in any of the studies.

In this sense, family treatment of problem poverty families suffers the same defects of evaluation that characterize the family therapy field in general (Wells, Dilkes, & Trivelli, 1972; Briar & Miller, 1971). Other kinds

111

of efforts with problem poverty families have been evaluated much more thoroughly and extensively. Geismar (1971) reviews the evaluations of effectiveness of a number of those projects. He concludes that effort to help such families must attend to the material as well as the interpersonal aspects of the family situation and that intervention which is multi-faceted has an edge over single-method efforts. Resources as well as treatment must be available. Though the facets he defines are not necessarily the same as the efforts we have described, we also advocate multiple modes or points of intervention. He concludes that intervention with problem poverty families has been shown to produce positive change. With this we also concur.

Without minimizing the need for further systematic evaluation of the family group approach, we do assert that the approaches we have described can be effective in producing change. The projects that have undertaken before-and-after assessment of the families offer one basis for such an assertion (Levine, 1964; Minuchin et al., 1967). There is a further basis in the report of Sager et al. (1968) that change to family system strategies resulted in greater continuance in treatment of the population served, though not necessarily of the same families.

Further research is needed to identify which aspects of theory and technique account for the usefulness of a family group approach. It should ascertain that successes are attributable to the theory and techniques rather than to the talent of particularly skilled practitioners who might have used other techniques with similar success. It also needs to isolate the characteristics of families that enable them to respond under these conditions of treatment. And finally, research should identify more explicitly the mix of external system change and internal family change that is needed to provide relief from poverty status and to improve in general the functioning of the family group and its individual members.

SUMMARY

The poverty families discussed in this chapter are those with multiple problems. The focus on the family as a group as it is affected by external systems differentiates our approach from much other work on this category of families. Problem poverty families are heavily affected by their negative position in relation to external systems. The failure of external systems to provide material or psychological support, status, or information leaves the family to its own resources, with negative effects on the relationships among family members. Parents experience losses in self-esteem, lack status with each other and with their children, and abdicate their leadership roles within the family. Generational boundaries become blurred, with children taking on parental roles. Communication processes do not contribute to problem solving. Both family structure and process are inadequate to the problem-solving effort.

Treatment for problem poverty families is a complex effort. Solving the family's problems and improving its means of problem solving are concurrent, not sequential, tasks. The social worker approaches the whole family so that each member can feel the worker's interest without having to vie for the worker's acceptance and recognition. The worker moves quickly to meet material as well as emotional needs. Home visits, participation with the family in a variety of activities, and talking are vehicles for interaction with the worker. The worker moves to strengthen the parental subsystem, to change communication patterns, and to enhance the family members' solidarity and cohesiveness, in the context of work on problems presented by the family. Since family members are often socially isolated, the worker helps connect them with the extended family, recreational resources, social contacts, and agency supports. Agency attitudes and practices frequently have a negative impact on the family, requiring the worker to serve as broker and advocate for the members.

Co-workers are recommended for the family because of the multiplicity of tasks for and with the family. Changed agency attitudes and practices are seen as necessary for effective intervention. The treatment procedures we outline have been tested in practice. However, there is a paucity of research about the effects of treatment for problem poverty families.

REFERENCES

Alexander, J. F., and Parsons, B. "Short-Term Behavioral Intervention with Delinquent Families." *Journal of Abnormal Psychology*, 81:219-25, 1973.

Angell, R. G. *The Family Encounters the Depression*. New York: Scribners, 1934.

Bandler, L. "Casework: A Process of Socialization." In E. Pavenstedt (ed.), *The Drifters*. Boston: Little, Brown & Co., 1967.

Barnes, G. G. "Working with the Family Group." *Social Work Today*, 4:65-70, 1973.

Billingsley, A. "Family Functioning in the Low-Income Black Community." *Social Casework*, 50:563-72, 1969.

Bowen, M. "Family Therapy and Family Group Therapy." In H. Kaplan and B. Sadock (eds.), *Comprehensive Group Psychotherapy.* Baltimore: Williams and Wilkins Co., 1971.

Briar, S., and Miller, H. *Problems and Issues in Social Casework,* Chap. 11. New York: Columbia University Press, 1971.

Cade, B. "Therapy with Low Socio-Economic Families." *Social Work Today,* 6:142-45, 1975.

Chilman, C. "Social Work Practice with Very Poor Families: Some Implications Suggested by Available Research." *Welfare in Review,* 4:13-21, 1966.

Chilman, C. "Families in Poverty in the Early 1970's: Rates, Associated Factors, Some Implications." *Journal of Marriage and the Family,* 37:49-62, 1975.

Freeman, H., Hoffman, M., Smith, W., and Prunty, H. "Can a Family Agency be Relevant to the Inner-Urban Scene?" *Social Casework,* 51:12-31, 1970.

Geismar, L. L. "Implications of a Family Life Improvement Project." *Social Casework,* 52:455-65, 1971.

Geismar, L. L., and Ayres, B. "Evaluating Social Functioning of Families Under Treatment." *Social Work,* 4:102-8, 1959.

Grosser, C. "Community Development Programs Serving the Urban Poor." *Social Work,* 10:15-21, 1965.

Hallowitz, D. "Counseling and Treatment of the Poor Black Family." *Social Casework,* 56:451-59, 1975.

Hess, R., and Handel, G. *Family Worlds.* Chicago: University of Chicago Press, 1959.

Hoffman, L., and Long, L. "A Systems Dilemma." *Family Process,* 8:211-34, 1969.

Holland, D. "Familization, Socialization and the Universe of Meaning." *Journal of Marriage and the Family,* 23:415-26, 1970.

Kaslow, F. W. "How Relevant Is Family Counseling in Public Welfare Settings?" *Public Welfare,* 30:18-25, 1972.

King, C. H. "Family Therapy with the Deprived Family." *Social Casework,* 48:203-8, 1967.

Laing, R. "Family and Individual Structure." In P. Lomas (ed.), *The Predicament of the Family.* New York: International Universities Press, 1967.

Lance, E. A. "Intensive Work with a Deprived Family." *Social Casework,* 50:454-60, 1969.

Levine, R. "Treatment in the Home." *Social Work,* 9:19-28, 1964.

Lewis, J. M., Beavers, W. R., Gossett, J. T., and Phillips, V. A. *No Single Thread: Psychological Health in Family Systems.* New York: Brunner/Mazel, 1976.

McAdoo, H. "Development of Self-Confidence and Race Attitude in Black Children: A Longitudinal Study." In W. E. Cross, Jr. (ed.), *Third Conference on Empirical Research in Black Psychology.* Washington, D.C.: U.S. Department of Health, Education, and Welfare, 1977.

McAdoo, J. "Relationships between Black Father-Child Interaction and Self-Esteem in Preschool Children." In W. E. Cross, Jr. (ed.), *Third Conference on*

Empirical Research in Black Psychology. Washington, D.C.: U.S. Department of Health, Education, and Welfare, 1977.

McKinney, G. E. "Adopting Family Therapy to Multi-Deficit Families." *Social Casework,* 51:327-33, 1970.

Minuchin, S. "Conflict Resolution Family Therapy." *Psychiatry,* 28:278-86, 1965.

Minuchin, S., and Montalvo, B. "Techniques for Working with Disorganized Low-Socio-Economic Families." *American Journal of Orthopsychiatry,* 37:880-87, 1967.

Minuchin, S., Montalvo, B., Guerney, B., Rosman, B., and Schumer, F. *Families of the Slums.* New York: Basic Books, 1967.

Mostwin, D. "Multidimensional Model of Working with the Family." *Social Casework,* 55:209-15, 1974.

Moynihan, S. "Home Visits for Family Treatment." *Social Casework,* 55:712-17, 1974.

Orcutt, B. "Casework Intervention and the Problems of the Poor." *Social Casework,* 54:85-95, 1973.

Orcutt, B. "Family Treatment of Poverty Level Families." *Social Casework,* 58:92-100, 1977.

Perlman, H. *Social Casework.* Chicago: University of Chicago Press, 1957.

Powell, M., and Monoghan, J. "Reaching the Rejects through Multi-Family Group Therapy." *International Journal of Group Psychotherapy,* 19:35-43, 1969.

Rabinowitz, C. "Therapy for Underprivileged 'Delinquent' Families." In O. Pollack and A. Friedman (eds.), *Family Dynamics and Female Sexual Delinquency.* Palo Alto, Cal.: Science and Behavior Books, 1969.

Reid, W., and Shyne, A. *Brief and Extended Casework.* New York: Columbia University Press, 1969.

Sager, C., Masters, Y., Ronall, R., and Normand, W. "Selection and Engagement of Patients in Family Therapy." *American Journal of Orthopsychiatry,* 38:715-23, 1968.

Satir, V. *Conjoint Family Therapy.* Palo Alto, Cal.: Science and Behavior Books, 1967.

Scheinfeld, D. R., Bowles, D., Tuck, S. J., and Gold, R. "Parents' Values, Family Networks, and Family Development: Working with Disadvantaged Families." *American Journal of Orthopsychiatry,* 40:413-25, 1970.

Stack, C. *All Our Kin.* New York: Harper & Row, 1974.

Umbarger, C. "The Paraprofessional and Family Therapy." *Family Process,* 11:147-62, 1972.

Wells, R., Dilkes, T., and Trivelli, N. "The Results of Family Therapy: A Critical Review of the Literature." *Family Process,* 11:189-207, 1972.

Wiltse, K. "The Hopeless Family." *Social Work,* 3:12-22, 1958.

CHAPTER **5**

Adult Children and Aging Parents

The composition of a family is usually considered to be centered around two adults (parents) and one or more children living in the same household. The parents are the oldest members of the family and are considered to be in charge and to carry some type of executive authority as part of their responsibility. However, this is not the only family composition social workers encounter in professional practice. Some families are headed by only one parent; others include relatives outside of the nuclear family, friends of long standing, and so on—all of whom interact with each other in predictable ways to form a functional unit.

One family makeup with which social workers are becoming increasingly involved consists of adult children and their aging parents. The members of this family may or may not live in the same household, and the oldest members do not usually carry executive responsibility for the system. In fact, the reverse is true, in that the adult children are considered responsible for planning and providing to meet the needs of their parents.

Working with adult children and their parents as a family unit is not a completely new experience for social workers. We believe it is an area of

The authors express appreciation to Dorothy V. Harris, Assistant Director of Social Work for Medicine and Emergency Medicine, The Johns Hopkins Hospital, Baltimore, for her assistance in developing this chapter.

practice which is deserving of more attention, however. There is increasing evidence that social workers are steadily becoming more involved in planning with elderly clients, within the context of a family which includes their adult children.

In examining families of this composition, this chapter will discuss prevailing attitudes toward the elderly, pertinent aspects of the aging process, and underlying dynamics of intergenerational family transactions. Some suggestions for intervention with adult children and their aging parents will also be considered.

ATTITUDES TOWARD THE AGED

The increased awareness of older citizens and their need to participate in society in meaningful ways is a positive trend, in our estimation. Underlying attitudes which are somewhat derogatory toward the elderly and the aging process persist, however. Many of these attitudes seem to grow out of a well-established belief in individuality, self-reliance, and productivity as symbolic of the preferred life-style in our society. This lends support to the value of youth and leaves less than sufficient room for reward to the aged who, for various reasons, no longer may be completely independent or able to make a substantial material contribution to society.

Studies have revealed a number of stereotypes about older persons in our society. Spence, Feigenbaum, Fitzgerald, and Roth (1968) found medical students perceived old people as "more emotionally ill, disagreeable, inactive, economically burdensome, dependent, dull, socially undesirable, dissatisfied, socially withdrawn, and disruptive of family harmony than youth or adults" (p. 979).

Wolk and Wolk (1971) report similar attitudes among student social workers and other professional practitioners.

Research, however, has found most negative stereotypes about the elderly to be untrue. For example, the belief that the aged person loses intelligence and cannot master the learning of new material was not substantiated by the findings of Dennis (1966) or Butler (1967). Some also hold that the older person is a nonproductive member of society. This was not supported by Soddy (1967) and others who have compared age and productivity. For example, most of the studies regarding age and output in the work situation have shown a slight positive relationship between output

117

and age, or none at all (Soddy, 1967, p. 87). The same was generally true with regard to such work-related factors as absenteeism, accidents, and illnesses.

The health of the aged is questioned by many who believe their physical condition renders them susceptible to frequent illnesses that limit most of their activities. In addition, it is widely assumed that the elderly are usually disengaged from their families and live in relative isolation. Neither assumption is supported by research findings. A National Health Survey (National Center for Health Statistics, 1964-65) showed that most persons in this group were able to perform in their major activity roles. And Shanas, Townsend, Wedderbrun, Friis, Milhoj, and Stehouwer (1968) reported frequent contacts between a large majority of older persons and their relatives.

Social workers and other professionals intervening in situations involving the elderly should be careful not to fall prey to these negative attitudes. Instead, they should view the aged differentially as individuals, the same as other clients, and proceed to meet their needs in the manner most appropriate for each situation.

THE AGING PROCESS

In order to work effectively with the family that includes adult children and their elderly parents, it is essential to have an understanding of the aging process and how it affects both parents and children. Although growing old is a normal phase in the individual life cycle, it is often the most difficult to accept by the older person who experiences it, as well as by their children who witness it. In various ways aging represents an ending process frequently associated with loneliness and dependency for the elderly. It is also a constant reminder of one's own mortality to younger persons who observe the aging of their elders.

The continuing desire to understand the aging process and its impact upon individuals and society has attracted numerous researchers. Havinghurst and Albrecht (1953), Cummings and Henry (1961), Tallmer and Kutner (1969), Lemon, Bengston, and Peterson (1972), and Maddox and Douglass (1974), to mention a few, have all addressed various aspects of the aging process. From these and other studies a number of theories have been suggested as a basis for understanding the process of growing old and the behavior shown by old people. While there is far from unanimous agreement among researchers, it seems fair to say that there is general agreement that older people display behavior which supports the belief that they tend to disengage from the interactional processes of society. However, the extent of disengagement and the casual factors underlying this process remain in question among researchers.

Up to this time most attention has been focused on two theories of aging: the theory of activity and the theory of disengagement.

Activity Theory

It is widely assumed that aged persons become increasingly less active and withdraw from some of the roles they have customarily fulfilled, or have these roles withdrawn from them. Many researchers have looked to activity among the aged for answers to the problems of adjustment in later life. Havinghurst and Albrecht (1953) studied the activity of this group and reported a positive relationship between social activity and satisfaction. A number of researchers have also reported corroborative findings. For example, Burgess (1954) found that persons with a high level of adjustment spent greater amounts of time in participation with social and voluntary organizations. Kutner, Fanshel, Togo, and Langner (1956) reported a significant relationship between high morale and a high level of activity.

Activity theory, as it relates to the aging process, grew out of these findings. It is based on the assumption that the social self is evidenced and sustained through interaction with others, as manifest in the performance of various life roles. It is specifically centered around the importance of social role participation as a means of realizing a satisfactory adjustment in later life.

More recent research by Lemon et al. (1972) tends to limit the applicability of activity theory. For example, their findings did not support all interpersonal and noninterpersonal activity as contributing to life satisfactions. They did not find a significant relationship between life satisfaction among the elderly and solitary activity such as watching television or reading a book. Social participation in formal organizations was also found to have no significant influence on feelings of satisfaction. However, significance was found between life satisfaction and informal activity with friends. This supports an earlier finding by Lowenthal and Haven (1968):

119

...it is clear that if you have a confidant, you can decrease your social interaction and run no greater risk of becoming depressed than if you had increased it. Further, if you have no confidant, you may increase your social activities and yet be far more likely to be depressed than the individual who has a confidant but has lowered his interaction level. Finally, if you have no confidant and retrench in your social life, the odds for depression become overwhelming. The findings are similar, though not so dramatic, in regard to change in social role: if you have a confidant, roles can be decreased with no effect on morale; if you do not have a confidant, you are likely to be depressed whether your roles are increased or decreased (though slightly more so if they are decreased). In other words, the presence of an intimate relationship apparently does serve as a buffer against such decrements as loss of role or reduction of social interaction. (pp. 26-27)

Therefore, based on more recent findings, it seems safe to assume that older people can benefit from access to someone in whom they can confide, and having a confidant is perhaps more important than engaging in activity per se.

Disengagement Theory

In studying the aging process, Cummings and Henry (1961) presented findings which indicated that the existence of older people was characterized by withdrawal from participation in the interactional processes of society. They defined this withdrawal as disengagement on the part of the aged, supported by the decreasing number of people with whom the aging individuals were involved and the amount of interaction they experienced with these associates. Underlying this decrease in involvement with others was a change in the personality of the elderly person which resulted in increased preoccupation with the self. This formal presentation by Cummings and Henry set forth the early framework of disengagement theory.

Over the years since these findings were reported, a number of researchers and writers have focused their attention on this theory. Bell (1976) is among those most recently concerned with the theory of disengagement, which he explains as follows:

By and large, the theory posits a functional relationship between the individual and society. The fact that individuals age and die and that society needs a continual replacement of "parts" is a fundamental tenet of the theory. In this view, both the person and society comprehend the necessity of the situation. As a consequence, the individual who can no longer produce effectively is expected to withdraw (i.e., disengage) from the on-going social life about him. . . . The disengagement processes which eventuate in a self-oriented personality are held to contribute to the maintenance of psychological well-being in late life. (pp. 31-32)

Thus, disengagement theory suggests that disengagement from active society by aging people is a natural phenomenon from which both the individual and society benefit. Society gets a "new part" which enables it to continue at an optimal level of functioning, and the disengaged individual finds satisfaction in a new self-centered role. It is further implied that social and psychological withdrawal by older people from active participation in the social life around them may be a necessary part of a successful aging process.

The suggestion that the elderly person wishes to withdraw from social life as a normal consequence of growing old has been challenged by other researchers, including Tallmer and Kutner (1969). They suggest that certain concomitant life stresses associated with aging could produce the withdrawal reported by Cummings and Henry. In replicating the Cummings and Henry study, they studied the relationship of three independent variables—ill health, widowhood, and retirement—to the disengagement process. Their data provided substantial evidence that disengagement is not caused by aging but is the result of the impact of stresses, physical and social, and these stresses may be expected to increase with advancing years.

Both activity theory and disengagement theory have claimed the attention of many researchers, but there is no consensus as to the relationships of various factors operating within the framework of these theories. Based on the research that has been done, we hold with the view that disengagement is a differential experience of older people which has a strong relationship to the conditions of life as experienced by the individual. In the case of activity theory the people involved, the nature of the activity engaged in, and the degree of confidence shared among the participants seems to be of paramount importance in promoting feelings of well-being among the aged.

While we will not undertake to examine further or clarify these theories, we will borrow from both in accordance with the above statement. Role theory will also be drawn upon later in the chapter to promote understanding of some of the dynamics of relationship and to consider intervention strategies.

LOSSES EXPERIENCED BY THE AGED

Underlying the disengagement process of the aged is the experience of loss in several areas of functioning. Schwartz and Mensh (1974) speak of natural losses which occur over time in a more or less gradual manner. This includes functional deterioration with regard to vision, hearing, central nervous system functioning, use of body muscles, and so on. They also mention "culturally determined and circumstantial losses such as the breaking up of one's social network, economic loss, loss of assigned roles, and loss of options and/or privacy" (p. 8). In order to understand older people in their situations, social workers must be familiar with these losses and their potential effect on the life circumstances of this group.

Physiological Aging

Physiological aging is an area of medical expertise involving biological processes of the body, and we will deal with it only briefly and in relation to a few physical changes that can be readily observed. This is a significant part of the life cycle and perhaps the most noticeable process of change among older people. Signs of physiological change may vary to some extent among individuals and are most noticeable as the body begins to be somewhat less efficient in the performance of its customary life-sustaining functions. Among these changes is a gradual dehydration of muscles and other deteriorations that affect the normal functioning of body organs. This is usually accompanied by a loss of physical dexterity and feelings of tiredness. Some increase in blood pressure may also be experienced. Recovery from injuries and the healing of wounds are relatively slower among the elderly. Visual and hearing impairment, together with central nervous system changes that can result in forgetfulness and some decline in mental alertness, may occur.

While these physiological changes are recognized as a part of the aging process, they do not indicate an automatic onset of illness or the need to curtail older persons' performance of major activity roles. To the contrary, most of them are able to continue their major activities in spite of physiological aging.

These losses are not unnoticed by the elderly themselves. They are painfully aware of these changes, which come at a time when they are usually involved with fewer people and less frequently than in earlier life.

It is well for the social worker to be aware that older people may mourn the loss of physiological functioning in the same manner they experience the loss of a relative, a position, or a status in life.

Studies (Bartko, Patterson, & Butler, 1971; Kannel, 1971) have also shown that good physical health is related to activity. For the elderly activity is at least one means through which they can maintain contact with the world around them; and good health may be the key to sustained activity.

Psychological Aging

The process of aging psychologically is not completely separate from the biophysical process of aging. Indeed, it is very closely related in many ways. Biophysical influences are recognized, for example, in the tendency of older people to show a decrease in memory for more recent events, while at the same time demonstrating vivid recall of events and experiences which occurred many years before. This shift in memory to past events usually reflects on a period in the life cycle of aging individuals when they perceived themselves as more successful. Since a number of changes occur in later years that tend to threaten the self-image of the older person, perhaps this is one way of connecting with the experience of usefulness.

Among the losses experienced by old people the most inevitable is the breakup of their social network. Schwartz and Mensh (1974) suggest that one of the prices for surviving into the later years of life is the likelihood that most friends and associates, and sometimes many family members, are eventually eliminated, for various reasons, from the network with which the elderly interacts. Included in this process are the disruptions usually brought on by retirement. The social network of the retiree as it relates to economics, status, and roles represents perhaps the most significant disruption. In terms of economic loss many older people, upon termination of gainful employment, are faced with a change in the standard of living to which they were accustomed. For those who were able to maintain barely an adequate standard of living while fully employed, the loss of income by retirement frequently plunges them into poverty with all of the psychological implications of this status. For example, the elderly couple who manages to live independently, by careful management of the husband's income, might find themselves needing to depend more upon their children for financial assistance after his retirement. This is likely to

123

interfere with feelings of independence and contribute to a sense of growing insecurity for the older people.

Certain social losses also accompany disengagement from gainful employment. The reality of retirement usually means the end of a number of social and collegial activities such as lunches, attending conferences, union meetings, picnics, and so on. The older person does not easily replace these associations and in many cases may well drift toward a life of increased loneliness.

The emphasis of society on a youth culture imposes some limitation on the coping ability of the aged population. Physical attractiveness, strength, and success in competition are important attributes of a youth-oriented culture. However, these attributes diminish with age, and the elderly can no longer compete successfully for rewards which demand these attributes. Bowman (1956), in pointing up the relationship between physical changes and emotions, suggests skin wrinkles, loss or greying of hair, and other physical indications of aging may contribute to inferior feelings. If there is a decrease in sexual capacity or less enjoyment from the sexual experience, this too can contribute to feelings of depression in aging individuals. However, there is considerable disagreement among researchers and writers with regard to change in the sexual capacity of older people.

Intelligence and learning receive a good deal of attention from those who study and work with the elderly. It is generally accepted that a close relationship exists between these attributes, but some studies of intelligence show a decline with age, some show no change, and still others show an increase in intelligence among older people. The reason for the disparity may be the measuring processes used. The instruments used to measure intelligence in the elderly in many situations have drawn much criticism. Carp (1973) suggests that one of the problems with existing instruments is in the standardization of intelligence tests, which are based on the results achieved by younger people. The aged do not share common experiences with the younger group on whom most tests are standardized. Therefore, they cannot be expected to respond in the same way to material drawn from the experiences of young people (Carp, 1973, p. 119). As a result, an accurate measure of intelligence among the elderly is not likely to be obtained by the use of such instruments.

Carp also found a general lack of interest among the elderly in taking intelligence tests. Most of them think these tests have very little intrinsic value. This usually results in low motivation for taking such a test, which is likely to have a negative influence on the outcome.

Thus we conclude that a true determination of change in intelligence among older persons has not yet been achieved. In regard to learning, there is little evidence of change in learning itself among the aged. Nevertheless, learning in older people may be affected by interest and motivation in relation to what is to be learned. In other words, the degree of learning may be reduced if the new knowledge or experience is not in keeping with individual interest. Learning scores are also reduced by a slower rate of responses, which might be caused by disease or other biological dysfunctions common to the aging process.

According to Botwinick (1973), role relationships between men and women change during later years, as evidenced by women demonstrating more assertiveness and men showing more of their submissive impulses (p. 66). It is well to keep in mind that such changes can be problematic, especially when they involve a marital relationship. Consider the case of a husband who retires from his employment after many years of working and providing for his family. His retirement income is much less than his previous earnings, so his wife accepts a part-time job as a nursing aide and becomes involved in her work and the collegial atmosphere of the hospital. In addition to elevating her status to that of employee and breadwinner, she is the beneficiary of social gains no longer shared by her retired husband. By reason of his own change in role and status, the husband may experience serious damage to his self-esteem, and this can find expression in a deterioration of the marital relationship. Often, the deteriorating marital relationships of aging couples somehow manage to involve one or more of the adult children. The struggle that is likely to follow can soon escalate to a point where the family can no longer cope with the conflict, and help is sought from outside the family group.

WORKING WITH THE FAMILY

The focus in this section is on family transactions as experienced by adult children and their aging parents and the underlying dynamics of the functioning of families of this composition. The interactions between adult children and their parents must be understood before intervention into the dysfunctional processes that may occur as a result of these interactions can be undertaken.

We cannot overemphasize that the elderly are members of families, and their problems can best be viewed in the context of family interactions. Contrary to popular belief, ties between parents and their adult children are not always severed. Instead, contacts between them are quite frequent in most cases. Therefore, family therapy involving adult children and their parents is not only appropriate but necessary in many situations where the aged members are experiencing difficulty.

We hold with Brody (1966), who believes adult children generally behave in a responsible manner toward their parents. When they do not, the situation is often complicated by a constellation of personal, social, and economic forces. Therefore, in order to work effectively with adult children and their parents, the social worker must make a careful assessment of the existing situational and emotional factors as they relate to the transactions occurring between the two generations.

Within the broad guidelines of this assumption, we will consider some of the forces operating in extended family relations.

Defining the Problem

The assessment begins with some notion of how the presenting problem might be viewed. Savitsky and Sharkey (1972) report that there is little difference in the way a family presents itself to the social worker when it comes for help, whether the problem is aged parents or a rebellious adolescent. In either case the problem presented is frequently not in itself the problem with which help is most urgently needed. This is not to say the worker should ignore the problem as initially defined by the family. It is obvious that what the family presents is what they have singled out as their present concern, and this must be addressed in a way that is acceptable to them. We are suggesting, however, that when the problem presented concerns the aged parents, the worker should not overlook other possible aspects of the problem. For example, aging parents can create a great deal of anxiety for their children as a result of their inability to function independently or to accept altered roles in relation to the children. Adult children may also be experiencing guilt over their own inability to meet the needs of their elderly parents effectively.

When such underlying concerns are interfering with the problem-solving process, it may be necessary to focus on these concerns as a way of helping the children find the true source of their discomfort, en route to a more appropriate view of the parents' situation. The following case from our files demonstrates what a family may bring to the worker and what often lies beneath their expressed concerns.

The daughter requested and was granted some time for herself and her husband with the social worker at the nursing home where her 76-year-old mother was recently admitted. They had been seen during the admissions process, at which time both expressed satisfaction with the care the nursing home purported to provide. Nevertheless, the daughter was now complaining vigorously, with support from her husband, about the care her mother was receiving. She described her mother as a very neat person who was accustomed to clean surroundings and having her food prepared as she liked it. The daughter reported that on her last visit she had found her mother wearing clothes that were not clean, and she did not finish her meal. She was sure the food had not been properly prepared.

Finally, the daughter wondered if it had not been a mistake to place her mother in the nursing home. When questioned about this she was able to reveal a great deal of fear and concern about her mother's poor health; the demands her presence in their home had made on both her and her husband; and how much they had tried to provide the care she needed but had failed in these efforts. Nevertheless, the daughter still felt responsible for her mother's care and was not sure they could entrust this responsibility to the nursing home.

There was no objective reason for the complaints offered by the daughter about her mother's care. Further exploration revealed the primary problem was not the mother's care in the nursing home, but the anxiety her disability had created for the daughter and the guilt generated around the family's inability to care for her. A part of the work to be done here was to help the daughter and her husband cope with their feelings about themselves in relation to the health and physical needs of the wife's aged mother.

Relationships

Knowledge of the relationship that exists between adult children and their parents is crucial in work with the extended family. This is so, regardless of the problem presented. The social worker will find it useful to obtain some sense of the kind of parent-child relationships experienced

127

during the developmental stages of the adult children, and how this relationship developed over the years. Leach (1964) suggests:

The quality of a person's childhood relationship with his parents strongly influences his feelings toward them throughout his life. If it promotes his independence while meeting his normal dependency needs, he is better able to resolve his conflict between dependence and independence and to move away from his parents without guilt and crippling anxiety. At the same time he has no need to renounce the relationship; it remains warm and friendly....A child so reared expects and wants to share his and his children's life with his parents and to plan with and for the parents whenever they need his help. (p. 146)

This means that if the adult son or daughter shared a relationship with his or her parents during the early years which provided for growth and was experienced as satisfactory, the current relationship is likely to be sufficiently strong to make constructive problem solving a successful undertaking. On the other hand, if the earlier parent-child relationship was characterized by conflict and this conflict was not resolved, efforts to work with them at a later time are likely to be very difficult. This past unresolved conflict may return and interfere with the adult child's ability to help the parents and the parents' ability to accept help from the child (Leach, 1964, p. 146).

Bringing the adult child and parent together in a therapeutic situation when earlier conflicts have not been resolved, therefore, can produce undesirable consequences. For example, the child may see it as a chance to get revenge for what were perceived as earlier injustices from the parent. And the parent might view the coming together as an opportunity to renew the struggle to control the behavior of a disrespectful child. Sometimes guilt is encountered over past failures on the part of both parent and child. In any case, when the aging parent cannot function independently and needs the assistance of the adult child, the worker must act to resolve the conflict, if at all possible, and provide the help needed by the elderly family member.

It is usually helpful in these situations to assist the family members involved to talk about past and present experiences in order to deal with the guilt and anger that have characterized their relationship, and to reach a level of understanding that will allow the necessary planning to take place. Care should be taken to prevent the encounter from becoming only an opportunity for each to blame himself or place blame on the other. We have found it helpful in such cases to encourage self-responsibility for all by focusing on the way each individual is experiencing the other and what each can do to help change the way they are relating to each other.

It is well to recognize that the prospect is not always good for resolving long-standing conflicts in relationships between parents and adult children. A major problem experienced by social workers in cases of enduring parent-child conflict is getting the children involved with the parent and the problem situation. This apparent lack of interest is a primary factor in maintaining the conflict. The following case example from our experience demonstrates resistance to involvement with a parent when conflict remains.

Mrs. O, formerly a very successful buyer for a large department store, had for many years spent much of her time away from her family. Her misunderstandings with her two daughters apparently began during early childhood when the demands of her job prevented their spending time together. To compensate for this Mrs. O frequently bought them expensive gifts. When the daughters started to demand more of her time in pursuit of a closer relationship, she interpreted this as unreasonable and showed her irritation by threatening to discontinue the expensive gifts. At other times she would picture herself as a "poor misunderstood mother" and threaten to harm herself if her daughters "did not love her." Her husband also got his share of the blame from Mrs. O for the daughters wanting to spend more time with her. She considered Mr. O inadequate as a husband and father whose income as a clothing store salesman was considerably less than hers. They seemed to live in constant disagreement, and their verbal battles were well known throughout the neighborhood. When the daughters graduated from high school both chose universities outside of the state, much to the mother's dismay, as she perceived this as "running away" from her. And she never permitted them to forget this "ungrateful act."

Soon after retirement, Mrs. O began experiencing serious health problems. Mr. O, who suffered from asthma and arthritis, had retired earlier and was experiencing a great deal of difficulty himself. However, they were able to manage for a few years, but finally sought help when Mrs. O's physician recommended specialized care, and preferably a warmer climate. Both daughters were now married and lived in an ideal climate for their mother's condition. When contacted to see if they could be of assistance in planning for her, one daughter stated her mother still blamed her for "leaving home" and "ruining her health." This daughter left no doubt that she did not want her mother to move to the area where she was currently living. She expressed the belief that whatever she tried to do would be misinterpreted by her mother, and she was not willing to undergo the emotional strain of further involvement. The other daughter thought any closer involvement with her mother would destroy her marriage, as Mrs. O thought she had married "beneath herself."

She said her husband and her mother "hated each other" and she saw no way of improving her own relationship with her mother. The daughters were not willing to be involved beyond making limited financial contributions, if this was needed, in providing care for their mother.

This represents a seriously damaged relationship between adult children and parent. Only minimal participation in planning can be expected from the children in such cases.

We agree with those who maintain that when the conflict is unresolved, aged parents and their children will not be able to live comfortably together. When living arrangements for a parent are involved, it would be ill-advised to consider the parents moving into the home of a child with whom there is long-standing unresolved conflict. This is not to say that all hope of improving the relationship should be abandoned. If any evidence of positive aspects of a relationship remains, the worker should try to revive and build on what is left. However, until some improvement is realized in such cases, living arrangements should be separate.

Role Reversal

In working with aging parents and their adult children, it is important to understand the role shifts that occur between them. Several authors, including Glasser and Glasser (1962), Rautman (1962), and Field (1972), have defined this shift in roles between the two generations as role reversal. In commenting on the process involved in this shifting of roles, Peterson (1974) suggests, "If middle-aged sons or daughters feel their parents are no longer capable of making decisions, the children will take over this role and become parents to their parents" (p. 225). In other words, the elder who has carried the accustomed role of protector and provider for the child at an earlier point in time now gives up this role to the adult child and becomes the receiver of these benefits.

It is necessary to point up the disagreement that exists with regard to the concept of role reversal involving adult children and their elderly parents. The literature reflects the views of some authors who do not accept role reversal as an appropriate definition of what takes place when the adult child assists, protects, and provides for the parent who is unable to plan appropriately and provide for her or his own needs. For example, Brody (1971) suggests:

130

There can be no true role reversal....The help and protection given by an adult child to an old parent cannot be equated with psychological relationships. In feeling, though the adult child may be old himself, he remains in the relationship of child to parent; he does not become parent to his parent. (p. 56)

She sees the adult child's activities on behalf of the parent as indicative of a mature adult's capacity to be depended on by his parent.

The aged parent does not make a complete psychological transition from the adult role to that of a child; nor does the adult child completely transfer from the role of child to that of parent to a parent. The fact that both have long experience and emotional investment in their previous roles makes a complete psychological transition of roles unlikely. Yet the adult child is frequently required to assume responsibility in relation to the aged parent that is normally associated with the parental role, and to this extent parent and child are operating in a role reversal position which can result in conflict for both participants. Consider the situation in which the adult child is required to make decisions that will affect the way the parent is to live for the remaining years of life. The child, especially one who has experienced a good relationship with the parent, is likely to perceive such action as causing the parent pain and will have a great deal of difficulty accepting the responsibility for making such decisions. In this context the concept of role reversal, which denotes a shift in role responsibility within the aged parent-adult child relationship, is appropriate.

Evidence of the difficulty experienced by both generations involved in role reversal is suggested throughout the literature. Rautman (1962) believes that once the individual reaches maturity and assumes the role of parent to a new generation, parents and children cannot step out of their respective roles, and continue their relationship, without experiencing a great deal of difficulty. Savitsky and Sharkey (1972) also see an impact on both sides of the relationship; they suggest: "When a crisis brings parents and children together, the latter's capacity to tolerate being a person depended upon by the parents is tested, as is the aged person's capacity to handle dependency feelings upon the children" (p. 5).

In our experience, role reversal frequently takes place amid a great deal of resentment on the part of parents, and much guilt is often evidenced by children. The parents are likely to view the takeover by children as another loss, which is met with a struggle to maintain as much control as possible over their own lives. On the other hand, children often perceive their actions in assuming decision-making power over their parents as degrading the persons for whom they have the greatest respect. Most children feel strongly that it is their duty to honor their parents with respect, rather than promoting within them feelings of helplessness by taking over control of their lives. The fact that this shift in roles comes at a time in the life cycle of the parents when they are less able to regain the decision-making function in their lives, and thereby may remain dependent upon the adult children, is likely to increase the burden of guilt for these children.

The child's ability to take an adult role in relation to the parent depends largely upon the degree to which separateness or individuality was established in the family at an earlier stage. When this has been realized, family members possess a differentiated self, and neither parent nor child needs to view the other as an extension of the self. As a result the adult child will be more likely to maintain objectivity in relation to the needs of the elderly parent.

Problems can occur for adult children in spite of their intellectual awareness of the parents' needs. Although children may realize that their parents are unable to function independently and a shift in roles may be necessary, they frequently need help in accepting the change on an emotional level. Parents may also need help in handling their feelings in relation to depending upon the children.

The giving up and taking on of responsibilities as inherent in the role reversal process is not limited to the two generations directly involved. The systemic properties of family functioning come into play, and family interactions at various levels are involved. Field (1972) says: "The assumption of increased responsibility for their parents' welfare may create for the children a serious dilemma, as they find themselves conflicted as to whether their responsibility to their parents interferes with the adequate discharge of their responsibility to their own children" (p. 131).

At the time added responsibility is brought on by the needs of aging parents, many adult children are still very much involved with their own nuclear families. For example, some may still have children in school or just beginning their careers who look to them for help at the same time as the elderly parents. It is also likely that many of these second-generation adults will be deeply involved in their own careers, and this too will claim a good deal of their attention. Role shifts involving aged parents under these conditions present the adult children (second generation) with quite a dilemma. In some cases they may need direct help in sorting out and establishing priorities that will allow them to continue functioning in their various roles. When there are also problems in relationships between these extended family members, the worker must understand the nature of the conflict and determine where changes are needed and can be realized.

Loss and Grief

It is important for social workers to consider grief and mourning over losses when working with aging persons and their families. Old people experience increasing difficulty in replacing losses due to diminishing inner and outer resources and may grieve over a loss that seems rather insignificant to young observers. There is little doubt that society fails to fully appreciate the dynamics of loss and, as a result, does not deal with it appropriately in many cases, especially where the aged are concerned. This is reflected in the reported perceptions children have about the experiences of their aged parents. Simos (1973) found that adult children recognized parental mourning most often when the loss involved significant others, such as spouses or children. Yet old people also may "grieve over the death of a pet, the loss of a job, a social role, self-esteem, independency, a lifetime home, or right to drive an automobile, or the failure of bodily functions or sensory activity" (p. 80).

As further evidence of children's misunderstanding of loss experienced by their aged parents, Simos (1973) reports:

Isolation and denial as defenses against the pain of loss were seen by children as lack of feeling on the part of the parents. Feelings of helplessness and despair, normal reactions to loss, were experienced as burdensome parental traits. A desperate attempt to hold on to remaining possessions or life styles was seen as stubbornness. (p. 80)

Social workers involved in work with adult children and their aged parents need to be especially alert to the possibility of loss among older members. The likelihood that children may misunderstand the impact of such losses must also be kept in mind. When this is indicated, intervention should include helping younger family members to relate realistically to the losses of the older members.

133

Life-Style

Knowledge of the life-style of old people also is useful in gaining an understanding of their social adjustment. The aging individual who has spent a lifetime actively involved in various activities may find it difficult to accept the inactivity to which older people are often relegated in later years.

Those whose primary activities during their most productive years were centered around work and family may be faced with loneliness and isolation when these supports are no longer available. Simos (1973) found that many elderly persons with such life-styles had developed such a narrow range of interests, coupled with poor social skills, that they were unable to engage in social activities. Others were able to respond socially only when the opportunity was provided by the initiative of other people.

Another problem frequently encountered in work with this type of extended family unit is the conflict resulting from the extreme dependency of the aging parent on the adult child. This usually develops when a parent who has enjoyed a very close and dependent marital relationship attempts to transfer dependency needs to a child in the absence of the spouse. In such cases the smoothness of the symbiotic interactions between the parents is likely to have hidden the existence of the prevailing dependency, and the children have been presented with a picture of independent functioning. This false perception on the part of the children can contribute to a misunderstanding of the parents' behavior with regard to fulfilling dependency needs through relationships with them during the latter years. In this case conflict is likely to develop between parent and child, necessitating help outside of the family to clarify the situation and provide both parent and child with a realistic basis for relating.

Social workers will find it helpful in alleviating conflict about the dependency of the aging parent on the adult child to gain some understanding of the relationship that previously existed between the parents. Awareness of the former life-style of old people is also useful in assessing their adjustment and intervening on their behalf.

Conflicts and Disagreements

Disagreements between children may be encountered in work with the multigenerational family. These disagreements may arise from misunderstanding, lack of information, rivalry between children, and so on. When failure to agree is centered around information deficits, often the situation can be corrected through improved processing and sharing of information among family members.

When rivalry between the children is involved, however, the problem is much more difficult. Not only are the principals in the rivalry situation adults, but many are also parents of adult children to whom the rivalry is likely to have been passed. When this is the case, the third generation may be involved in the problem. A tremendous amount of energy has usually been invested by the second-generation adults in relation to various forms of competition and difference over the years. As a result, their responses are influenced by a lifetime of thoughts, feelings, and experiences based on these unresolved rivalries. When these adults are seen in relation to problems involving aged parents, they are likely to have relatively fixed positions. Each child is interested primarily in working his or her own will successfully. The struggle between these adult children can easily reach the level where the parent's needs become secondary to the children's need to prevail.

In such situations each side may seek additional support and gain momentum as the struggle continues. Spouses and children frequently become involved in the conflict, and sometimes other relatives and friends lend their support to one of the sides. The following case summary reflects the difficulty that can be encountered when disagreement about planning for an elderly parent is based on rivalry between adult children.

The patient, a frail man of 75 years, was brought to the Adult Consultation Clinic by his daughter, who explained her difficulty in continuing to maintain him in her home. As a result she was seeking help in planning for a new living situation for her father. The father did not take kindly to the possibility of residing in a special-care facility and wanted to contact a son with whom he thought he could live. The daughter was obviously distressed at the mention of her brother's involvement but gave in to her father's wishes. Soon after the father's contact with his son the son called the clinic to arrange an appointment and requested all consideration of his father entering a residential facility be discontinued.

In the following weeks several members of this extended family were involved. The "tug of war" between the son and daughter was readily seen. Charges and countercharges relative to respective efforts to gain control of the patient's finances and other properties were heard from both. Each pulled in other relatives who were sympathetic to their respective views, and these relatives were as firmly fixed in their opinions as the children. Although the son could not arrange for his father to

135

live with him and presented no alternative plan, he could see his sister "getting her way" and "maintaining an advantage with their father." He suggested the possibility of court action to protect what he perceived as his own interests, and his sister was also willing to battle with him through court proceedings. It was obvious that the aged father's needs were being ignored as the struggle intensified between the children, and the extended family's energies were now also being spent in the contest.

The social worker must keep in mind the needs of the aged parents and refrain from becoming completely consumed in the struggle between the children. This kind of struggle usually neutralizes efforts to plan for the parents, and significant change in the rivalrous relationship between the children is likely to require long-term intervention. Therefore, in the interest of the parent, it may be necessary to make clear to the children the way the worker is experiencing their struggle, which will not be dealt with specifically until an acceptable outcome has been realized on behalf of the parent. In this case the focus of intervention is removed from the children's struggle with one another to the needs of the parent and what can be done in this regard.

Role of the Spouse

It is also important to understand the role of the spouses of adult children when aging parents are included in the family group, both relationships between this adult pair and relations between the spouse and the parent. If the adult child and spouse enjoy a satisfactory relationship, work involving the aged parent will most likely proceed without representing a serious threat to the relationship of this subsystem. However, when the spouse relationship is characterized by disagreement and tension, the strain of involvement with the aging parent is likely to escalate the conflict. The resulting struggle between the spouses will interfere with the social worker's efforts to intervene on behalf of the elderly parents. If, in addition to a good relationship between the adult child and spouse, relations between the spouse and the parent-in-law are also good, the intervention process usually proceeds without major conflicts or disruptions, and outcomes are likely to be acceptable to all concerned.

When there is conflict between the spouse and the elderly parent, the work to be done will be difficult. This conflict creates the likelihood of disruption in other family relationships, especially between adult child and spouse and sometimes between the adult child and the parent, as the reciprocal aspects of relating within the family system take over.

In most situations these types of relationships are readily identified, and the strategies commonly used by social workers in dealing with relationship problems are usually sufficient. Nevertheless, the fact that problems can develop out of what appears to be satisfactory relations between adult children and spouses should not be overlooked. This outcome is not uncommon, especially in cases where one of the principals in the relationship has adapted to a deficit in the functioning of the other, and this adaptation is taxed by closer involvement with an extended family member such as an aging parent.

For example, consider the spouse who over the years has adapted to the necessity of meeting the dependency needs of the husband or wife and gives the appearance of enjoying a satisfactory relationship. When the parent is brought into the picture, the role of this spouse may be required to expand to the point of meeting the needs of not one but two dependent people. This is especially so if the aged member needs assistance with routine maintenance or in the area of decision making. The dependent spouse will usually have trouble carrying executive responsibility relative to these needs of the parent as indicated by the following case summary:

Mr. and Mrs. J had been married for 15 years without children when Mr. J's father came to live with them. Mrs. J was the strong member of this marital pair, and her authority and overall assertiveness in relation to family matters were accepted by Mr. J, who preferred to remain in the background. It soon developed that the aging father required a great deal of supervision with regard to his behavior and personal hygiene but was resistive to any effort to control his activities. The burden of responsibility increased considerably for the wife, as she found her husband unable to provide any direction for his father. In various ways he deferred decision making and care for the aging parent to his wife. When they were unable to work this out, Mrs. J asked for help. Although she was very fond of her father-in-law and had not objected to his moving in with them, she had not anticipated the problems he brought into their lives, especially her husband's reactions to his father's needs. In retrospect, Mrs. J could see that she had, in some ways, been a "mother" to Mr. J but was unwilling to "add a new baby" at this stage of her life.

This situation represented a real threat to the marital relationship, and this relationship was crucial in meeting the needs of the aging father. The social worker chose to focus on the interactions between the marital pair as it related to roles, expectations, and so on. While alternative plans for Mr.

137

J's father were discussed, neither wished to have him placed outside of their home, and Mr. J was gradually able to take on some of the responsibility for his father.

Encounters of this type clearly indicate the importance of the role assumed by the adult child's spouse and the necessity of understanding the spouse's relationship within the family unit. Social workers will find it very useful, in working with families in which elderly parents are members, to pay special attention to the spouse without kinship ties to the parents. If this individual experiences conflict in existing family relationships or is unwilling to accommodate to the intervention process, the realization of desired outcomes from such activity will be difficult.

SUMMARY

Working with the extended family concerning care for the oldest generation is becoming more widely recognized in social work practice. More and more adult children are seeking help in planning for their elderly parents or with conflicts in family relationships resulting from the pressures of interacting with them. We have presented in this chapter some guidelines for a beginning understanding of the aging process and how it affects older people themselves, as well as those who for various reasons are involved with them. Some problems encountered in work with families composed of adult children and their elderly parents have been examined, and suggestions for intervention have been offered.

Since working with the type of family unit described in this chapter is still in the process of refinement, additional knowledge and skill will be forthcoming and made available to practitioners in the future. In the meantime, we hope that the information presented here will enable social workers to help meet the needs of our increasing elderly population from a family-centered perspective. Practitioners who engage in this work should be well aware of their own perception of the aging process and their attitudes toward old people. We believe this will help reduce subjectivity and displacement and enhance the outcome of intervention.

REFERENCES

Bartko, J. J., Patterson, R. D., and Butler, R. N. "Biomedical and Behavioral Predictors of Survival among Normal Aged Men: A Multivariate Analysis." In

E. Palmore and F. C. Jeffers (eds.), *Prediction of Life Span*. Lexington, Mass.: D. C. Heath Co., 1971.

Bell, B. D. *Contemporary Social Gerontology*. Springfield, Ill.: Charles C Thomas, Publisher, 1976.

Botwinick, J. *Aging and Behavior*. New York: Springer Publishing Co., 1973.

Bowman, K. M. "Mental Adjustment to Physical Changes with Aging." *Geriatrics*, 2:139-45, 1956.

Brody, E. M. "The Aging Family." *The Gerontologist*, 6:201–6, 1966.

Brody, E. M. "Aging." In *Encyclopedia of Social Work*, 16th Issue, Vol. I, pp. 51-71. New York: National Association of Social Workers, 1971.

Burgess, E. W. "Social Relations, Activities, and Personal Adjustment." *American Journal of Sociology*, 59:352-60, 1954.

Butler, R. N. "The Destiny of Creativity in Later Life." In S. Levin and R. Kahana (eds.), *Psychodynamic Studies on Aging*. New York: International Universities Press, 1967.

Carp, F. M. "The Psychology of Aging." In R. R. Boyd and C. G. Oaks (eds.), *Foundations of Practical Gerontology*. 2nd ed. Columbia: University of South Carolina Press, 1973.

Cummings, E., and Henry, W. E. (eds.). *Growing Old*. New York: Basic Books, 1961.

Dennis, W. "Creative Productivity between Twenty and Eighty Years." *Journal of Gerontology*, 21:1–8, 1966.

Field, M. *The Aged, the Family, and the Community*. New York: Columbia University Press, 1972.

Glasser, P., and Glasser, L. "Role Reversal and Conflict between Aged Parents and Their Children." *Marriage and Family Living*, 24:46–51, 1962.

Havinghurst, R. J., and Albrecht, R. *Older People*. New York: Longmans Green, 1953.

Kannel, W. B. "Habits and Heart Disease Mortality." In E. Palmore and F. C. Jeffers (eds.), *Prediction of Life Span*. Lexington, Mass.: D. C. Heath Co., 1971.

Kutner, B., Fanshel, D., Togo, A., and Langner, S. W. *Five Hundred Over Sixty*. New York: Russell Sage Foundation, 1956.

Leach, J. M. "The Intergenerational Approach in Casework with the Aging." *Social Casework*, 55:144–49, 1964.

Lemon, B. W., Bengston, V. L., and Peterson, J. A. "An Exploration of Activity Theory of Aging: Activity Types and Life Satisfaction among In-Movers to a Retirement Community." *Journal of Gerontology*, 27:511–23, 1972.

Lowenthal, M. F., and Haven, C. "Interaction and Adoption: Intimacy as a Critical Variable." *American Sociological Review*, 33:20–30, 1968.

Maddox, G. L., and Douglass, E. B. "Aging and Individual Differences: A Longitudinal Analysis of Social, Psychological, and Physiological Indicators." *Journal of Gerontology*, 29:555–63, 1974.

National Center for Health Statistics. *National Health Survey.* Series 10. Washington, D.C.: U.S. Government Printing Office, 1964–1965.

Peterson, J. A. "Therapeutic Intervention in Marital and Family Problems of Aging Persons." In A. Schwartz and I. Mensh (eds.), *Professional Obligations and Approaches to the Aged.* Springfield, Ill.: Charles C Thomas, Publisher, 1974.

Rautman, A. L. "Role Reversal in Geriatrics." *Mental Hygiene,* 56:116–20, 1962.

Savitsky, E., and Sharkey, H. "The Geriatric Patient and His Family: A Study of Family Interaction in the Aged." *Journal of Geriatric Psychiatry,* 5:3–19, 1972.

Schwartz, A. N., and Mensh, I. (eds.). *Professional Obligations and Approaches to the Aged.* Springfield, Ill.: Charles C Thomas, Publisher, 1974.

Shanas, E., Townsend, P., Wedderbrun, D., Friis, H., Milhoj, P., and Stehouwer, J. *Old People in Three Industrial Societies.* New York: Atherton Press, 1968.

Simos, B. G. "Adult Children and Their Aging Parents." *Social Work,* 18:78–85, 1973.

Soddy, K. *Men in Middle Life.* Philadelphia: J. B. Lippincott Co., 1967.

Spence, D. L., Feigenbaum, E. M., Fitzgerald, F., and Roth, J. "Medical Students' Attitudes Toward the Geriatric Patient." *Journal of the American Geriatrics Society,* 16:976–83, 1968.

Tallmer, M., and Kutner, B. "Disengagement and Stresses of Aging." *Journal of Gerontology,* 24:70–75, 1969.

Wolk, R. L., and Wolk, R. B. "Professional Workers' Attitudes toward the Aged." *Journal of the American Geriatrics Society,* 19:624–39, 1971.

CHAPTER **6**

Interactions and Treatment in Child-Abusing Families

The professional literature on abusive families has been prolific. A recent annotated bibliography on child abuse from the National Clearinghouse for Mental Health Information lists over 330 items. The literature covers a wide range of concerns, including the search for causes of violence to children, the organization and delivery of social services, the role of public prosecutors and court decisions, and the incidence of unreported cases.

Information about interpersonal transactions among family members is our particular concern in this chapter. We have also sought definitions of "family" in which something more is meant than the abused child and the abusive parent, since references to the family of the abused child often turn out to mean only the abusive parent.

Several aspects of the literature are of particular relevance for these purposes. First is the attempt to identify the psychological characteristics and life history of the abuser. Often these characteristics are seen as cause, though not necessarily sole cause, of the abuse. Second, the characteristics of the abused child are identified. It is suggested that certain qualities may make the child more vulnerable to abuse by the parent. Third, there are other causal explanations that take into account the situational elements of family life, such as the family's socioeconomic and material status, size of

141

family, circumstances of birth of the abused child, age of parents, marital conflict, family isolation from relatives and the community, and stresses such as changes in family membership or roles, illness, or loss of employment.

What we wish to emphasize, however, are the transactional elements and systemic properties of the family, which are generally neglected in the literature. While the characteristics of the child and the abusing parent are undoubtedly important, we will draw attention to the kinds of interactions that may occur between the principals. Information about these dynamics yields understanding of both the relationship and the abuse. We also broaden the understanding of "family" beyond the parent-child dyad to include other relationships within the family. The interaction of parent and child takes place, not in isolation, but within the context of the parent's relationship with a spouse (or other significant adults), or the lack of such relationships, as well as the parent's relationship to other children in the family. Beyond this, current stresses affect the relationships among all family members. This view directs attention to current relationships, transactions, and events in the life of the family, and their interactive effects as a means for understanding why the abuse occurs and to provide clues about corrective action that might be undertaken.

Rather than providing an exhaustive explanation of child abuse, or even of the functioning of abusive families and their members, this chapter synthesizes some of the existing knowledge about these families with concepts about the family as a system. Particular attention is drawn to instances in which this way of conceptualizing the family has been utilized and found to be helpful. The synthesis draws heavily on family systems concepts that have been developed in the family therapy field. Family therapists have not been prolific in producing studies addressed to the child-abusing family, nor have helpers of the abusive families made much use of systems understanding and treatment orientation. Our effort to draw together both of these bodies of information should be useful to social workers and other practitioners.

Barnes, Chabon, and Hertzberg (1974) suggest the importance of utilizing the time-tested clinical and treatment information which has been at our disposal over the years.

It is not easy to move beyond the symptom of child abuse into the dynamics which have led to it. When this process becomes possible, what emerges is that often these families have experienced lives similar to any seriously dysfunctional family. Taking primary attention off the symptom and carefully reviewing known causal variables and present stress factors will, more often than not, yield fruitful results." (p. 609)

In support of their position, these authors draw attention to available knowledge and theory in social casework, ego psychology, and parenthood. Because their case example reveals how second- and third-generation family characteristics can influence the occurrence of abuse, their position applies to the available knowledge about family systems and family group treatment.

DEFINITION OF ABUSE

We define the child-abusing family as one in which children have been subjected to nonaccidental physical injury. Given this brief definition, we have excluded a number of kinds of maltreatment of children from discussion.

Sexual abuse, for example, is included in the legal definition of abuse in many states, but is excluded from this discussion, since the dynamics appear to be different from physical abuse situations. Incestuous relationships between siblings and between parents and children, as well as sexual relationships between children and other adults responsible for their care or involved in a social relationship with the family, are defined as sexual abuse. It is differentiated from molestation of children by persons peripherally known or totally unknown to the family. Family dynamics in cases of sexual abuse are problematic. Revelation of its occurrence has been found to be even more problematic for the family (James, 1977).

Another topic excluded is abuse which is not physical but is administered verbally and is psychological in effect. This does not fall within most statutory definitions, however much it may concern helping professionals. Psychological abuse includes a broad range of parent-child interactions and results in a variety of outcomes for children; it may, for example, stunt physical growth to the extent of producing dwarfism (Goodwin, 1978).

Neglect also is not considered child abuse, although the separation of abuse situations from neglect situations is not always easy, since neglect readily appears to abuse the child. The issue is most clearly demonstrated in "failure to thrive" children, who may suffer physical ills due to parental

143

neglect. While some of the family dynamics which lead to neglect may appear similar to those found in families of physically abused children, our attention will be on the physically abused child.

Within the physical abuse category there can be great variation. Physical abuse ranges in severity from surface bruises or injuries, to internal injuries, to death. In frequency it may be confirmed on the basis of a single incident or of repeated incidence over extended periods of time prior to actual reporting. Thus, both "mild," single incidents and severe, repeated incidents are reported and confirmed as physical abuse. The dynamics of specific cases may be described within this range of differences, but the same set of dynamics clearly does not apply to all cases.

Other elements complicate the effort to discuss the dynamics of abuse situations. The abuse of one child involves different conceptualizations of family processes than the abuse of several children in the same family. In some situations abuse is inflicted by a sibling rather than a parent. Parents are also involved in the dynamics of such a situation, but in a different way than when the parent inflicts the injury directly. Other forms of violence may not be unrelated to situations in which the child is abused. Sometimes children inflict bodily injury or death on a parent. Sometimes spouses abuse each other. Though there may be common family processes in all these forms of family violence, we will not attempt to account for all of them. Our discussion focuses on physical violence directed at children by parents.

A MODEL FOR UNDERSTANDING THE OCCURRENCE OF VIOLENCE TOWARD CHILDREN

A natural reaction to child abuse is to wonder how a parent could behave in such a destructive way toward a child who is helpless or at least relatively powerless in the relationship with the parent. One common theory holds that a parent who injures a child must be emotionally unbalanced or mentally disturbed. In this linear, cause-and-effect relationship, the disturbed parent's behavior is traced to internal psychological conflict due to a deprived and destructive childhood of her or his own. Typically, the abusing parent was an abused child. As we shall see, there is merit to this position, but it does not by itself explain the occurrence of abuse. Why does violence occur at some times and not at others, and why is one child in a family injured when others are not?

144

Other theories take a more comprehensive view of child abuse. Gelles (1973) sees the psychopathology of the parent as an insufficient explanation because it allows for only a single cause. Abuse is more complex. The sex, age, and social position of the parents and the family also must be taken into account. Though abuse occurs in all socioeconomic strata, for example, it occurs more frequently in lower SES families. This is certainly true of the abuse that is reported. It is possible that in higher SES families injured children will be seen by private physicians, who are less likely to report abuse than clinics or emergency rooms, where lower SES families are more frequently seen. Thus there may be some distortion in the reported figures, but even with correction for this discrepancy, child abuse probably occurs more frequently in lower SES families.

In this expanded model for understanding child abuse, the economic and social stresses experienced by the family are seen as contributors to the occurrence of such abuse. Like Gelles, Gil (1970) also sees the stresses on the family as a contributory factor. Beyond this he points out that the cultural view of children and prevailing child-rearing practices in some sense sanction violent behavior toward children. There is general acceptance of violence within the culture as a means of dealing with conflict. Until recently, children have not been seen as needing special protection. The right of parents to control and discipline children has not been restricted, and physical punishment, even severe punishment, has been acceptable. These aspects of the attitudinal orientation of parents also contribute to the occurrence of abuse.

In addition to the cultural, economic, and social situation of the family which impinges on family functioning, stresses that are situational and transient may also contribute to the occurrence of abuse. A classification of crises in families was introduced in Chapter 2. Some that have been found to be in evidence in studies of abusive families include unwanted or unexpected pregnancies, large family size, loss of family members through death or desertion, marital stress, illness, role changes, and other more immediate stresses such as criticism or disappointment.

The characteristics of the abused child are another element in a model which seeks to account for abuse. Children who are sickly, unresponsive, aggressive, retarded, or otherwise unrewarding to the parent have been more subject to abuse than other children.

Green, Gaines, and Sandgrund (1974) define the etiology of child abuse as "based upon an interaction among three factors: the personality traits of

145

the parents that contribute to 'abuse proneness'; the child's characteristics that enhance his scapegoating, and the increased demand for child care exerted by the environment" (p. 886). We concur that the characteristics of parent and child and the elements in their current situation interact to bring about the abuse, but we leave the more general situational elements in the background in order to focus on the nature of these interactions. In the case of child abuse, "interaction" may mean, as we understand Green et al. to mean, that the parent under situational stress responds negatively to some identifiable characteristic of the child. There is little doubt that this occurs, but we suggest further that a negative cycle of interactions proceeds from these beginnings and results in the physical violence. Violence does not occur just because these three elements are present; an ensuing process is also necessary.

The following sections draw on the existing literature to identify data and events that are needed for understanding the various elements and the interactions among them. We offer our conceptualization of the process that occurs and identify treatment methodology that has been developed to disrupt the negative processes and to promote the well-being of the abused child, siblings, and parents.

CHARACTERISTICS OF THE ABUSED CHILD

A whole array of characteristics of abused children has been reported. Children of both sexes and all ages are abused. According to a recent report of the National Institutes of Mental Health (1977), male and female children are abused in about equal numbers. Some studies report that more younger children than older children are abused, but it is not clear that this is generally true, since many investigations have focused on younger children. Gil (1970) reports that almost half of the children were over 6 years of age. A recent study by Janzen (1978) found cases equally distributed over the 1 year and the 6–16-year age range, with smaller numbers in the 2–5 age category. Thus, sex and age as characteristics of the child do not appear to be factors in vulnerability to abuse. Birth order or sibling position may be a factor. Only child, oldest child, or youngest child have all been identified in various studies as more subject to abuse (Janzen, 1978; NIMH, 1977).

Physical illness appears to make children more subject to abuse. Lynch (1975) compared abused children with nonabused siblings and found

146

statistically significant differences in the amount of illness (including illnesses which require hospital admission) experienced by abused children and their unabused siblings during the first year of life. Fomufod, Sinkford, and Lowy (1975) and Pasamanick (1975) report similar findings and concerns. These troubles appear to antedate the neonatal period, since Lynch also reports that the period of pregnancy with the later-abused child was often characterized by complications requiring investigation or hospitalization, or by denial of the pregnancy or refusal of prenatal care. During the prenatal period, also, there were significant differences between the abused child and the normal sibling group.

Other studies have reported that the abused child may have a physical defect or be retarded, may be colicky or irritable, or may manifest poor impulse control (Green et al., 1974). Johnson and Morse (1968) report that the children failed to respond to care, to thrive, and to show normal growth and development. Children under 5 were described as whiny, fussy, listless, demanding, stubborn, unresponsive. Children over 5 were hyperactive or listless, boisterous or silent, immature, and overly dependent for their ages. Ounsted, Oppenheimer, and Lindsay (1974) describe a condition of "frozen watchfulness" which appears to be unresponsiveness to contact.

Other characteristics of the abused child appear to be important only because they produce certain images in the minds of the parents. The child may represent to the parent a hated parent, spouse, paramour, or sibling because of certain physical features, sibling position, or circumstances of conception and birth. These characteristics are of the order of those Vogel and Bell (1968) have reported as important in the selection of the family scapegoat and may thus help to account further for the selection of the child to be abused.

Steele and Pollock (1972) conclude that in the possession of these characteristics the child contributes unwittingly to the abuse. It is not clear from any studies to date, however, that the characteristics were always existent prior to the abuse. Possibly they appeared after the abuse occurred. Lynch's (1975) data on physical illness during early months would suggest the illness as a precursor, but she also produces data about the condition and attitudes of the mother during pregnancy which complicates the picture. Premature birth has also been mentioned as a characteristic of the abused child. However, one study (Hunter, Kilstron, Kraybill, & Loda, 1978), which compared abused and nonabused children

147

who were born prematurely, found differences in their families and not in the children themselves. Corey, Miller, and Widlak (1975), in a study of two years of hospital admissions, compared children admitted because of battering and those admitted for other reasons. They also found more differences in the families than in the children themselves. Such reports suggest that some child characteristics, including physical illness, may be responsive to parental behavior. The inability to determine which comes first, the child's characteristics or the parents' responses, implies that parental perceptions and the interactive process may be more important than the characteristics of the child by themselves.

CHARACTERISTICS OF THE ABUSER

The catalog of characteristics of the parents who abuse their children is lengthy. Social class is one of these characteristics. The National Institutes of Mental Health (1972) found that "Among reported cases, low-income, low-skill, and low-education families are over-represented" (p. 132). Smith and Hanson (1975) found that many of the personal characteristics and attitudes attributed to abusers are confounded by social class, but they do not appear to differentiate abusers from nonabusers when controls for social class are instituted. One characteristic they do identify as differentiating abusive parents, when social class is controlled, is their tendency to use physical punishment, which suggests that "they are under-controlled rather than over-controlled aggressors." Since social class may be viewed as a characteristic of both the parent and the social situation, it may be that social situational stresses, rather than personality characteristics, are the significant aspect of class which contributes to the perpetration of abuse. Thus any emphasis on the personality characteristic of the parents needs to be tempered by awareness of social class characteristics.

Green et al. (1974) characterize abusive mothers as relying on their children to gratify their dependency needs, having poor impulse control, feeling worthless, suffering from shifting self-identifications, using projection and externalization to defend their self-esteem, and projecting their own negative attributes onto their children. Ounsted et al. (1974) found various mental disturbances were present, but they do not elaborate statistically, since that would be more "likely to mislead than to clarify." We agree that it is not particularly helpful to identify categories of mental illness as a characteristic. Ounsted et al. describe the mothers as feeling "trapped, unwanted, unloved and unequal to their roles as children, as spouses and as parents." Johnson and Morse (1968) describe both parents as anxious, hostile, depressed, and untrusting. The parents studied responded inappropriately, impulsively, and excessively to events and sought love, gratification, and fulfillment in their children. Physical deficiencies (Blumberg, 1974) and low frustration tolerance (Gayford, 1975) have also been observed in abusive parents.

There is almost universal agreement that parents who abuse their children were themselves as children deprived and subject to parental violence (Steele & Pollock, 1972). Thus they suffer from an intense need for love, acceptance, and self-affirmation. There is also general agreement that abusive parents are lacking in parenting skills and in clear images of what can reasonably be expected from their children (Tracy & Clarke, 1974). Their own childhood histories suggest that their family models prepared them inadequately for their roles and behavior as parents and contribute to their maltreatment of their children. Since most abusing parents give evidence of such a childhood history, there is reason to be concerned that the presently abused child will become an abusive adult. There are, however, no firm data from longitudinal studies that support the contention that all abused children will become abusive parents (Jayaratne, 1977).

Many of these characteristics are attributed to both parents of the abused child, not only to the overt perpetrator of the abuse. Mothers do not abuse children significantly more often than fathers (NIMH, 1977; p. 135). In a given situation one parent may be the overt abuser while the other is an accomplice who accepts, condones, and sometimes abets it (Steele & Pollock, 1972). The fact that a disproportionate share of abuse appears to occur in female-headed families (NIMH, 1977) somewhat complicates this picture, but there is evidence that even in these families, a male is sometimes the abuser, or at least at the scene.

FAMILY INTERACTIONS

Dyadic Interaction

The particular characteristics of parent and child in child abuse situations set up conditions for a relationship which is likely to be unsatisfying to either of them. For example, a small child who is sickly and in need of a great deal of care and attention is likely not only to be unsatisfying to the parents but also to place additional demands on them. Parents who in their own development lacked both needed nurturance and a clear understanding of their needs may find the neediness of the child overwhelming, and this may result in unresponsive neglect or an aggressive response. In either case the child may respond with more of the same crying and parent-requiring behavior, rather than less of it, resulting in more of the same response from the parent. In other instances, the infant may not possess any particular physical or mental characteristics, but the circumstances of birth or some other element that prompts a negative image of the infant in the mind of the parents may prompt the negative parental response.

For an infant, the behavior cannot in any sense be thought of as premeditated, but only as an expression of the needs of the child and thus an "unwitting" contribution to the situation. Older children have their own ways of expressing their need for a positive parental response. Both their withdrawn and unresponsive and their aggressive behaviors may be means of seeking such response, but neither is likely to be perceived by the parents as rewarding their own need for a positive response from others. When they respond negatively to the child's behavior and thereby fail to meet the child's need for positive response, they also do not dispose the child to friendly behavior in return. The negative response of each to the other becomes more extreme until violence to the child results or something else happens to interrupt this sequence. Such sequences are defined as symmetrical escalations by Watzlawick, Beavin, and Jackson (1967). In older children violence toward the parent may also in some instances be a consequence.

Family Triads

The dyadic interaction of parent and child does not take place in isolation from other forces and events. A number of factors contribute to its occurrence and perhaps, occasionally, to its interruption. Among the more significant of these situational factors is the relationship between the parents.

The studies of abusive families are rich with data about the problems in these relationships. Blumberg (1974) says that:

150

. . . the hostility that one parent feels toward the other but cannot express because of fear can be displaced onto the child. A similar mechanism can play a role concerning one parent's child by a previous partner . . . . In the case of an unmarried mother, or when the husband or paramour deserts the home, the mother with a poor ego structure and a vulnerable personality may resort to battering her child when she is faced with a stressful situation. (p. 25)

Steinhausen (1972) also sees the child as a substitute for the partner who, in a dominant-submissive marital relationship, cannot be attacked. In a study of battered wives, Gayford (1975) found that the women in many instances discharged their frustration on their children. In a study of the battered child syndrome, Bennie & Sclare (1969) found that in the weeks prior to abuse of a child the marriage of the abuser had been in a turbulent state. One form of filicide is done deliberately to bring suffering to the marital partner, according to Resnick (1969). Moore (1974) describes abused children as "pawns in marital wars" who are injured in trying to defend one parent in a battle with the other. Jealousy by one parent of the other parent's feelings toward a child is seen as a factor in abuse by Ounsted et al. (1974). In one of their cases the father tore the baby from his wife's breast and threw it across the room, saying, "Those breasts are mine." Situations in which the abused child is seen by the mother as competition for the father's love are also reported by Lansky and Erickson (1974).

Some of the subtleties of these interactions are described by Steele and Pollock (1972). A spouse who very much needs to please may be instigated to abuse a child by the other parent's comment that the child is spoiled or needs more discipline or by critical comments about the spouse's handling of the child. Alternately, an overwrought parent may instigate the other parent's violent response with a "You do something" attitude (Kempe & Kempe, 1976). In other instances a nonabusing parent may attempt to compensate the child for negative treatment by the other parent, giving rise to jealousy and further hostility on the part of the abusive parent. In an instance in our experience, the father insisted that the adolescent child needed a firm hand and discipline to compensate for the mother's tendency to overlook the child's negative behavior. The mother felt she needed to be kind and loving to compensate for the father's abusing, rejecting behavior. A reduction in the abusive behavior of one parent also has consequences for the other parent; Steele and Pollock (1972) report that the nonabusing parent may become abusive when the previously abusing parent becomes more tender. Again, the jealousy of the other parent is evident. Vogel and

Bell (1968) report that the marital relationship becomes more stormy when the attacks on the child subside.

In family triads, therefore, three different dynamics are likely. The first is that the child is a scapegoat for the hostilities which the parents do not direct at each other for fear of disrupting their relationship with each other. Second, love and attention given to the child are seen as being subtracted from what one parent has to offer the other, which gives rise to jealousy and a consequent attack on the child. The child is seen as depriving the spouse of desired and needed affection. Finally, the attack on the child is also a means of pleasing the spouse in response to a critical comment. In a stable husband-wife relationship, according to Blumberg (1974), "both parents share the responsibilities of child rearing in one way or another. Frustrations can be communicated and solutions or advice can be forthcoming." This is obviously not the situation in the relationships between an abusive parent and a spouse. Their relationship with each other does not meet their needs for love and affirmation, and is not seen as doing so. They are in no position to be supportive of each other as spouses and thus do not offer a base for effective parenting. Smith and Hanson (1975) found that abusive mothers reacted more negatively to difficulties with their husband than to difficulties with their child, that the behavior toward the child "is based not on a rejection of the child as such, but on a rejection of their unsatisfactory social, marital, and parental roles." According to Newberger (1973), "We are coming to see that the essential element in child abuse is not the intention to destroy the child, but rather the inability of the parent to nurture his offspring, a failing which can stem directly from ascertainable environmental conditions." (p. 327)

Siblings

There is amazingly little documentation of the position of siblings of the abused child in the occurrence of violence. In some instances siblings are also abused (Johnson & Morse, 1968), sometimes worse than the child whose abuse was first reported. If the abused child is removed from the home, another child is sometimes scapegoated by being singled out for abuse. In other cases, a sibling may ally himself or herself with the parent in attacking a child or even become the means of the parent's attack on the child, similar to the way a spouse can be provoked to attack a child. And a sibling who is neither victim nor perpetrator may live in fear that what

152

happened to the abused child may also happen to him and may doubt the parents' love. In some instances siblings feel they are somehow responsible for the abuse, and they should have protected the abused child (Beezley, Martin, & Alexander (1976). Whatever their role, their participation in the family will be affected. Treatment also should attend to these various aspects of the siblings' experience, both to enable their own growth and to improve the functioning of the family group.

OTHER SITUATIONAL ELEMENTS

Illness in the parents, like illness in the abused child, can be a factor in abuse. Parents who are ill are limited in ability to meet the child's need and may be frustrated because they are deprived of meaningful roles, either within the family or outside it. Galdston (1965) notes that illness or disability sometimes deprives parents of a meaningful role outside the home as a breadwinner and thrusts them into a more direct but unaccustomed child-caring role when the spouse goes to work. Their inability to adapt to the illness or disability, plus the thrust into the undesired role, both serve to upset whatever balance in relationships existed prior to the illness. Underlying or together with all of these factors may be the frustrations in some families brought about by poor housing and limited resources.

Losses of relationship also appear to be a significant situational element. Losses may be barely discernible, as when the nonabusing parent leaves the house or is unavailable when needed or desired by the child-caring parent. Other losses may be more obvious. The withdrawal of a boyfriend from a relationship or the separation of a spouse can serve to undermine the parent's ability to respond positively to a child. Baldwin and Oliver (1975) report "frequent changes of adults in charge of the children as spouses, cohabitees and relatives came and went." Family change and instability both appear as situational elements contributing to abuse.

Illness and losses might be manageable if the family had other supports. But Holland (1973) reports that abusive families are isolated, including isolation from social agencies to which they had in the past gone to seek to have their needs met. Bennie & Sclare (1969) found "lack of support of parents and parents in-law was often evident, sometimes because of religious conflict, more frequently because of psychopathic attitudes. The management of the deprived home devolved upon one individual, usually the assailant." There is in such situations little relief from child-caring responsibility, or any support when other stresses such as illness, change of housing, loss of employment, or intrafamily conflicts occur.

The combination of limited parental coping capacity, the care-requiring characteristics of the child, the tenuously balanced relationships between pairs or triads of family members, and situational stress appear to set the stage for abuse of the child. In some instances material means may discourage violence by allowing relief through the hire of child care services or making the parent feel rewarded with treats or purchases. Such relief is not available to the economically deprived family. Newberger (1973) points out that welfare programs offer inadequate help in such stressful circumstances. Nor does such relief always serve to avoid violence, as is evident in more affluent families in which abuse occurs. In other instances a responsive environment in the form of an empathetic circle of friends or a caring extended family might be helpful. But where these are not available or helpful, other means of treatment are necessary.

TREATMENT EFFORTS

While interdisciplinary treatment teams and concrete services are both useful and necessary in work with abusive families, our discussion of treatment will draw on the three elements of the model proposed above for understanding the occurrence of violence toward children and the interactions between these elements: characteristics of the child, characteristics of the parents, and the situational effects of the environment in which the interactions take place. We also will not consider the authoritative aspects of involvement, though we recognize that in these cases the use of authority and questions about who uses it and how it is used are extremely important and difficult, particularly in the initial stages of contact with abusing families. (See Chapters 3 and 4 for further discussion of the use of authority.)

The characteristics of the parents and of the child in child-abuse situations, as described above, are vulnerabilities that they bring to the interaction. Some of the treatment efforts considered here serve to help parents and children deal with these vulnerabilities, and thus to interrupt the negative cycle of interaction that takes place between them and to set their relationship on a course likely to be more satisfying to both. Insofar as the relationship between the parents—assuming two-parent families, or

154

the parent and significant other adults in one-parent families—is a factor in the situation, treatment efforts should be designed to enable parents to find other ways of coping with their difficulties. Some treatment efforts to be described are directed to this end. Other efforts are directed to other elements of situational stress, necessitating both hard and soft services.

Interventions with Parents

Meeting Parents' Needs. The worker with abusive parents needs first of all to convey that he or she is there to understand care, and help rather than to threaten or criticize. A nonjudgmental attitude is essential (Roth, 1975). The worker responds to the parents' strong dependency needs and to their need for a parenting, caring person in their lives. Consistency in this accepting and caring position is important because the parents' own feelings of guilt and their previous life experience may lead them to find such an attitude unbelievable and perhaps even frightening. Ounsted et al. (1974), who work in a residential setting with mothers and children, observed a "second day packing" phenomenon—a wish to flee—that results from these feelings. Most workers have found that concern about the parents' own needs and feelings should be emphasized with the parents, rather than concern about the child, and this concern should be for the needs of both parents. By this approach, the worker avoids arousing the same feelings of jealousy and neglect that have characterized the family's internal interactions. The applicable principle from conjoint family treatment is the worker's ability to focus on the interactions, to identify with each member present, and to avoid siding with one family member against another.

The worker's ability to identify with both parents is not only critical in conjoint sessions, it is also necessary in separate individual sessions. For some workers this may be particularly difficult, at least initially, in relation to the overt perpetrator of the abuse. Blumberg (1974) notes that some spouses are not able to share the worker and that conjoint sessions should come later in the work with the family. Individual sessions may be necessary, especially early in the case. Separate workers from the interdisciplinary treatment team appear in these instances to be particularly useful.

The giving, nurturant approach is manifest first of all through the workers' attitudinal orientation, but giving comes in more concrete forms also. The residential program described by Ounsted and Lynch (1976) provides complete care for mothers and children. Tuszynski and Dowd (1978) describe a day care program which children attend five days a week and in which parents participate two days. In neither of these programs is the child separated completely from the family, but the parents are given relief from child care and the opportunity of observing how others care for children. In other programs parent aides offer assistance to the parents in their own homes, working with the parents and providing support, companionship, and relief from child care. In still other programs, children may be left for short periods of time with child care staff so that the parent has relief from this responsibility. Services which meet family needs for income maintenance, housing, employment, and medical care are also provided.

The NIMH review (1977) notes that some programs consider nurturance to the parents sufficient in itself, since it meets deep needs of the parents which have in the past been unmet and thereby enables them to be more giving to their children. In our view, as in that of the NIMH study of programs, no program can be effective without this base; other elements of treatment may not begin until parents experience an alliance with the worker. However, other components implicit in the nurturance can be made more explicit and thereby more helpful. Specifically, parenting skills must be developed, the parents' denial and guilt need to be dealt with, and the social isolation of the family should be ended.

Teaching Parenting. Providing parents with the opportunity to observe how others care for their children offers them the chance to learn new skills in child care and to overcome the deficits in their own parental role models. Seeing how others approach a colicky, unresponsive, stubborn, insistent, or otherwise difficult child enables them to learn other, more useful responses. These can be substituted for their own aggressive responses in order to arouse a positive reaction in the child. These opportunities are provided in residential and day care programs but also constitute an aspect of parent-aide activity. Opportunities of this nature may also be provided by social workers during parental visits with children who are temporarily separated from the family.

In addition to modeling parenting skills, some programs teach specific aspects of child care and offer parents instruction about what can reasonably be expected of children of a given age. Their own experience and models have not provided this knowledge, which is particularly crucial.[1] Instruction is sometimes given individually to parents, sometimes in classes. It may be given by social workers or by other members of a treatment team.

Attempts have also been made to teach specific modes of interaction with children. Beezley et al. (1976) have found Parent Effectiveness Training to be useful but in need of modification because in its original mode it seems too advanced for abusive parents. Other approaches which modify the behaviors of both parent and child have been found to be effective. Jeffrey (1976) shows parents how to give positive reinforcement and teaches them to communicate, to play, to give positive attention, and to adapt the house to the child. She also helps parents draw up behavioral contracts with children and demonstrates how to deflect both their own and their children's aggressive responses.

Work with a mother who had held her 17-year-old child's hand over a fire revealed that she was giving intermittent reinforcement to the child's negative behavior (Palakow and Peabody, 1975). She was taught to identify the child's positive behaviors and reinforce them instead through the provision of allowances or attention. Tracy and Clark (1974) suggest that parents should try to "catch the child being good" and then offer rewards for the behavior. Treatment for a mother who had tried to suffocate and drown her child, but who had subsequently withdrawn from interaction to avoid further violence, involved incremental steps toward reengagement which were likely to be rewarding to both child and parent (Gilbert, 1976). The husband was involved in rewarding the wife for positive steps between the treatment sessions. Gilbert proceeds on the assumption that behavior change can precede changes in feeling but will lead to changes in interaction and in the feelings of the participants toward each other. By these means mothers in a program conducted by Tracy, Ballard, and Clark (1975) "improved their techniques for controlling the children, using less physical punishment. In addition, by increasing the parents' sense of competence as parents and adults, consistent improvement was shown in other areas of family functioning."

---

[1] This lack of parental knowledge and experience may help to account for the fact that in some studies "only" children or "oldest" children, no matter of what age, appear to be more frequent victims of abuse. Some learning of child care may have taken place by the time the second and later children appear.

Modeling, teaching parenting skills, providing knowledge about the expectable behaviors of children are all useful in giving parents models and skills they can use to alter parent-child interaction. The negative cycle can be changed to a cycle of interactions that is more rewarding to both. The effort to alter parents' responses to their children, however, can take place only in the context of a relationship in which the parents can clearly experience concern for themselves as persons, and not only as instruments to meet their childrens' needs. Thus, their learning occurs in the context of being given to and nurtured. The modeling of care-giving behavior has teaching value because it provides parental relief from child care. Learning can occur when teaching is experienced not as a criticism but as a means of achieving a more rewarding relationship with a child.

Parent skills training serve to develop more realistic and consistent responses of parent to child and a clearer expression of parental expectations. This makes the child more clear about the rules and less likely to deviate from parental expectations, so that less demand is placed on the parent for direction and supervision. It also makes the child feel more comfortable, positive, and responsive to the parent. A changed interaction pattern should follow. In giving attention to the dyadic interactive process, the worker needs to bear in mind the balance of relationships throughout the family. This avoids rearousal of jealousy between parents and children and prevents its appearance between family members and the worker or workers on the treatment team.

Encouraging Parental Acceptance of Responsibility. Parents also can be helped to move from a defensive denial of responsibility for the child's injury to ownership of responsibility, to concern for the child's welfare and recognition of their own wish to be better parents. In the context of a giving and nonjudgmental relationship, it becomes possible for them to do so. They are often relieved to reveal the assault and to talk about their emotions at the time and how they felt afterward. These sessions, timed rightly, can be individual with one parent or conjoint with both. Ounsted et al. (1974) found that parents can set for themselves the task of breaking the cycle of violence that has been characteristic of their families for generations. The worker's questions about their own childhood family experiences help them become aware of this cycle and make it more possible for them to break the hostile identification with their own parents. Increasing the individuation of the parents, and their separateness from their own parents, helps to establish a separate identity and increases

158

confidence and competence. In instances in which the child is scapegoated because in a parent's eyes he or she is representative of some other hated person in the life of the parent, the displacement has to be recognized and the original feelings about those persons need to be resolved.

These interventions, which are of a psychotherapeutic nature, may occur in individual or conjoint sessions with parents. Group treatment has also been found to serve this purpose productively (Oppenheimer, 1978). But they may also occur when time is allowed in visits to day care centers, in sessions in which plans are made for visiting a child who is separated from the home, or interspersed in parent skills training sessions.

The mix of the various interventions with parents—nurturance, parent skills training, and psychotherapy—will be different for different parents. The readiness of the parents to engage in parent training or emotional abreaction will come at various stages of contact, depending on their ability to trust the worker's acceptance and caring for them. The mix of interventions depends also on the family's material status and needs and the agency's ability to provide services such as day care, parent aides, and other needed services in support of the parents and their parenting efforts. Worker assessment and reassessment of needs and readiness must be continuous.

Treatment of the Abused Child

The NIMH (1977) study of treatment programs notes with approval the great amount of effort devoted to nurturing abusive parents as family leaders, which enables them to fulfill themselves and their functions as parents. It also notes, with some sadness, the widespread neglect of treatment for the children who are abused. These children also need help, of course, and for some of the same reasons as the parents. Beyond immediate physical care, their emotional needs must be met, and their interaction with their parents needs to be changed.

The child's need to be given to and attended to can take many forms. At a minimum, physical injuries and health problems must be cared for. When the child feels physically well, the demands on parents for care are reduced, and child and parents can feel more friendly to one another. Caring attention can release the child from "frozen watchfulness," unresponsiveness, or withdrawal, and from the opposite behaviors of hyperactivity and unregulated or hostile responses. New behaviors appear first with substitute caretakers while the child is receiving residential or day care, and only tentatively in contacts with the child's own parents. But as parents learn to respond to the child's changed responsiveness, the child's responsiveness to parents continues to improve. The changed interaction between parents and child is made possible initially through meeting each party's individual needs, and then through the more reasonable and explicit structure provided by the parents. Jeffrey's (1976) effort to teach children how to respond shows promise of promoting positive interactions between parent and child.

Beyond these efforts, play therapy or psychotherapy may enable abused children to cope with their feelings about injuries and illnesses, and about their parents and siblings. The hurts and rejection they have experienced will no doubt be alleviated by the changed behavior of the parents and the new interaction pattern which will result. But play therapy or psychotherapy can remove further blocks to children's growth and development and make it possible for them to behave in relationship-seeking ways which are rewarding to them and to the parents.

Marital Treatment

The treatment of the parents and the abused child described thus far is designed to help them as individuals and to change their interactions. However, the dyadic interaction between parent and child occurs in the context of other relationships, some of which do not involve the child's participation but which nevertheless result in child abuse. These relationships also need correction and alteration. As Blumberg (1974) says, treatment should meet the needs of parents as persons before it focuses on marital problems. The NIMH (1977) report suggests this sequence of treatment activity for the family.

While we agree that a focus on marital problems in general may be out of place in the early stages of treatment, we suggest that marital relationships as they affect behavior toward the child can be considered early in the contact. Once the parents have acknowledged their violence to the child, the relationship between spouses may be considered as a situational element in the *specific* act of abuse—what was going on at the time, how the spouse behaved, and how the abuser felt about these events. The parents can be encouraged to express not only feelings of anger and rejection, but also their views of what was wanted from spouses and others and what would have been helpful. These feelings, and the responses of the spouse to the abusing parent, can be elicited in conjoint sessions. The worker is in a position to acknowledge the needs of each, to note the expectancies of the other that give rise to disappointment, jealousy, and scapegoating behavior. The spouse's ability or inability to respond, his or her wish or unwillingness to do so can be made explicit and can then be taken into account in the further development of the child care plan and of the marital relationship.

The problem to be solved at this stage of treatment is the occurrence or avoidance of further abuse. The task of the family adults is to find a way, if they can, of helping each other to achieve avoidance of further abuse. At this stage of the treatment the parents can learn what each needs from the other to achieve this goal.

These efforts may move them, over time, to deal with many aspects of their relationship, so that in the long run they can depend on each other rather than on their child for positive responsiveness and affirmation. Alternatively, they may have to accept the knowledge that the dependability they seek will not be forthcoming, and they can learn to avoid further disappointment by looking to their own strengths or elsewhere for the support they need.

In addition to the clarification of roles and expectations, couples can benefit from help in learning how to communicate in ways that promote positive relationships. Communications that are vague or ambiguous, and sequences of communications that do not result in clarity, can be corrected by means we have suggested elsewhere (see especially Chapter 4, on problem poverty families). Work on communications not only facilitates the clarification of roles and expectations, it can also help to resolve differences and disagreements so that they do not build into reservoirs of ill will which might eventually spill onto spouse or child.

Our underlying assumption is that solid relationships between the parents or between a single parent and other supportive adults or agencies reduce parental dependence on positive responses from the child as a means for affirming parental identity and self-worth. These adult relationships, therefore, ought to be fostered and enhanced. The relationships of one or both adults to external systems may also need to be encouraged, changed, or enlarged, so that these systems can be supportive of the nuclear family group.

161

Treatment for the Family, Including Siblings

The literature on child abuse is almost totally silent on family therapy, except to note that it is strange in a field in "which the focus is on the family, that so little family therapy is offered" (NIMH, 1977). Most of the treatment is directed toward change in the behaviors of individuals which is designed to lead to changes in interaction. Beyond these efforts, workers may find it possible to promote negotiated change between family members. Older children and their parents often can be helped to jointly negotiate behavior changes and the rewards that may follow. They can also be engaged in mutual training for improved communication. While such conjoint treatment is extremely difficult in early stages of contact with the family, it can be undertaken profitably at later stages.

So little commentary is available on siblings in child-abuse situations that they seem to have been excluded from treatment. Since they are recognized as being affected in some way, however, they should be included, and there is the possibility that both they and the family could benefit from their participation. Often family realignments and changes take place during treatment sessions (Lehigh University Center for Social Research, 1976), with the expectation that the new behaviors can be transferred to the family's experience at home.

Work with the Extended Family

In some cases it is useful to help an abusive mother work on her relationship with her own mother, to resolve the disappointment, fear, and ambivalence that characterize the relationship (Steele and Pollock, 1972). We see the need for both parents to achieve greater separateness and detachment from their families of origin and to define an identity of their own. This work on differentiation of self is characteristic of the family therapy field. It may be accomplished by direct work on these relationships in contacts with members of the extended family (Bowen, 1971), or by asking individuals or couples to describe relationships in their families of origin. In these ways they may become aware of the origins of their expectations for current relationships, and this awareness can relieve them of the need to continue these relationships and enable them to negotiate new kinds of interaction.

In instances in which the parents' relationships with their own parents

162

and with siblings are characterized less by hostility, ambivalence, and lack of differentiation and more by simple lack of contact, it may be possible for the worker to enable the extended family to be more of a resource for the parents. This can provide the parents with avenues of social contact or, in some instances, emotional or tangible support.

Coping with Situational Stress

While relationships with spouses, paramours, and the extended family are one form of situational stress, other crises may also require intervention. These stress situations include pregnancy or birth of another child; loss of employment or other change in financial situation; illness of an adult or child, or loss of an immediate or extended family member. Any of these stresses can disrupt whatever balance has existed in the give and take of family relationships. They may overwhelm a child-caring parent or thrust the parent into an undesired role. New expectations can arise for all family members.

Workers should be available at such times to family members, either individually or as a group, to help them deal with feelings and find ways of coping. Tasks must be defined and agreement reached as to how they are to be accomplished and by whom. Where external resources are needed, the worker needs either to make arrangements for them, with family members' consent, or to serve in a broker or advocate role for the family. The worker's availability at times of crisis seems particularly important in this group of families, where the balance of relationships and personal and social resources is often precarious.

The social isolation of the family is another aspect of situational stress, or, more specifically, a factor in the lack of relief from situational stress. Inputs from the extended family are, of course, one way of reducing the isolation. Initially, however, the treatment agency is the chief avenue for reducing social isolation. The agency provides the family with new feedback about its operations and supplies it with specific means of support and help. Treatment in groups, in residential settings, or even in weekend camps (Oppenheimer, 1978) can open up new personal contacts for the family. These new experiences can provide them with the skills needed in interactions with individuals outside the immediate family group and offer them a bridge to relationships in the larger community. Referral to Parents Anonymous, a self-help group of abusive parents, can serve to reduce isolation and provide support.

A NOTE ABOUT THE ORGANIZATION OF SERVICES

The kind of connectedness of the agency to the family that we have described requires considerable outreach, substantial time in contact, and a variety of modes of helping and giving. These are not always available. Certainly, it is not enough to assign a single worker to a huge caseload of families. The literature refers repeatedly to the necessity for interdisciplinary teamwork, both for diagnosis and treatment. This provides a variety of modes of helping and meets the need to work with all members of the family, not only with the person who has physically inflicted the abuse.

There is a great need to broaden and strengthen the range and availability of services to include all of these elements, if families in which abuse has occurred are to be successfully helped. Treating agencies will increase their effectiveness to the degree that they are organized toward these ends.

SUMMARY

In this chapter we have taken note of some specific characteristics of abusing parents and abused children and have observed how these characteristics give rise to negative patterns of interaction. We have noted that the interaction of abusive parent and abused child does not take place in isolation but is affected by other interactions in the family and events in the family's situation. The relationship between the parents is seen as particularly crucial, perhaps as crucial as the relationship between parent and child. There has been relative neglect in the field of the experiences of siblings of the abused child, and the family as a whole is seen as likely to be isolated from external supports, or in difficult relationships with extended family. Unlike other writing on child abuse, which focuses primarily on the abused child and the overt perpetrators of the abuse, we have emphasized the transactions between family members and with the larger family system.

The treatments described are designed to help family members as individuals and in their interactions with others, and to alter relationships within and beyond the immediate family. The efforts include nurturance of the parents, imparting skills and knowledge for parenting, help in dealing with feelings, and recognition of reactions to members' own behavior and that of others. These activities are useful in interrupting old patterns and

164

initiating new behaviors, and thereby altering interactional patterns. Enabling the parents to alter their relationships so that they can support each other in child-caring and parenting activities is an important means of helping the child, as well as providing greater satisfaction for the parents themselves. Where other situational stresses affect the balance of family relationships, agency action is needed to provide relief and support.

The range of services encompassed requires comprehensive care which cannot be provided by a single worker assigned to a huge caseload. Thus, the interdisciplinary teams which are widely noted in the literature, and services to the entire family, are valued and needed in effective programming for families in which abuse of the child occurs.

REFERENCES

Baldwin, J., and Oliver, J. "Epidemiology and Family Characteristics of Severely Abused Children." *British Journal of Preventive and Social Medicine*, 29:205–21, 1975.

Barnes, G., Chabon, R., and Hertzberg, L. "Team Treatment for Abusive Families." *Social Casework*, 55:600–11, 1974.

Beezley, P., Martin, H., and Alexander, H. "Comprehensive Family Oriented Therapy." In R. Helfer and C. Kempe (eds.), *Child Abuse and Neglect*. Cambridge, Mass.: Ballinger Publishing Co., 1976.

Bennie, E. H., and Sclare, A. B. "The Battered Child Syndrome." *American Journal of Psychiatry*, 125:975–79, 1969.

Blumberg, M. L. "Psychopathology of the Abusing Parent." *American Journal of Psychotherapy*, 28:21–29, 1974.

Bowen, M. "Family Therapy and Family Group Therapy." In H. Kaplan and B. Sadock (eds.), *Comprehensive Group Psychotherapy*. Baltimore: Williams and Wilkins Co., 1971.

Corey, E., Miller, C., and Widlak, F. "Factors Contributing to Child Abuse." *Nursing Research*, 24:293–95, 1975.

Fomufod, A., Sinkford, S., and Lowy, V. "Mother Child Separation at Birth: A Contributing Factor to Child Abuse." *Lancet*, 2:549–50, 1975.

Galdston, R. "Observation on Children Who Have Been Physically Abused and Their Parents." *American Journal of Psychiatry*, 122:440–43, 1965.

Gayford, J. "Wife Battering: A Preliminary Survey of 100 Cases." *British Medical Journal*, 5951:194–97, 1975.

Gelles, R. "Child Abuse as Psychopathology: A Sociological Critique and Reformulation." *American Journal of Orthopsychiatry*, 43:611–21, 1973.

Gil, D. *Violence against Children; Physical Child Abuse in the United States*. Cambridge, Mass.: Harvard University Press, 1970.

Gilbert, M. "Behavioral Approach to the Treatment of Child Abuse." *Nursing Times*, 72:140–43, 1976.

Goodwin, D. "Dwarfism: The Victim Child's Response to Abuse." *Baltimore Sun*, September 24, 1978.

Green, A., Gaines, R., and Sandgrund, A. "Child Abuse: Pathological Syndrome of Family Interaction." *American Journal of Psychiatry*, 131:882–86, 1974.

Holland, C. "An Examination of Social Isolation and Availability to Treatment in the Phenomenon of Child Abuse." *Smith College Studies in Social Work*, 44:74–75, 1973.

Hunter, R., Kilstron, N., Kraybill, E., and Loda, F. "Antecedents of Child Abuse and Neglect in Premature Infants: A Prospective Study in a Newborn Intensive Care Unit." *Pediatrics*, 61:629–35, 1978.

James, K. "Incest: The Teenager's Perspective." *Psychotherapy: Theory, Research and Practice*, 14:146–55, 1977.

Janzen, C. *Child Abuse Families in Baltimore County*. Report to the Inter-Agency Child Abuse and Neglect Committee of Baltimore County, 1978.

Jayaratne, S. "Child Abusers as Parents and as Children: A Review." *Social Work*, 22:5–9, 1977.

Jeffrey, M. "Practical Ways to Change Parent/Child Interaction in Families of Children at Risk." In R. Helfer and C. Kempe (eds.), *Child Abuse and Neglect*. Cambridge, Mass.: Ballinger Publishing Co., 1976.

Johnson, B., & Morse, H. "Injured Children and Their Parents." *Children*, 15:147–52, 1968.

Kempe, R., and Kempe, H. "Assessing Family Pathology." In R. Helfer and C. Kempe (eds.), *Child Abuse and Neglect*. Cambridge, Mass.: Ballinger Publishing Co., 1976.

Lansky, S., and Erickson, H. J. "Prevention of Child Murder: A Case Report." *Journal of the American Academy of Child Psychiatry*, 13:691–98, 1974.

Lehigh University Center for Social Research. "Treatment of Families Exhibiting Violence Toward Children." Mimeo report, 1976.

Lynch, M. "Ill Health and Child Abuse." *Lancet*, 2:317–19, 1975.

Moore, J. "YoYo Children." *Nursing Times*, 70:1888–89, 1974.

National Institutes of Mental Health. *Child Abuse and Neglect Programs: Practice and Theory*. Washington, D.C., 1977.

Newberger, E. H. "The Myth of the Battered Child Syndrome." *Current Medical Dialogue*, 40:327–34, 1973.

Oppenheimer, A. "Triumph over Trauma in the Treatment of Child Abuse." *Social Casework*, 59:352–58, 1978.

Ounsted, C., and Lynch, M. "Residential Therapy: A Place of Safety." In R. Helfer and C. Kempe (eds.), *Child Abuse and Neglect*. Cambridge, Mass.: Ballinger Publishing Co., 1976.

Ounsted, C., Oppenheimer, R., and Lindsay, J. "Aspects of Bonding Failure: The Psychopathology and Psychotherapeutic Treatment of Families of Battered Children." *Developmental Medicine and Child Neurology*, 16:447–56, 1974.

Palakow, R., and Peabody, D. "Behavioral Treatment of Child Abuse." *International Journal of Offender Therapy and Comparative Criminology,* 19:100–103, 1975.

Pasamanick, B. "Ill Health and Child Abuse." *Lancet,* 2:550, 1975.

Resnick, P. J. "Child Murder by Parents: A Psychiatric View of Filicide." *American Journal of Psychiatry,* 126:325–34, 1969.

Roth, F. "A Practice Regimen for Diagnosis and Treatment of Child Abuse." *Child Welfare,* 54:268–73, 1975.

Smith, S., and Hanson, R. "Interpersonal Relationships and Child Rearing Practices in 214 Parents of Battered Children." *British Journal of Psychiatry,* 127:513–25, 1975.

Steele, B., and Pollock, C. "A Psychiatric Study of Parents Who Abuse Infants and Small Children." In C. Kempe & R. Helfer (eds.), *Helping the Battered Child and His Family.* Philadelphia: J. B. Lippincott Co., 1972.

Steinhausen, H. Sozialmedizinische Aspekte der Korperlichin Kindes-mishandlung [Social-Medical Aspects of Physical Maltreatment of Children]. *Monatschrift fuer Kinderheilkunde,* 120:314–18, 1972.

Tracy, J., Ballard, C., and Clark, E. "Child Abuse Project: A Followup." *Social Work,* 20:398–99, 1975.

Tracy, J., and Clark, E. "Treatment for Child Abusers." *Social Work,* 19:338–42, 1974.

Tuszinski, A., and Dowd, J. "An Alternative Approach to the Treatment of Protective Service Families." *Social Casework,* 59:175–79, 1978.

Vogel, E., and Bell, W. "The Emotionally Disturbed Child as the Family Scapegoat." In N. Bell & E. Vogel (eds.), *A Modern Introduction to the Family.* New York: Free Press, 1968.

Watzlawick, P., Beavin, J., and Jackson, D. *Pragmatics of Human Communication.* New York: W. W. Norton & Co., 1967.

167

CHAPTER 7

Intervening With The Black Family

By OLIVER C. HARRIS and PALLASSANA R. BALGOPAL

Much has been written about the black family in our society, but little, by comparison, has been said about the therapeutic encounter with this group. There are probably many reasons for the limited reporting of work with black families. Nathan Ackerman points up one of the most significant factors, a lack of knowledge:

> One citizen treats another. One group treats another. And we don't understand enough of the spontaneous kind of therapy that emerges in this world of the black people, in the immediate everyday relations within the family members and the community. This is a kind of spontaneous psychotherapy that we know nothing about (quoted in Sager, Brayboy, & Waxenberg, 1970, p. 152).

There are probably many other reasons for this limited reporting. We suspect that one reason is that work with black families has been included in

---

Note: The authors wish to acknowledge Salvadore Minuchin's work with black families.

the reports of intervention with other groups, such as hard-to-reach families, multiproblem families, low-income families, and problem poverty families. Another likely reason is that black families, other than those from the low socioeconomic group, have not been extensively involved in family therapy. And, of course, it is also possible that the clinicians who have written about their work are not aware of a significant difference between work with black and other minority families and work with white families. In this case there would be no compelling reason to address either group specifically in discussing family treatment.

Be this as it may, there is a dearth of information on treating black families. We share the opinion of those who believe that the similarity of all families as a social system is much greater than the differences among them. Yet we suggest that what is different about the black family is of sufficient significance that it should be considered in making an assessment of the family upon which to base effective intervention efforts.

Therefore, we will consider these differences and the meaning they have for the functioning of black families, and offer some ideas about intervening with this group. Although we may refer to both lower and upper socioeconomic classes, the main thrust of the chapter is toward the black, middle-class family. The literature already provides some information relative to work with low-income families, minority and nonminority. And the upper-class black family is not likely to use a social work agency, the primary operational structure in which the social workers' therapeutic activity takes places.

The assessment of any family must include the gathering of sufficient information about family transactions to enable the therapist to put the problem to be worked on into proper perspective, while helping the family to see and relate to the problem appropriately. As in preceding chapters, the focus of intervention with families is on the interactions among family members. The primary objective of the therapeutic encounter is to alter dysfunctional interactional patterns in such a way as to improve family functioning. While this process applies to work with black families, some variations in emphasis and strategy are necessary.

To assist those who intervene with black families, we will discuss some of these necessary variations later in this chapter. However, we begin by identifying the black middle class in contemporary society, presenting its family structure, and discussing some aspects of family functioning.

THE BLACK MIDDLE CLASS

The foundation of the black middle class can be traced to the rural South and the institution of slavery. The conditions of servitude to which blacks were subjected under the system of slavery and its impact on family life have been documented. Historically, the black man was denied the opportunity of being the responsible head of his family, while the black woman was allowed to surface in this role. For various reasons, this continued to be the dominant perception of black family structure long after slavery was abolished. It has served to perpetuate a myth prominently presented in much of the literature.

There is evidence of a large increase in the number of blacks who have achieved middle-class status within the past decade. There is also evidence that the black middle class of today does not fit the description of a group struggling to imitate the white middle class, as suggested by Frazier (1962) and others. A more recent study by Kronus (1971) presents the black middle class as a group with its own identity. This class is highly family oriented, and the families are usually small. Family orientation indicates a kind of togetherness, with members spending time and engaging in activities together as a functioning unit, which was not often recognized by earlier researchers.

The black middle class of today does not stand in awe of its white counterpart and in many cases welcomes the opportunity for competition. Self-determination appears to be the dominant theme among the black middle class, as indicated by increasing demands for input in the areas of education, employment, politics, and so on. As a group, they are no longer focused only on issues pertaining to the middle class but assume a strong posture relative to improving the position of blacks in general. This seems to reflect greater security for this group, although the degree of status security may vary within the group.

The black middle class of the eighties is composed of well-educated persons who are interested in the welfare of family members. The majority of families include both parents. There is little desire for what might be considered the superficial aspects of life, including expensive and flashy automobiles or clothes. Education is seen as an important means of access to the economic opportunity structure. As a group members of the black middle class tend to live within their means and to accept responsibilities to their families, their employers, and to their communities. In sum, the black middle class is a self-determined, responsible group which participates in a pluralistic society.

FAMILY STRUCTURE AND FUNCTIONING

When using a social systems approach to provide an appropriate framework within which to assess family functioning, it is necessary to consider the totality of interactions and interdependencies that influence the family's behavior. In keeping with this approach, this chapter views the middle-class black family as a system composed of subsystems. The family itself is seen as a subsystem within the broader network of the black community and wider society.

The typical black middle class family of today consists of two parents and two or three children sharing the same household. The husband-father carries the primary provider role for the family, although it is likely that the wife-mother also is employed. The father is very much involved in the rearing of children, and the household usually does not include extended-family members.

As a social system, the black family interacts with and is influenced by both the black community and the wider society. These two systems have different expectations and different behaviors are required in order to succeed and earn status in them. The reference group in the wider society is the conjugal white family, usually of middle-to upper-middle-class status, and this status is determined by employment, education, and income. In the black community status is based more on consumption patterns and other visible achievements than on employment, education, and income. As a result, different life-styles emerge in each situation. This difference in life-style between the black community, in which black families are rooted psychologically, regardless of where they reside physically, and the wider society, in which they must also participate, places an extremely heavy demand on the black family in its effort to adapt to both systems. The situation also has tremendous impact on the socialization of black children, whose parents must try to prepare them to deal successfully with both experiences. It is necessary for the black family to incorporate the values of two different reference groups with two distinct lifestyles if its members are to participate successfully in the American

171

dream and compete for the rewards available through this process. White families need not engage in this type of socialization process to prepare their children to function in society.

In the attempts of black families to meet the requirements of the wider society while satisfying the needs of family members, an interchange of customary roles is not uncommon. The widely accepted rule that the husband-father performs the instrumental functions while the wife-mother carries out the expressive function is, as suggested by Billingsley (1968), "far too simplistic a framework for examining the functioning of black families" (p. 25). It is well established that the black wife-mother frequently plays a major role in the execution of instrumental functions, but it is not so well known that the black husband-father performs many expressive functions. This pattern of functioning within the black family is tied to a history in which the black female had greater access to the economic opportunity structure of society than the black male did. Both husband and wife generally accept this way of contributing to the well-being of the family. We are not suggesting that instrumental and expressive functions are necessarily mutually exclusive in any case, but the black husband-father is likely to be much more involved in performing expressive functions and the wife-mother in performing instrumental functions than their white counterparts are.

This departure from the widely accepted norm of family functioning should not be interpreted as deviant behavior or an automatic source of conflict in family relationships, however. Social workers should take into account the life-styles which have emerged from the experience of black people in America. Attempts to assess black family functioning by using only the norms of the white family may result in something less than accurate measurement.

Spouse Relationship

One of the keys to understanding family interactional patterns is knowledge of family relationships, such as those between husband and wife. In the wider society, Scanzoni (1971) suggests:

...the relationship between husband and wife in modern society can be thought of in terms of a reciprocal exchange of role duties and rights. The more fully the husband fulfills his chief role obligation as provider, the more fully the wife is

172

motivated to fulfill her chief obligations as "expressive agent," or "socio-emotional hub" of the conjugal family. (pp. 199-200)

This suggests that the relationship between husband and wife is significantly influenced by the rewards provided by the husband. Occupational status, education, and income are primary factors in the husband's ability to provide these rewards. Scanzoni found that among white families, the greater the husband's claim on these three status symbols, the more rewards he provided to his wife, and the more positively both husband and wife considered their primary relations. This was not the case with black families. An increase in these indicators of social position and the provision of greater rewards to the black wife did not bring a corresponding increase in her positive perception of her relationship with her husband.

Scanzoni contends that the concept of relative deprivation as suggested by Pettigrew (1964) may be responsible for this difference between the two groups. This concept is based on the fact that even though the black family now has greater access to the opportunity structure and claims more rewards from it than ever before, the rewards are not equal to those received by white families of similar educational levels. At the same time that black family rewards are increasing, the expectations of black families are increasingly based on the opportunity structure's standard of rewards to their white counterparts. As a result, there is an inevitable comparison between the lesser rewards they receive and the greater rewards received by whites, which produces a feeling of deprivation on the part of blacks.

In connection with the idea of relative deprivation, we suggest the black wife's failure to show an increase in positive feeling for her husband as a result of his provision of increased rewards is in no way an attempt on her part to punish him. Neither does it reflect a lack of appreciation for the increased rewards. Instead, the black wife's expression is a reflection of her dissatisfaction with the opportunity structure's double standard of distributing rewards. In addition, there is an awareness on her part that the opportunity structure is controlled by whites, which is a strong reminder that the black family is not in complete control of its middle-class status. Therefore, a certain tentativeness is associated with the increased rewards the black husband provides, and the wife with a history filled with uncertainties does not allow herself to fully experience rewards that can be denied by powers beyond her control.

The black wife is also supportive of her husband and ascribes to him the role of primary provider for the family. Her failure to increase or decrease expressive responses in direct proportion to the provision of status rewards is likely to be reassuring to her husband, who does not completely control the rewards he is able to provide. This also frees the husband from fluctuation in his wife's affections toward him. It follows, then, that the quality of the black husband-wife relationship is not dependent on the amount of status rewards he can provide. Therefore, social workers might find it useful in the intervention process to gain knowledge of the extent of mutuality in the perception of roles between the black husband and wife, as well as the extent of satisfaction experienced in relation to their role performances.

Another consideration in viewing the black husband-wife relationship is the often-implied interference resulting from the wife's employment. Contrary to the notion that the white wife is "allowed to work" by her husband, the black wife's employment is generally considered normal and is usually accepted by her and her husband. This is probably helped along by the black wife's history of greater accessibility to the economic opportunity structure, while the husband has been denied an equal opportunity to participate. However, it is customary for the black wife to keep a low profile in relation to her working and performing instrumental functions within the family. It is probably fair to assume that both the wife's history of participation in the labor market, and her deemphasis of the role of her employment in family functioning, are largely responsible for the absence of threat to the husband's provider role. Hence her employment offers little threat to their relationship. While the possibility of conflict arising from the wife's employment should not be ignored in working with the black family, it is unlikely to be the primary source of disruptive forces.

The distribution of power between the black husband and wife is another key to understanding their relationship. The social worker intervening with the black family can no longer approach the task with the traditional view of the family as a matriarchy. Neither can the worker apply the popular conceptualizations relative to the distribution of power and authority that have been found to exist within the white family. For example, Scanzoni (1971) found that the black wife did not attribute more power and authority to the husband out of deference for increased status rewards he could provide (p. 205), but the white wife tended to respond in proportion to the rewards received. In fact, the black family operates in an egalitarian power structure, which is to say that power and decision making are shared equally by husband and wife.

It is important that the relationship between the black husband and wife be viewed within the context of the black family experience. Workers intervening with black families should have some knowledge of the cultural heritage of black people. We also suggest caution in drawing conclusions about black husband-wife relationships; they should not be based solely on variables known to influence the relationship of white husbands and wives. An exploration and differential evaluation of the specific attitudes of each black husband and wife toward their own roles and the roles of the other party will enhance workers' understanding of the conflict.

Socialization of Children

One of the primary functions of any family is the socialization of the children. Usually we think of this process as teaching the child values and expectations in keeping with the dominant society. Billingsley (1968) concludes that the socialization process in the black family has a dual purpose, in that children must be taught "not only to be human, but how to be black in a white society" (p. 28). This is applicable to both the low- and high-income black family. It involves preparing black children for successes and disappointments. The latter, particularly, may be more closely related to race than to competence.

Black parents also seem to be aware of the particular vicissitudes that may arise in their children's transactions across family boundaries, as a result of their being black and relatively disadvantaged. Consequently, they try to communicate to them the values and specific role obligations that will enable them to cope with the greater stresses that inevitably face the members of black families (Scanzoni, 1971, p. 82).

McAdoo (1974), who seems in general agreement with Billingsley and Scanzoni, suggests that the socialization of black children requires them to become a part of the dominant culture while also internalizing the values of the black community. This socialization process, which prepares the child to function successfully in two different social systems, places a heavy burden on the child. It should be taken into consideration by workers and others seeking to understand the child's behavior.

Black parents also expect their children to earn greater rewards from the opportunity structure than they themselves were able to achieve. This

175

requires, among other things, holding on to middle-class status and taking advantage of opportunities to move up the socioeconomic ladder. One of the proven ways of socioeconomic advancement is education, which makes access to the opportunity structure less difficult. Black parents therefore emphasize the need for their children to obtain educations which prepare them for participation in the dominant culture with middle-class status. In many cases the parents select the best schools for their children, sometimes at great personal sacrifice, in the hope of enhancing their opportunities for success. Scanzoni also found that many black middle-class parents warned their children of the consequences of associating with people who might interfere with their social and economic advancement.

This kind of intensity of purpose may result in parent-child conflict in some situations, with the child struggling to differentiate from a family that is seen as far too controlling. In this case the worker needs to examine family boundaries and other systemic aspects of family functioning. As in the case of any other family, adjustments to allow for greater individuation among family members must be considered.

There is a likelihood, however, that a congruence exists between the perceptions of the black parent and child with regard to these socialization activities. There may be a mutual understanding and acceptance of roles and behaviors. This can be a result of the parent's communicating to the child her or his difference as it relates to the majority population and teaching the child how to cope with the consequences of being different. When this understanding is present it minimizes the likelihood of confrontation and conflict centered around socialization activities. Cooke (1974) offers support for this conclusion in her reference to the socialization of the black male, in particular. She suggests the lesson usually learned by the black male child is that "the often ambivalent role of polarities projected by his parents, especially his mother, when rearing him is preparation for his later subordinate role in a white society" (p. 81).

Therefore, behavior which in a different set of circumstances might be perceived as a likely conflict-producing situation, involving an overactive parent and a rebellious child, should not be so viewed in black parent-child interactions. Social workers should proceed cautiously in reaching a decision relative to the implications of this behavior. It will be useful to determine the extent to which a congruence of perceptions exists in the parent-child relationship before planning specific intervention strategies.

Support Systems

In the American population as a whole, demographic factors of age, occupation, and education account for much of the differences in mobility among individuals. As blacks have made some progress in closing the gap between themselves and whites in terms of education and occupation, it is likely they will have greater geographical mobility. Such mobility often places individuals and families in unfamiliar surroundings that result in a disruption of opportunities for feedback about themselves and validations of their expectations of others (Caplan, 1974). In other words, geographical mobility often severs the family's connection with its support systems.

While this is applicable to any family, black families are likely to find the loss of social support systems more disruptive than white families do. The black family uses the white family as a reference group in relation to the achievement of rewards from the dominant society, but it also has expectations which are framed in terms of the black community and the family's own previous experiences. This means the black family requires feedback and validation from the black community as well as from the wider society. White families are not faced with this duality since, as a rule, they seek validation only from sources within the dominant culture. Therefore, they experience less difficulty than blacks in moving from one location to another and maintaining or establishing the pattern of ties necessary for preserving their psychological and physical integrity.

Cassel (1973) also suggests that there are differences among the reactions of people to incomprehensible feedback (support disruption). The risk involved is not shared equally by all who experience breakdown in feedback regarding expectations and evaluations of behavior which serve to support and guide actions. For example, Cassel posits the existence of a dominant-subordinate factor in which a position of dominance tends to minimize the effect of experiencing loss of support, while a subordinate position tends to increase the effect. When we consider that the black family occupies a subordinate position to that of the white family in the dominant society, we believe it holds with Cassel's finding to assume that the black family will experience greater difficulty when their support systems are disrupted.

The role of black culture as a source of support for the black family must not be overlooked. Chestang (1976) states that the function of black culture is to deal with environmental threats in such a way as to guarantee the

177

survival, security, and self-esteem of black people (pp. 99–100). We agree, and suggest further that black culture is tied to the institutions of the black community which serve as a resource for the survival and security of the black family. It is within the context of this culture that black people get a sense of what Billingsley describes as we-ness, or peoplehood.

When feedback through familiar cultural channels is limited or disrupted for any reason, the black family's perception of itself as a viable unit is likely to suffer. For example, a breakdown in the supportive network of the black family may occur when it moves from one geographical location to another, leaving behind friends, relatives, familiar institutions, and accustomed ways of relating. The effect of the breakdown is most likely to surface when the family experiences a threat to its integrity. Such a threat may be brought on by conflict among family members, or it may result from transactions with systems outside family boundaries which necessitate the use of resources beyond those customarily used by the family for support and assistance in performing tasks. In the absence of familiar sources upon which to draw for help, the family may find itself, as Caplan suggests, unfamiliar with the communication signals that enable it to perceive the expectations, friendliness, or hostility in their immediate surroundings. As a result, family members, unable to feel safe and valued, are more likely to become susceptible to a crisis in functioning.

GUIDELINES FOR INTERVENTION

Theoretical Perspective

From a theoretical point of view, a systems perspective is necessary in work with black families, as it is with all families. We find symbolic interaction theory especially useful in viewing the functioning of the black family. This frame of reference addresses not only the concepts of status (or position) and role but also questions of socialization and personality. While status and role are important considerations in work with black families, socialization and personality are essential in understanding their behavior. In our view, socialization refers to "the process by which the human organism acquires the characteristic ways of behaving, the values, norms, and attitudes of the social units of which he is a part," and personality is "the development of persistent behavior patterns" (Stryker, 1964, p. 133).

178

These patterns of behavior are the result of experiences over time and should be viewed in this context when working with black families.

In the final analysis, Blumer (1969, p. 2) suggests symbolic interactionism rests on three basic premises:

1. Human beings act toward things on the basis of the meanings that the things have for them.
2. Meanings are derived from, or arise out of, the social interactions that one has with one's fellows.
3. These meanings are handled in, and modified through, an interpretative process used by the person in dealing with the things he encounters.

In applying these guiding principles of symbolic interactionism to work with black families, we favor a sociological-psychological approach to the explanation of meanings attached to experiences. We do not overlook the importance of the meaning of things toward which the members of black families act. However, we suggest that the meanings they attach to these things are influenced by a history of experiences common to black people. For this reason the meaning given to an experience in the context of social interaction is not only an expression of what black family members derive from the experience itself, it also reflects the disappointments, successes, happiness, and fears of earlier times. For example, when the black mother expresses dissatisfaction with her child's poor grades in school, the meaning she attaches to this experience comes from her own observation of the difficulty she and her people have had in earning rewards from the opportunity structure of the wider society. She also realizes that education is at least one way of making access to this structure less difficult, and poor grades mean a greater struggle for success.

Consider also the black husband who adapts to his wife's working by accepting increased responsibility for child care and housekeeping chores, and who shows little concern over the equal distribution of power that exists between himself and his wife. The meaning this has for him is shaped by his awareness of the difficulty long associated with the black males' access to employment and the greater opportunity for black females. Therefore he reacts not only to what is encountered physically—that is, his wife's working—but also to this experience as modified through an interpretative process which is influenced by his previous experiences. The husband responds to a symbolic environment created in part by his own internal processes.

179

A symbolic-interactionist conceptualization of human behavior lends itself to exploration and understanding of the uniqueness of the black family experience. It suggests the likelihood and significance of individual reactions to a symbolic environment that is derived from the meaning the person attaches to what is experienced. We suggest that the experience of black people in American society shapes the meaning they give to what they encounter in various transactions with their environment. And their response to other persons and situations, based on this meaning, will influence the way others respond to them. We believe that viewing black family interactions within a systems-interactionist framework allows for the most complete understanding of the family's transactions, member with member, and members with the world outside of family boundaries.

Intervening with the Family

The primary objective of family intervention is to alter dysfunctional interactional patterns between family members. Many family therapists believe this can be accomplished while obtaining only a minimum of history information from the family. We agree with this approach for the most part, but we believe an exception is necessary when intervening with black families. Among the reasons for this shift in emphasis is the cultural heritage of black people in general, which is distinctly different from other racial or ethnic groups. The circumstances surrounding the development and maintenance of the black family in America also have resulted in a variation of life-styles among these families. Therefore, in order to make a differential assessment of family functioning and to plan for effective intervention, the worker needs to examine selected aspects of the family's history, depending on the difficulty experienced.

Not only is history information important in understanding the functioning of black families, but certain kinds of history information are essential. Our concern is for more experiential information rather than strictly chronological-developmental data. The experiences of the parents as children growing up in their families of origin; their coming together as a couple; their ideas about raising their own family; and the impact social, economic, and political forces have had on their lives are all important experiences which usually prove to be profitable areas for exploration. However, social workers must keep in mind the specific problem being presented by the family and develop the necessary information around this difficulty, instead of routinely developing generalized information about the family.

For example, if the problem is presented as the parents' frustration over the child's apparent lack of interest in school, it would hardly be necessary or profitable to explore in detail how the parents became interested in each other and what each wanted from the marriage. Instead, it would likely be most productive to examine what they want for their child and how they arrived at these expectations. A better understanding of the situation might also be realized by obtaining some idea of what their own parents had expected of them as children and their vision of possible obstacles to the child's participation in the economic opportunity structure.

When the parent-child relationship is the target of intervention, it will be helpful to explore socialization patterns, including the parents' own experiences with the socialization process in their families of origin. While this information is useful in work with nonminority families as well, it has special significance in intervening with black families. The black child undergoes a unique and demanding socialization process which incorporates the values and expectations of two different cultures, as we have noted. Socioeconomic success is also an important family value that is imparted to the black child as he is taught to participate successfully in the economic opportunity structure of the wider society. Although the socialization experience of black children does not automatically produce a pathological situation, it does have the potential for problem development and should be fully explored when parents and children are experiencing difficulty in communicating and relating to each other.

With many families, especially those who come for help after a recent change in geographical location, we suggest an examination of the family's support systems. Hansell (1976) has suggested a number of attachments to various resources as instrumental in helping people cope with the kind of distress that is usually experienced in the loss of social supports. Although he was concerned primarily with the individual, some of his ideas are also applicable to families and can provide direction for social workers intervening with black families, especially where a breakdown in sources of support has been established. The following points are extrapolated from Hansell's suggestions (p. 33):

1. The family must be attached to appropriate sources of information. The family in unfamiliar surroundings may not have sufficient access to sources of information, in which case the worker can connect the family

with individuals, groups, or organizations with which they can communicate and from which they can receive necessary information.

2. There should be attachment to resources that will enable the family to realize its identity as a functioning unit. If the family has lost its connection with familiar resources that have customarily fed back to them what is expected and how well they are meeting these expectations, the worker must provide for new sources of validation. This can often be realized by helping the family establish interdependent connections with other families, or other persons outside its boundaries, with whom members can share mutual interests and activities and can develop trust. This attachment will allow the exchange of suitable information and increase feedback to the family about its operations.

3. It is essential that the family be attached to groups of people who regard it as belonging. These might include religious groups, political groups, and so on, which have the capability of assisting the family with various tasks.

When support systems are disrupted the worker should examine the family's attachment to these resources and plan to effect connections where indicated. The primary objective is to connect the family with others who will be able to "speak their language" and with whom family members can feel comfortable, build trust, and gain a sense of self and a feeling of security.

When viewed as a social system, the similarities between the black middle-class family and the white middle-class family are far greater than the differences. However, if we are to understand the black family we must examine its functioning within a framework that allows us to view what is different and determine what, if any, impact this difference has on family transactions. Billingsley (1968, pp. 150–51) has suggested a set of guidelines for understanding the black family which we believe are essential. First, he suggests the black family should be viewed as a social system interacting with a number of other systems. Second, a historical perspective of the black family is necessary in order to best understand its structure and functioning. Third, it must be realized that black people operate with a differentiated set of social structures which should be considered in viewing their behavior. In other words, differences exist between black families in the same way as differences exist between white families, and differential assessments and intervention strategies are necessary in work with different families. Fourth, black family structure should be perceived as an adaptation to a set of conditions existing in the family's wider social environment which is related to its efforts to meet the needs of its members and the demands of society.

It is also well to remember that self-determination is very important to black families. This determination is likely to be reflected in the family's transactions with other systems, and social workers must be prepared to deal with this. In addition, we suggest that workers take into consideration the local and national sociopolitical climate at the time of the therapeutic encounter, as the struggles of the black middle-class family may be related to these phenomena.

SUMMARY

Working with black families is not a completely different experience from working with other families. The similarities are greater than the differences. Nevertheless, there are a few differences which are significant, and social workers should take them into consideration when planning change with black families.

It is important to recognize the cultural heritage of the black family in America, society's perception of the family, and the family's perception of itself. The basis of relating between husband and wife, the socialization of children, the importance of support systems, and the impact of the prevailing sociopolitical climate are important areas for consideration in work with this group.

A systems-symbolic interactionist approach is a useful framework within which to view black family functioning. Social workers must also remember that there are differences between black families, and a differential use of treatment techniques and strategies is necessary.

REFERENCES

Billingsley, A. *Black Families in White America.* Englewood Cliffs, N.J.: Prentice-Hall, 1968.
Blumer, H. *Symbolic Interactionism: Perspective and Method.* Englewood Cliffs, N.J.: Prentice-Hall, 1969.
Caplan, G. *Support Systems and Community Mental Health.* New York: Behavioral Publications, 1974.
Cassel, J. C. "Psychiatric Epidemiology." In G. Caplan (ed.), *American Handbook of Psychiatry.* Vol. 2. New York: Basic Books, 1973.

Chestang, L. "The Black Family and Black Culture: A Study of Coping." In M. Sotomayor (ed.), *Cross Cultural Perspectives in Social Work Practice and Education.* Houston: University of Houston, Graduate School of Social Work, 1976.

Cooke, G. "Socialization of the Black Male: Research Implications." In L. E. Gary, (ed.), *Social Research and the Black Community: Selected Issues and Priorities.* Washington, D.C.: Institute for Urban Affairs and Research, Howard University, 1974.

Frazier, E. F. *Black Bourgeoisie.* New York: Collier Books, 1962.

Hansell, *The Person in Distress.* New York: Human Sciences Press, 1976.

Kronus, S. *The Black Middle Class.* Columbus, Ohio: Charles E. Merrill Publishing Co., 1971.

McAdoo, H. P. "The Socialization of Black Children: Priorities for Research." In L. E. Gary (ed.), *Social Research and the Black Community: Selected Issues and Priorities.* Washington, D.C.: Institute for Urban Affairs and Research, Howard University, 1974.

Pettigrew, T. F. *A Profile of the Negro American.* Princeton, N.J.: D. Van Nostrand Co., 1964.

Sager, C. J., Brayboy, T. L., and Waxenberg, B. R. *Black Ghetto Family in Therapy.* New York: Grove Press, 1970.

Scanzoni, J. H. *The Black Family in Modern Society.* Boston: Allyn & Bacon, 1971.

Stryker, S. "The Interactional and Situational Approaches." In H. T. Christensen (ed.), *Handbook on Marriage and the Family.* Chicago: Rand McNally & Co., 1964.

Minuchin, S., Montalvo, B., Guerney, B., Rosman, L., and Shumer, F. *Families of the Slums.* New York: Basic Books, 1967.

CHAPTER **8**

Family Treatment for Alcoholism

By CURTIS JANZEN

The increasing use of family therapy in the treatment of alcoholism raises questions about the relationship between the problems of the family and the problem of alcoholism. If family treatment is to benefit the entire family, not just the alcoholic, it is necessary to clarify the relationship between both sets of problems. This article will attempt to clarify the nature of the family relationship as it has been described in the social work literature and to discuss the ways in which this understanding has been used by various treatment programs (Hill & Blane, 1967; Emrick, 1974, 1975).

A second goal is closely related to the first. Although the literature has reported extensively on services to members of the alcoholic's family, this discussion has too frequently been unrelated to the various perspectives of family therapy. Ideas from these two areas will be brought together in a way that may be helpful to professionals working with families of alcoholics.

Reprinted from *Social Work*, 23:135-41, 1978, with permission of the publisher and the author. Copyright 1978, National Association of Social Workers, Inc.

The author's frame of reference emphasizes the view that families of alcoholics are transacting systems. Because this perspective is only implicit in the review, the article concludes with an explanation of how family systems theory can be better applied to treatment of an alcoholic's family relationships.

FAMILY RELATIONSHIPS

In the studies under review, there is wide recognition that the problems of alcoholics and the problems of their families overlap significantly. Alcoholism is seen as either the cause or the consequence of the pattern of family life. This issue is discussed first from the point of view of the relationship between the alcoholic and the spouse and then with regard to the involvement of other family members.

Who Controls Whom?

Three separate but related views of the spouse's relationship to the problem of alcoholism are present in the literature. The first perspective emphasizes the need of the spouse to have the alcoholic continue drinking. Needs for dependency, feelings of inadequacy, and sexual anxieties are all emotional disturbances that might prompt a wife to wish to "control" her husband and increase his sense of inadequacy. Such actions, in turn, increase her sense of adequacy, calm her anxieties, or meet her needs for affirmation and nurture. There is, however, considerable disagreement as to the existence of emotional disturbance in the spouse (Fox, 1956; Krimmel, 1971; Rae, 1972).

Other studies suggest that if the wife is disturbed, the disturbance originates as a consequence of the drinking and is not its cause. Bailey (1968), Cohen and Krause (1971), and Kogan and Jackson (1965) report improvement in one spouse as the other's drinking subsides. In their article, Edwards, Harvey, and Whitehead (1973) review numerous studies about the wives of alcoholics and draw similar conclusions.

The second perspective is taken from Ballard (1959), who made an extensive study of the Minnesota Multiphasic Personality Inventories of alcoholic men and their wives. He concludes: "Even if there were no problems of alcoholism, the marriage in the experimental (alcoholism) group was of the sort where marital conflict was likely to develop." A similar point of view is taken by the Al-Anon Family Group (1967): "Troubled wives and alcoholics often take it for granted that their marital discords are due entirely to alcoholism, whether the alcoholic is sober or is still drinking. Yet alcoholism itself rarely creates all these problems and sobriety itself usually does not cure them" (p. 3).

In a comment on how difficult it is to face issues concerning relationships, Esser (1968) reports that the alcoholic sometimes brings up a problem of marital stress at one treatment session, but then resumes drinking before the next session. In this way, he diverts attention away from the marital difficulty and onto the drinking problem. This tactic seems to suggest that the drinking is used to avoid facing real problems in family relationships.

The third perspective is represented by Gorad's (1971) view of the way both the husband and wife in alcoholic marriages attempt to gain control of the relationship. In interpersonal exchange they are more competitive than spouses in normal marriages, practicing a continual game of one-upmanship. Gorad notes that although withdrawn, dependent behavior is not usually seen as controlling, such behavior, in fact, does serve to control the relationship. Thus, the wife, who seems strong in relation to the alcoholic, does not dominate the alcoholic any more than he dominates her. In addition, behaviors of a sharing or self-revealing nature are less frequent among these couples than among others. The attempts on each side at mutual control are self-defeating and only serve to perpetuate the problem. Similarly, Krimmel (1971) points out that the wife's attempts to control her husband's drinking are futile. He adds: "A wife cuts the power her alcoholic husband has over her by no longer needing or attempting to control him. This is not easy, because the alcoholic has a variety of weapons to perpetuate the emotional ties, however unhealthy they may be" (p. 104).

All three perspectives focus on the interactional process between spouses. The problem of alcoholism not only affects the functioning of the individuals involved; it becomes, in itself, a means of coping with and regulating the relationship. The focus of the treatment will be determined by which of these perspectives is believed by the therapist to have priority.

The perspectives drawn from the literature on alcoholism conform to a remarkable degree with the range of family treatment orientations delineated by the Group for the Advancement of Psychiatry (1970). At the risk of gross oversimplification, one type of family therapist works with the entire family but tends to see the focus of difficulties as residing in its

187

individual members. The family therapists at the other end of the range locate the source of the difficulty in the functioning of the family system, in the role problems, and in the relationships between roles and communication among the various individuals. The third type of family therapist works both with the members' internal problems and with the system's difficulties. Beels and Ferber (1969) offer a different way of categorizing the range of orientations to family treatment.

Interpersonal Payoffs

This chapter has thus far emphasized the disturbance in the marital relationship as opposed to the disturbance in the individual partners. There are various ways of viewing the patterns of relationship. Steiner (1969) observes that repetitive behavior sequences are transacted between the alcoholic and other family members and that the motive for engaging in these "is the production of certain interpersonal payoffs." The alcoholic, for example, may invite control from others and, depending on the response, allow himself to get angry at their attempts to tell him what to do. In this vein, Ward and Faillace (1970) comment:

> If the wife is forgiving, the husband has learned that forgiveness for being drunk can be obtained, provided he is appropriately remorseful and very sick. If she punishes him for his behavior by criticizing him, his guilt and shame are relieved and he feels considerably less anxious. In either case the pattern cannot be understood except in terms of the total sequence. (p. 686)

Ward and Faillace limit their discussion to the interaction between spouses. However, these transactions do not operate solely between husbands and wives but are present between any two persons in the family.

A second perspective on the disturbed relationship focuses on the failure of the spouses to define their separate selves. Al-Anon writings point out the danger of the idea that "being married to a man puts us in charge of him. We are so deeply involved that we treat those closest to us as though they were part of ourselves" (Al-Anon Family Group, 1967).

According to Bowen (1974), one consequence of this failure to differentiate is that one spouse overfunctions and the other underfunctions. He writes that in most marriages it is easier for the overfunctioning spouse to become more passive than it is for the underfunctioning spouse to become more active. Therefore, he suggests that the therapist work with that spouse to produce initial change in the interaction. If the wife ceases to overfunction, angry repercussions may ensue on the part of the alcoholic. However, because he is allowed to function freely as a separate self, anger may be followed by relief and positive change.

The foregoing discussion is based on alcoholic husbands and nonalcoholic wives. Nonalcoholic husbands interact somewhat differently with their alcoholic wives (Auger, 1973; Bailey, 1961; Krimmel, 1971; Meeks, 1970; C. Smith, 1975; and Wenberg, 1973). For one thing, husbands are less likely to endure the situation as long as wives are. In addition, it appears that the damage done to children differs as well, because husbands are not in as good a position as are wives to protect the children.

The review thus far suggests that altering the family's pattern of interaction can bring about a change in the alcoholic's drinking. However, it is also true that if the alcoholic stops drinking, thus initiating the change, further behavioral adaptation is required on the part of both spouses (Jackson, 1956). By the time the alcoholic begins to alter his drinking behavior, he has been excluded by the family. Now the family is required to change in order to bring the nondrinking alcoholic back into the family, to make room for his contributions, to learn to behave with less suspicion and fear, and to avoid remembering past failures. Other problems of the past, such as behavior on holidays and sexual relationships, need to be faced in a new way by both spouses. Thus, family roles, attitudes, and behaviors vary according to the stage of the crisis.

Role of Children

In considering the total functioning of the family, it is necessary to realize the role of the children. Numerous authors have drawn attention to the effect of alcoholism on the children involved (Auger, 1973; Chafetz, Blane, & Hill, 1971; Cohen & Krause, 1971; Sloboda, 1974). According to Bosma (1972), one of the long-term consequences is that children of alcoholics are more likely to marry alcoholics than are other children. Clinebell (1968) lists four factors that produce damage in the lives of the children of alcoholics: (1) the shift and reversal of parental roles, (2) the inconsistent and unpredictable relationship with the alcoholic, (3) the inadequacy of the nonalcoholic parent because of his or her own unmet needs, and (4) the interference in their relationships with their peers.

Krimmel (1971) states that children are exploited by both parents and are pressured to take sides in the parental battles, which serves to intensify rather than to alleviate the conflict. In this way, not only are children victims of the drinking problem but, because they have been caught up in the demands of the system and forced to take sides, they also contribute to the continuation of the problem. Thus children, like spouses, are a reciprocating part of the system that perpetuates both the alcoholism and the family's difficulties.

TREATMENT AND CHANGE

Before proceeding to a discussion of the ways in which concepts about family relationships are used in treating the alcoholic, a brief review is warranted of how the family is involved in the different treatment programs. Some programs are intended primarily for family members and serve the alcoholic only secondarily (Cohen & Krause, 1971; McDowell, 1972). Many programs are for outpatients alone and include alcoholics who have or have not been hospitalized previously (Bullock & Mudd, 1959; Preston, 1960; Woggon, 1972). Some family treatment services are offered during the alcoholic's hospital stay, and others require the residence of key family members during all or part of the residential phase (Binder, 1971; Brown-Mayers, Seelye, & Brown, 1973; Corder & Laidlaw, 1972; Catanzaro, 1973). A few programs treat the family at home (Esser, 1968, 1971; Pattison, 1965).

In some programs, spouses are seen separately, either individually or in groups, whereas others operate only as groups (C. G. Smith, 1969; Gliedman, 1956). In other programs, both spouses are seen conjointly or occasionally in groups with other couples (Berman, 1966, 1968; Burton & Kaplan, 1968). Many programs use several treatment methods (Ewing & Fox, 1968; Preston, 1960). In some instances, children are included in the family treatment interviews (Esser, 1968, 1971; Meeks & Kelly, 1970). Bowen and Esser recommend that to the extent that members of the extended family are accessible, they should be included in treatment as well (Bowen, 1974; Esser, 1968).

These variations in treatment procedures, although numerous, have all had success. On the basis of the available studies, it is not possible to state unequivocally that family treatment is better than other forms of treatment. It is clear, however, that family treatment can bring about a degree of growth and change that might not be possible with other

190

methods. Gerard and Saenger (1966) have documented that even one contact with the spouse can have a significant effect on the likelihood that the alcoholic will continue in treatment.

Spouses in Treatment

The reviewed studies note that change in the families of alcoholics begins to take place when members alter their pattern of responses to the alcoholic's behavior. Mueller (1972) states that the wife's attempts to control and threaten often serve to aggravate the alcoholic's guilt, self-hatred, and feelings of rejection and inadequacy and thus help to defeat her efforts to change him. Treatment should teach the wife to accept alcoholism as an illness—not as a weakness or as vindictive behavior. She needs to recognize that

> . . . she did not cause the illness and that she is not capable of or responsible for curing it. Once freed of that burden, she can drop her ineffective coping and rescue operations. She can learn to stop nagging, making threats without carrying them out, and protecting her husband from the consequences of his drinking. . . . Her consequent lack of action should not emanate from anger and retaliation but rather, so far as possible, from a sense of objectivity and detachment . . . surrender and release. (Mueller, 1972, p. 82)

With such a change in the wife's behavior, the alcoholic has less reason to blame others and to behave resentfully for their attempts to "run his life." The responsibility for control rests on the alcoholic alone.

With this in mind, Cohen and Krause (1971) trained social workers to teach wives of alcoholics the concept of alcoholism as a disease. In this way, the wives could learn to feel less responsible for their spouse's behavior and thus be able to alter their own behavior. Cohen and Krause point out that this group of social workers produced positive change in the alcoholic's drinking habits and in family behavior, but that these results were not significantly better than those of social workers who had not received special training. The researchers suggest that this may be because the treatment orientation focuses on goals of self-fulfillment and self-determination for each family member but minimizes the necessity for family members to sacrifice themselves for one another. This author would point out that although instruction in disease concepts is useful, it is not an end in itself. Rather, it is a means of helping the wife to desist from her regulatory

191

efforts, to value herself more highly, and to seek more successful routes to a satisfactory life.

Finlay (1966) has shown that "role network pressure" is useful in bringing the alcoholic to face his drinking problem. He writes: "A disruption that is seriously threatened by either spouse or employer, and which is imminent unless the alcoholic makes appropriate use of help, is indicated" (1966, p. 77).

In addition, Finlay (1974) advises that the family must be convinced that if the alcoholic is protected from the direct consequences of his drinking, he will be less likely to seek treatment. Such change on the part of the wife may be possible only after she views the problem from a different perspective or after she experiences an increase in her self-esteem. The inference here is that when she responds differently, the relationship pattern is altered and constructive change can take place. Decreased drinking, improved family relationships, or marital separation may all be indications of positive change.

Children in Treatment

The way in which children are involved in the alcoholic family's destructive pattern of relationships has been noted. However, although treatment would appear to be indicated, there is little documentation as to the method that would benefit them or the family most. Clinebell (1968) writes that the best way to help the children is by helping their parents. Mueller (1972) suggests that the wife must learn to accept alcoholism as an illness and be able to explain it as such to the children. In addition, the wife must be helped to recognize the children's problems and provide emotional support for them. Referring children to a program such as Alateen can be useful as well.

Ward and Faillace (1970) outline the benefits of referral as follows: "It encourages moves toward independence from the conflict-ridden family by documenting the uselessness of rescue or persecution attempts. The guilt about helplessness is turned toward constructive education goals" (p. 688). In other words, children tend to see the fault as lying in one parent or the other and ignore the faulty pattern of interaction between the two.

An additional problem is that the child of an alcoholic is not free to be a child or to concentrate on growing up. Too often he is called on to protect or advise his parent or parents (Press, 1975). Putting the child in the role of scapegoat or peacemaker does not resolve the family's difficulties. One of the goals of the therapeutic process, then, must be to help the child remove himself from the center of his parents' conflict.

Cohen and Krause (1971) note that an additional advantage in having children participate in family interviews is that the alcoholic will become aware of the effects of his behavior on them. For example, the alcoholic may realize that it is because of his behavior that the children no longer bring their friends home. To this point, Esser (1968) writes:

> In the family of an alcoholic, children get the impression that they may not ask questions. Questions might lead to undesirable discussions of the drinking habit, and the parents are too upset about that to discuss it openly. The children try to explain, but come to incomplete or incorrect conclusions. (p. 180)

Presumably family interviews should improve communication to the extent that children are permitted open expression of their feelings and comments on family problems (Meeks & Kelly, 1970).

The discussion thus far has assumed that the alcoholic member of the family is one of the adults. This is not to deny the existence of alcoholism among adolescents. However, to date there is a dearth of research on treatment for families of adolescent alcoholics.

Treating the Extended Family

In the existing literature there is only limited comment on the significance of including the extended family in the treatment of alcoholism. Esser (1968) notes that it is important to involve members of the extended family in treatment because they often "play an important role in maintaining the homeostasis within the family unit." This suggests that members of the extended family are frequently drawn into the conflict between the spouses, much as the children are urged to take sides. Bowen's (1974) discussion of triangles made up of members of the extended family indicates that this takes place when the tension between the spouses becomes too great. Disputes between spouses concentrate on the role of this or that relative, ignoring the anxieties and differences in their own marital relationship. Therapists need to be aware that the spouses draw their relatives into the conflict, and relatives whose own anxieties are aroused often inject themselves in defense of one spouse or the other.

Neither spouses nor relatives readily relinquish the involvements that have existed over long periods of time, but it is important that therapy induce them to do so.

One factor in the continued involvement of members of the extended family may be the unresolved attachment of spouses to their parents that interferes with their marital adaptation. Bowen (1974) observes: "The person who later becomes an alcoholic is one who handles the emotional attachment to his parents, and especially his mother, by denial of the attachment and by a super-independent posture which says, 'I do not need you. I can do it myself ' " (p. 118). The present author would suggest that the alcoholic and the spouse have equal difficulty in loosening close parental ties. In turn, both parents may have a problem loosening the bonds between themselves and their children.

The net effect of these views seems to be that two and three generations are involved in the creation and perpetuation of the problems of alcoholism. As Meeks and Kelly (1970) point out, the involvement of more than one generation in the treatment process is important not only because this may be a continuing source of difficulty, but also because changed behavior on the part of family members can be a source of healing and help to all concerned. Thus, positive change initiated by any one member in the family system produces positive growth and change in other members of the system as well.

A SYSTEMS STATEMENT

It is evident from the review that the only definition of family treatment is that it is treatment that involves the family of the alcoholic. Furthermore, no unitary conception of the relationship between alcoholism and the problems of the family is apparent. Nonetheless, a family systems approach seems to offer a comprehensive framework for resolving the apparent disparity.

A view of the family as a system implies that a family needs to be viewed as a whole; that the alcoholic cannot be considered in isolation from the social group of which he is a part. The family system, rather than the alcoholic alone, becomes the patient. The alcoholism is only a symptom of the system's malfunction. The alcoholic role is one role, but other family members have other definite roles within the system. Over time, role relationships become stabilized, and the behavior of members of the family can be predicted. A change in role behavior on the part of any family member precipitates crisis in the system as a whole. The change may be the result of inputs in the family system from some other social system—employers, friends, the police, the children's school, or some therapeutic agency—and will require new behavior on the part of other members of the system. This view helps to account for change in the drinking habits of the alcoholic when, in fact, it was other family members, and not he himself, who were being treated. It also helps to account for the fact that when the alcoholic changes, new adaptations are required of other family members in order for the family to achieve new balance and stability.

Finlay (1974) summarizes such developments as follows:

A more recent concept appearing in the literature on alcoholism regards excessive drinking from the viewpoint of communications, interactions, and transactions within the social system. Within this general framework, the problem for solution is defined in interactional terms, and the target for change becomes not simply the alcoholic but the interactional system in which he is involved.

Excessive drinking or drunkenness is recognized as one facet of a life-style in which the person avoids responsibility on a global scale. This style is actively reinforced by the interactional style of others—that is, the style is allowed to become stronger and more habitual because significant others do not constantly and effectively challenge or disrupt the alcoholic's modus vivendi. (p. 398)

Behavior within the family unit is a way of coping not only with internal stresses but with the behavior of others as well. Each person's response is a response to the response of others, which, in turn, was a response to some previous behavior. Over time, these responses assume a pattern. Each person develops characteristic responses to the characteristic behavior of others. One's own responses will alter when the responses of others are altered. The family is thus seen as a homeostatic system in which the members are engaged in a mutual effort to keep behavior in the family on a certain course. In commenting both on the systems effect and on the implications for treatment, Mulford (1970) observes: "If becoming a problem drinker is a product of social interaction, then becoming a recovered problem drinker is likewise a product of social interaction. To effect recovery is a reintegration process involving other persons, usually those involved in the process when he became a problem drinker." (p. 8).

Not only does an individual's behavior have an effect on the behavior of others, there are also consequences for the continuing identity formation and self-esteem of both parents and children. Individuals who continue to berate and deprecate each other contribute to a person's formation of a negative self-image. Although this is readily seen in the case of parent-to-child interaction, it is also present in parent-to-parent interaction and in children-to-parent interaction. The images that others have about an individual and that are conveyed through verbal and nonverbal behavior have a profound effect on the continuing personality development of the alcoholic, the spouse, and the children. Lofland (1969) writes: "Other things being equal, the greater the consistency, duration, and intensity with which a definition is promoted by others about an actor (person) the greater the likelihood that an actor will embrace that definition as truly applicable to himself." Individuals who act in accord with negative self-image will engage in behavior that is simultaneously self-destructive and that reinforces the other's negative image of him. Family members must be extricated from this cycle of negatively reinforced interaction.

Regardless of who the patient is, the important thing in treatment is to clarify the nature of the interaction among the dyads and triads in the family group. In this way, previously established destructive patterns can be interrupted and changed. Since conflict in a family is to be expected, the goal of therapy is to help family members find new ways of resolving such conflict. This may mean teaching them to communicate their own needs directly and clearly instead of by their control of the other persons. It may also mean learning how to respond differently to the communications of others. Finally, it may mean enabling a current conflict between two persons to remain and to force its resolution, rather than allowing it to be interrupted and diluted by a third person. This is what happens when a child is allowed to enter into his parents' conflict.

Although it would seem desirable to involve as many relevant family members as possible in the learning process, it is not always possible to do so. Learning can take place in the presence of the entire family group, but it can also take place with pairs of members working with each other or even with one individual working with the caseworker. Or, learning may come about through the group participation of one or more family members. An example of this might be a child's participation in Alateen, where he can be taught to stay out of parental conflict as much as possible. No matter which person begins to change his way of relating to the family, treatment for the entire family has begun. Although change can be resisted, it cannot be ignored. Other family members must find new ways of behaving when one of the members changes his ways.

REFERENCES

Al-Anon Family Group. *The Dilemma of the Alcoholic Marriage.* New York, 1967.

Auger, R., Bragg, R., Corns, D., and Miller, M. "Preliminary Assessment and Prognostic Indicators in a Newly Developed Alcohol Treatment Program." *Newsletter for Research in Mental Health and Behavioral Sciences,* May 1973, pp. 21–24.

Bailey, M. B. "Alcoholism and Marriage: A Review." *Quarterly Journal of Studies on Alcohol,* 22:81–97, 1961.

Bailey, M. B. *Alcoholism and Family Casework.* New York: Community Council of Greater New York, 1968.

Ballard, R. G. "The Interaction Between Marital Conflict and Alcoholism as Seen Through MMPI's of Marriage Partners." *American Journal of Orthopsychiatry,* 29:528–46, 1959.

Beels, C. C., and Ferber, A. "Family Therapy: A View." *Family Process,* 8: 230–318, 1969.

Berman, K. "Multiple Family Therapy: Its Possibilities in Preventing Readmission." *Mental Hygiene,* 50:367–70, 1966.

Berman, K. "Multiple Conjoint Family Groups in the Treatment of Alcoholism." *Journal of Medical Society of New Jersey,* 65:6–8, 1968.

Binder, S. "Newer Therapeutic Procedures for Alcoholics." *Zeitschrift fuer Psychotherapie und Medizinische Psychologie,* 21:239–47, 1971.

Bosma, W. "Children of Alcoholics: A Hidden Tragedy." *Maryland State Medical Journal,* 21:34–36, 1972.

Bowen, M. "Alcoholism as Viewed Through Family Systems Theory and Family Psychotherapy." *Annals of the New York Academy of Sciences,* 233:115–22, 1974.

Brown-Mayers, A., Seelye, E., and Brown, D. "Reorganized Alcoholism Service." *Journal of the American Medical Association,* 224:233-35, 1973.

Bullock, S. C., and Mudd, E. H. "The Interrelatedness of Alcoholism and Marital Conflict." *American Journal of Orthopsychiatry,* 29:519–27, 1959.

Burton, G., and Kaplan, H. M. "Group Counseling in Conflicted Marriage Where Alcoholism Is Present: Client's Evaluation of Effectiveness." *Journal of Marriage and the Family,* 30:74–79, 1968.

Cadogan, D. A. "Marital Group Therapy in the Treatment of Alcoholism." *Quarterly Journal of Studies on Alcohol,* 34:1187–94, 1973.

Catanzaro, R., Pisani, V., Fox, R., and Kennedy, E. "Familization Therapy." *Diseases of the Nervous System,* 34:212–18, 1973.

Chafetz, M., Blane, H., and Hill, M. "Children of Alcoholics." *Quarterly Journal of Studies on Alcohol,* 32:687–98, 1971.

Clinebell, H. J., Jr. "Pastoral Counseling of the Alcoholic and His Family." In R. Catanzaro (ed.), *Alcoholism: The Total Treatment Approach.* Springfield, Ill.: Charles C Thomas, Publisher, 1968.

Cohen, P., and Krause, M. S. *Casework with Wives of Alcoholics*. New York: Family Service Association of America, 1971.

Corder, R. F., and Laidlaw, N. D. "An Intensive Treatment Program for Alcoholics and Their Wives." *Quarterly Journal of Studies on Alcohol*, 33:1144–46, 1972.

Edwards, P., Harvey, C., and Whitehead, P. "*Wives of Alcoholics:* A Critical Review and Analysis." *Quarterly Journal of Studies on Alcohol*, 34:112–32, 1973.

Emrick, C. "A Review of Psychologically Oriented Treatment of Alcoholism, I: The Use and Interrelationships of Outcome Criteria and Drinking Behavior Following Treatment." *Quarterly Journal of Studies on Alcohol*, 35:523–49, 1974.

Emrick, C. "A Review of Psychologically Oriented Treatment of Alcoholism, II: The Relative Effectiveness of Different Treatment Approaches and the Effectiveness of Treatment Versus No Treatment." *Quarterly Journal of Studies on Alcohol*, 36:88-108, 1975.

Esser, P. H. "Conjoint Family Therapy with Alcoholics." *British Journal of Addiction*, 63:177–82, 1968.

Esser, P. H. "Evaluation of Family Therapy with Alcoholics." *British Journal of Addiction*, 66:251–55, 1971.

Ewing, J., and Fox, R. "Family Therapy of Alcoholism." *Current Psychiatric Therapies*, 8:86–91, 1968.

Finlay, D. "Effect of Role Network Pressure on an Alcoholic's Approach to Treatment." *Social Work*, 11:71-77, 1966.

Finlay, D. "Alcoholism: Illness or Problem in Interaction." *Social Work*, 19:390–405, 1974.

Fox, R. "The Alcoholic Spouse." In V. Eisenstein (ed.), *Neurotic Interaction in Marriage*. New York: Basic Books, 1956.

Fox, R. "Treating the Alcoholic's Family." In R. Catanzaro (ed.), *Alcoholism: The Total Treatment Approach*. Springfield, Ill.: Charles C Thomas, Publisher, 1968.

Gallant, D. M., Rich, A., Bey, E., and Terranova, L. "Group Psychotherapy with Married Couples: Successful Techniques in New Orleans Alcoholism Clinic Patients." *Louisiana State Medical Society Journal*, 122:41–44, 1970.

Gerard, D.L., and Saenger, G. *Outpatient Treatment of Alcoholism: A Study of Outcome and Its Determination*. Toronto: University of Toronto Press, 1966.

Gliedman, L., Rosenthal, D., Frank, J., and Nash, H. "Group Therapy of Alcoholics and Concurrent Group Meetings of Their Wives." *Quarterly Journal of Studies on Alcohol*, 17:655–70, 1956.

Gorad, S. L. "Communicational Style of Alcoholics and Their Wives." *Family Process*, 10:475–89, 1971.

Group for the Advancement of Psychiatry. *The Field of Family Therapy*. New York, 1970.

Hill, M., and Blane, H. "Evaluation of Psychotherapy with Alcoholics: A Critical Review." *Quarterly Journal of Studies on Alcohol*, 28:76-104, 1967.

Jackson, J. K. "The Adjustment of the Family to Alcoholism." *Marriage and Family Living*, 18:361–69, 1956.

Kogan, K. L., and Jackson, J. K. "Stress, Personality, and Emotional Disturbance in Wives of Alcoholics." *Quarterly Journal of Studies on Alcohol*, 26:486–95, 1965.

Kranitz, L. "An Alternative Treatment of Alcoholism." *Newsletter for Research in Psychology*, 13:21, 1971.

Krimmel, H. (ed.). *Alcoholism: Challenge for Social Work Education*. New York: Council on Social Work Education, 1971.

Loescher, D. A. "Time Limited Group Therapy for Alcoholic Marriages." *Medical Ecology and Clinical Research*, 3:30–32, 1971.

Lofland, J. *Deviance and Identity*. Englewood Cliffs, N.J.: Prentice-Hall, 1969.

McDowell, F. K. "The Pastor's Natural Ally against Alcoholism." *Journal of Pastoral Care*, 26:26–32, 1972.

Meeks, D. E., and Kelly, C. "Family Therapy with the Families of Recovering Alcoholics." *Quarterly Journal of Studies on Alcohol*, 31:399–413, 1970.

Mueller, J. F. "Casework with the Family of the Alcoholic." *Social Work*, 17:79–84, 1972.

Mulford, H. *Meeting the Problems of Alcohol Abuse: A Testable Action Plan for Iowa*. Cedar Rapids, Iowa: Iowa Alcoholism Foundation, 1970.

Pattison, E. M. "Treatment of Alcoholic Families with Nurse Home Visits." *Family Process*, 4:74–94, 1965.

Press, L. "Treating the Family." *Maryland State Medical Journal*, 24:32–35, 1975.

Preston, F. B. "Combined Individual, Joint, and Group Therapy in Treatment of Alcoholism." *Mental Hygiene*, 44:522–28, 1960.

Rae, J. "The Influence of Wives on the Treatment Outcome of Alcoholics." *British Journal of Psychiatry*, 120:601–13, 1972.

Sloboda, S. "The Children of Alcoholics: A Neglected Problem." *Hospital and Community Psychiatry*, 25:605–6, 1974.

Smith, C. Personal communication, February 26, 1975.

Smith, C. G. "Alcoholics: Their Treatment and Their Wives." *British Journal of Psychiatry*, 115:1039–42, 1969.

Steiner, C. "The Alcoholic Game." *Quarterly Journal of Studies on Alcohol*, 30:920–38, 1969.

Ward, R., and Faillace, L. "The Alcoholic and His Helpers." *Quarterly Journal of Studies on Alcohol*, 31:684–91, 1970.

Weinberg, J. "Counseling Recovering Alcoholics." *Social Work*, 18:84–93, 1973.

Woggon, H. A. "The Alcoholic Unit at Broughton Hospital." *Inventory*, 22:18–19, 1972.

CHAPTER **9**

Family Treatment In A Medical Hospital Setting

By JUDITH FINE

Chronic illness profoundly changes the lives of those it affects. It changes the quality of life for individuals and families and affects both individual and family self-images. It alters the developmental course of the family group and the attainment of family and individual goals. The consequent need to face, integrate, cope with, and adapt to changes in finances, work, marital and parental roles, and life satisfactions and plans utilizes a great deal of the patient's and family members' energies and often requires outside help.

The frequency and impact of chronic illness are bringing social workers, both in hospitals and in the community, into increasing contact with affected individuals and families. Social workers in acute-care medical settings need an organized framework which permits them to help patients and their families achieve the following goals: lessen emotional pain, learn to handle ongoing tensions, make role changes, and identify remaining

Note: The author wishes to express appreciation to Dr. Rosalynde K. Soble, Assistant Professor, University of Maryland School of Dentistry, for extensive review and suggestions in the preparation of this chapter.

areas of pleasure and satisfaction or discover new ones. The framework should be flexible enough to accommodate to the variety of chronic diseases, personality types, and family structures the worker encounters.

The course of chronic illness in the patient is progressive, is accompanied by exacerbations and remissions, and is incremental in its effect on the patient's social functioning and physical mobility. Using the course of the chronic illness as the organizing concept makes it possible for social workers and others to make certain predictions about the points when stress will be the greatest on the patient and on family life. (See Abrams, 1974, and Cotter, 1978.) At these points of stress, such as the time of diagnosis or hospitalization and other exacerbation periods, psychological stress is the greatest, and social functioning deteriorates for both the patient and the family. At these times, the need to make changes to accommodate to the increased psychological stress and the necessary role shifts is most pressing.

The chronic illness concept, in conjunction with a conceptual framework for organizing aspects of differences in individual and family functioning, permits the social worker to evaluate the vulnerable areas of particular kinds of families and of the ill persons in those families. The worker can then assess the structural characteristics which may be most sensitive to stress and change for a particular type of family group. This type of framework for assessment enables the worker to identify and predict problems and conflicts which may develop and to plan ahead for ways to assist the patient and the family when the stress and the concomitant need for changes occur.

FAMILY REACTION TO CHRONIC ILLNESS

The recognition that stress and disorganization are inevitable is of major importance and is well documented in the literature. Nagi and Clark (1964) studied a total of 294 respondents who had been married prior to the onset of disability. Of these, 236 remained married and 58 separated or divorced. The picture which emerges is that people who are older, more educated, and more geographically stable continue in marriages after disability occurs. Since only demographic variables were studied, the quality of life in the continuing family relationships is not known. However, other studies do evaluate the quality-of-life component. Wishnie, Hackett, and Cassem (1977), in their study of 24 middle-class postmyocardial infarction males, found that "interpersonal friction" followed the infarction even in previously stable families, and that preexisting family problems worsened. Kaplan, Grobstein, and Smith (1976) conducted a study of 40 families, in each of which a child had died of leukemia. They found that "only 12 percent of the families managed to emerge intact from the illness experience . . . without multiple problems among the survivors." Of the remaining group, 5 percent divorced, 18 percent separated, and 70 percent reported serious marital problems (p. 75). In another study, Fink, Skipper, and Hallenbeck (1968) examined the long-term effects of disability on marriages of 30 21-to 60-year-old women who became disabled after marriage. The authors found that the more limited the woman was in both physical mobility and ability to participate in activities, the more likely the husband was to feel dissatisfied because his need for companionship was not being met.

Several other studies highlighted the impact of illness on roles. The results of Klein, Dean, and Bogdonoff's (1967) study of married patients with a chronic illness implied that the role failure which occurs when a spouse becomes chronically ill ultimately leads to interpersonal tension and somatic symptoms. This is also supported by the findings in Wishnie et al. (1977). Bromberg and Donnerstag (1977), who worked extensively with heart disease patients, found that for these patients a reactive depression was accompanied by a loss of self-esteem or confusion in role and identity.

Data from other studies suggest that in cases of terminal illness, family tension, problems, and grief reactions begin at the time of diagnosis. In the Kaplan et al. (1976) study of families with a leukemic child who had died, data were collected during the first few weeks following diagnosis and three months following the child's death. The authors found a correlation between the average number of problems identified for each family shortly after diagnosis and the level of coping after the child had died. They concluded that professional intervention would be most effective during the period immediately following diagnosis. In a study of children whose parents had died, Cohen, Dizenhuz, and Winget (1977) found that 35 percent would have liked more "help" at the point the diagnosis of the terminal illness was made.

The literature makes it clear that with the onset of chronic illness, needs that were previously met are not always accommodated in the new situations; tensions and symptoms increase; and dependency issues can become exacerbated. Although there may be divorces and separations, the data indicate that far more families stay together, living with the increased tensions and role strains.

Family systems normally have ways of handling and maintaining the balance of needs among family members. With the advent of a chronic illness, the balance between the needs of the ill member and the remaining well members becomes more delicate. With the progression of the illness in the patient, "unbalancing" tends to occur at stress points. The need to restore the balance is an ongoing process and calls for enough restructuring to permit the family group to reorganize at specific stress points. The restructuring should be aimed at strengthening the vulnerable areas. At each successive juncture as the illness proceeds in its course, the risk increases that the family will not be able to accommodate, that the needs of individuals will predominate, and that the family members will physically separate.

BASIS FOR SELECTION OF FOCUS OF INTERVENTION

Because stressful situations crop up quickly in the course of an illness (e.g., sudden hospitalizations or exacerbations), hospital-based social workers need to know how to select the most effective focus for intervention. Accurate identification of the specific vulnerability increases their ability to develop and implement a focused, goal-directed treatment plan. Thus, social workers need a tool to assess the "weak links" reflected in the patterns of coping responses and behaviors presented by the family unit and individual members. A model of differential family functioning is an aid to evaluation and assessment of predictable behavior in families who are struggling to cope with an illness or disability.

Generally, the family's style of coping with, and adapting to, the illness is an outgrowth of its ongoing system-maintaining processes, which have been forged out of its own history, personalities, culture, neighborhood, and socioeconomic class. Each family has its own unique structural aspects and style. Nevertheless, it is possible to classify these families through identification of gross differences in system structure and categorization of ongoing system-maintaining processes, functions, and style. By learning to identify the characteristics of specific types of family systems, social workers and other health care professionals can improve their ability to assess and evaluate families.

In addition to increased accuracy in assessment and prediction, employing a classification of family systems also improves the worker's accuracy in determining the focus of intervention and degree of change possible. The skills needed to intervene and help patients and families cope with stress and change are also improved.

CLASSIFYING QUALITIES OF FAMILY FUNCTIONING

A family systems classification which can be adapted by social workers and other health professionals in medical hospital settings is described in a study by Lewis, Beavers, Gossett, and Phillips (1976). Their research attempted to evaluate five specific "qualities of family functioning" to determine if there were significant differences in these qualities among different types of family systems.

The study, focusing on "psychological health in family systems," evaluated the quality of functioning of a group of 23 patient and nonpatient families on the five qualities of family functioning which the authors considered important in the development of capable, adaptive, healthy individuals. These are: (1) power structure, (2) perception of reality, (3) affect, (4) degree of family individuation, and (5) acceptance of separation and loss. Families in the study were then grouped and characterized in relation to these qualities as (1) severely disturbed, (2) midrange, or (3) healthy.

Significantly, the differences found in each of these qualities for the various family types all reflect the basic difference, along a continuum, in the degree to which the system is open or closed. The more disturbed families tend to show more general, overall rigidity in all qualities and structures than did the healthy families, who were more open. Midrange families appeared to be at midrange along the continuum.

Adaptation of Findings to the Medical Hospital Setting

The findings of the Lewis et al. (1976) study are presented in Sections I through V below, which describe the characteristic behavior for each quality of family functioning for the three types of families. My own assessment of behaviors which characterize these different family types when they present in medical hospital settings is also given, and the differential characteristics that distinguish families similar to the family types are identified. These can be used by the hospital-based social worker to increase accuracy in assessment, prediction, identification of vulnerabilities, determination of degree of change possible, and choice of treatment interventions at the various stress points in the course of the chronic illness.

Each section begins with a discussion of the Lewis study findings regarding a specific quality of family functioning. This is followed by examples of the social worker's approach to evaluation and treatment of families similar to these types of families as they might present in the medical hospital setting.

I. THE FAMILY POWER STRUCTURE

In comparing family power structures, Lewis et al. (1976) found that the leadership structure was most vaguely defined among the severely disturbed families. In those families there was little or no mutual support between the parents; the father had little power, and what power he did have frequently was undermined by a coalition between the mother and one of the children.

Lewis et al. found two characteristically different styles within the broad midrange category, which they identified as centrifugal and centripetal. These styles appeared to influence differences in the formation of the family power structure. Members of families with a centrifugal style tended to pull away from the family group, while those in families with a centripetal style tended to remain very involved with and enmeshed in the family group. (Lewis et al. also observed that centripetal-style families tended to produce "neurotic" children, and centrifugal-style families tended to produce children with "character disorders.")

Centrifugal-style and centripetal-style families had power structures that differed in the following ways. Centrifugal families had no stable, clear-cut power structure, so that neither parent was clearly and consistently in control. Additionally, each parent would form transient coalitions with different children. This type of shifting, changing power structure, with its lack of consistency, clear expectations, and predictability, encouraged manipulation and exploitation of family members by one another. Centripetal families were able to establish stable power structures and had hierarchies in which one parent was viewed as being in charge. Control was more effective, and limits were set on manipulation. However, neither of these family styles permitted much spontaneity, and neither permitted much negotiation or compromise.

The healthy family had the most clearly defined power structure, with father accepted as the leader by all family members. The coalition between parents was strong, and mother was clearly viewed by all family members as the second most powerful person. Children were included in family decision making and perceived themselves as able to influence outcomes. These families tended to be cooperative and effective in problem solving and decision making.

Application of Power Structure Findings in the Medical Hospital Setting

How the power structure of the various types of families affects the family's behavior and the approach of staff in their interactions in the medical hospital setting is examined in Table 1.

An analysis of the power structure is important for several reasons. First, the hospital-based social worker and other professionals need to identify the family's usual decision-making patterns in order to be able to work within that structure, if at all possible. It is important not to overburden an already stressed system by trying to change preexisting patterns. One important factor that is useful in assessing the quality of family decision making is the degree to which the family externalizes and involves others in the decision-making process. Families who behave in ways to "force" hospital staff to constantly push them for decisions are usually functioning at a lower level than those who naturally carry out this process within their own internal structure, with a minimum of assistance from outside.

Second, professionals in the health care system need to know which family members should be included in decision making and information sharing, especially at points where there is a change in the illness which will cause changes in the family's functioning.

Third, it is useful to understand how willing and able family members are to take responsibility and to act on suggestions made by the social worker and others. Further, it is helpful to both professionals and families when the social worker can anticipate the nature of their decision-making process.

Fourth, as the patient member of the family deteriorates in functioning and realistically needs to increase dependence on family members, it is important for the social worker to be able to anticipate the shifts in leadership and their effects on family structure and stability.

TABLE 1
Power Structure

Family Type (Lewis, et al.)	Family Characteristics	Family's Behavior In Interaction with Health Care Professionals	Approach of Staff
Severely disturbed	1. Little or no mutual support between parents. 2. Father has little power. 3. Coalitions between mother and child to undermine father's power.	The family may: 1. "Dump" patient member and disappear. 2. Be elusive to contact with staff. 3. Be hard to contact. 4. Be difficult to involve in planning.	Staff need to: 1. Be direct and specific in presenting information. 2. Define their roles specifically. 3. Accurately assess patient's and family's understanding of what they think needs to be accomplished and with what tasks they are willing to follow through. 4. Be ready to accompany patient and family members to assist in task completion. 5. Refer to home visiting agencies for follow-up, when indicated. 6. Have appropriate expectations of this family type's capacities and abilities.
Centrifugal	1. Neither parent clearly and consistently in control. 2. Each parent forms transient coalitions with dif-	The family may: 1. Employ "buck-passing." 2. Be argumentative, challenging, and provocative. 3. Challenge authority. 4. Have difficulty taking final re-	Staff need to: 1. Be comfortable in setting limits for these families. 2. Clearly convey limits, goals, and expectations for behavior and tasks. 3. Outline for family members the con-

	The family:	Staff need to:
(continued)	ferent children. 3. Shifting, changing, inconsistent power structure. 4. Lack of clear expectations. 5. Manipulation and exploitation. 6. Lack of spontaneity. 7. Inability to negotiate and compromise. ...sponsibility and following through on task completion.	sequences of their behavior. 4. Be able to handle their own anger when these family members become provocative and difficult. 5. Adopt an attitude of noninvestment in these families' decision-making outcomes.
Centripetal	1. Ability to establish stable power structure. 2. Have hierarchies, with one parent viewed as being in charge. 3. More effective control. 4. Family limits set on manipulation. 5. Lack of spontaneity. 6. Inability to negotiate and compromise. **The family:** 1. Usually will be able to make and follow through on decisions related to treatment and planning but may vacillate during the process. 2. May make decisions by "old rules" even in new and changed situations. 3. May make decisions which prove to be dysfunctional for coping with illness-related changes.	**Staff need to:** 1. Discuss family's view of problem(s) and proposed solutions. 2. Identify changes and differences between past situations and current situations and consequences of applying old problem-solving methods to the new situation. 3. Assess whether family members can perceive and accept differences. 4. Help families talk about ambivalence, fear, and guilt, if possible, and to separate the feelings associated with past experiences from their attachment to the current reality. 5. Help families consider new and different approaches to take in illness situation.

Healthy

The family

1. Most clearly defined power structure.
2. Father accepted as leader by all family members.
3. Mother viewed as second most powerful person.
4. Children included in family decision making.
5. Families tend to be cooperative and effective in problem-solving and decision making.

1. Will have the greatest ease in decision making.

Staff need to:

1. Communicate openly.
2. Share cognitive information freely.

Power Structure in the Severely Disturbed Family, and the Social Worker's Approach. Severely disturbed families are described as having a vague power structure and as being unable to negotiate issues among themselves. In medical settings, families with similar decision-making behavior may "dump" the patient at the hospital's door and seem to disappear. Family members often visit late at night, "flit" in and out of the hospital, or are very hard to reach by telephone. Social workers in medical settings find it difficult to involve them in planning.

With these families, the social worker's approach needs to be direct and specific, and a well-defined structure should be provided. Information on which decisions are to be based should be presented simply, accompanied by diagrams and pictures. Workers need to clearly define their roles to these families. They must determine which tasks the patient and family members think are necessary, and on which ones both the worker and the family can follow through. They need to help the family recognize the importance of other tasks and information which they may choose to ignore. All the instructions given by the social worker or other staff regarding the care of the patient or expected changes in the patient's functioning should be given in a clear and precise manner. Family members should be told gently and firmly what will happen and should be asked for their input as to what they think will be required to deal with changes.

In this type of family, a family member should be seen with the patient at clinic visits. The social worker should help educate staff to repeat information at each visit. It is appropriate to refer these families to community nursing agencies with home-visiting capability, in order to reinforce and further instruct the patient and family, if the family is willing to accept the referral. It is helpful if the social worker and other staff do not have high expectations of the ability of these families to make judgments and decisions on their own. Family members should be accompanied when they contact other agencies, as they often need this support to follow through.

Lewis, et al. indicated that the coalitions in severely disturbed families are generally weak. There may be times when the goal of the social worker is to bring about changes in coalitions within the family or to strengthen the power position of one member. With a family whose power structure is similar to the severely disturbed family, the selection of this goal has to be very carefully considered when there is physical illness. The behavioral changes required for any patient and family in the process of receiving medical care are stressful and anxiety provoking. They are more intense for families similar to the more disturbed families, and it is inadvisable to introduce major structural changes which place additional demands on family members, especially at stress points in the illness where decision making is required. At these times, the worker should rely on existing coalitions, the existing power structure, and the normal decision-making processes.

Decision making in a family similar to a severely disturbed family in an illness situation is exemplified in the following case history, taken from my files. (All case histories in this chapter are from my own files or files of supervisees. They were selected on the basis of their similarity to behavior of different types of families described in the Lewis et al. study.) In this case, the old decision-making patterns could not be altered during a period of stress.

This family was poor, black, and living on public assistance. Mrs. S, an asthmatic, was extremely dependent on others. She was separated from her husband and was totally responsible for the care of several children. She consistently had difficulty taking responsibility for the care of her children. Her fifteen-year-old son, Ed, had leukemia. During the course of treatment, Ed was given the usual drugs used in the treatment of this disease. After many exacerbations and remissions, it became apparent that the standard drugs were no longer effective. A decision had to be made as to whether or not to use a highly experimental drug with life-threatening side effects.

It was hard to commit Mrs. S to a specific time to discuss this situation. Her visits to Ed in the hospital were infrequent, unpredictable, and quick. Finally, a joint conference was held with the physician, the social worker, mother and patient. Mrs. S refused to make the decision, saying that she didn't want to be responsible "if anything happened." The responsibility for deciding fell to Ed, who became depressed but decided to reject treatment with this drug. The mother then supported his decision.

Power Structure in the Centrifugal-Style Family, and the Social Worker's Approach. The centrifugal-style family lacks a clearly defined leader, and neither parent is clearly and consistently in control. Usually, neither one wants to assume the final responsibility for decision making, and frequently both change their minds after decisions are made. Buck-passing is common behavior in these families; members are argumentative, challenging, and provocative. In joint decision-making conferences involving the patients, family members, and health care staff, families with decision making behavior similar to this type of family seem to respond well only to supportive but firm use of authority by health care professionals. Consequently, families whose behavior is similar to the centrifugal midrange family are more difficult for the social worker to influence and work with than families whose behavior is similar to that of the centripetal style family.

One helpful guideline for staff to follow is to be comfortable in setting limits with these families. They should be united and convey clear expectations in order to prevent manipulation by members of families with these behaviors. They need to make these family members clearly aware of the consequences of the family's behavior (e.g., that the hospital cannot keep the patient beyond the point when acute care is no longer needed).

Staff members who become argumentative with these family members or respond with anger to the family's provocative behavior lose the ability to guide the process. The most difficult aspect of transactions with these families for the staff is management of their own anger. The social worker needs to clarify the process for other staff and help them deal with their anger in more productive ways. The hardest task for the professional is to adopt an attitude of noninvestment in the outcome of the decision-making process. If members of this type of family sense that the professional is invested in the outcome, they begin to argue and struggle against the "opponent." The responsibility for, and investment in, the outcome of decision making about plans for the patient must rest squarely on the patient and family.

An example of decision making in a family with behaviors similar to those of the centrifugal-style midrange family is seen in the following situation. In this case, the patient demonstrated that, with help, he could be flexible in changing his decision-making pattern.

Mr. Q, a 70-year-old black man who lived alone, had been a religious leader in his church and community. He was hospitalized with crippling arthritis. The medical assessment was that he could no longer care for himself. Although the patient very much wanted to go home and definitely did not want to go into a nursing home, he also realized that he could no longer live on his own and that he required help from others. He contacted a son in another state, with whom he felt he would be able to live. That son agreed, but kept delaying the date of discharge and kept making promises to his father, but could not make firm plans.

During this time, the existence of other children, also living out of state, became known to the involved social worker. The worker began to contact the other children, who followed essentially the same pattern of first offering to take their father and then backing off from the decision. In addition, the children variously sided with and then turned against each other, so that the worker had no stable "ally" with whom to work toward discharge planning. There was still no firm plan by the time the patient was medically ready to leave the hospital. Although sad, the only option was a nursing home, if only on a temporary basis.

At that point, the patient became angry and said that the hospital staff were forcing him to make a decision. Although the worker felt angry with the patient, she avoided getting into a struggle with him. She calmly but firmly stated that because he would not make a decision, it was he who was forcing the staff to put pressure on him. She further noted that the staff had been very cooperative in letting him try to work out other plans up to that point. The patient remained angry but became subdued. At that point, the worker left the room to give him time to think about what he wanted to do, again avoiding a struggle. With this approach, the patient was able to decide to go into the nursing home.

Power Structure in the Centripetal Family, and the Social Worker's Approach. In the case of Mr. Q, family members had severe difficulty making decisions. This might not be a problem in a family with characteristics of the centripetal-style family, in which one family member is perceived as being in charge of the situation. The problem which can arise in these families, however, is related to the ambivalence and rigidity which characterize the family style. Frequently, family members either vacillate or make decisions by the "old rules," even when the situation is changed or the presenting problem has not been experienced previously. The result of this behavior is frequently that family members make decisions which prove to be dysfunctional for coping with the illness-related changes in family life.

If the social worker can enter the situation early enough (i.e., prior to the act of decision making), she or he may be able to intervene to prevent this process from occurring. The intervention consists of the following steps:

1. Discussion of the family's view of the problem(s) and proposed solutions.
2. Identification of the reality-based differences between the current illness-related problem or situation and past experiences and the consequences of applying old problem-solving methods to the new situation.
3. Discussion to elicit whether family members can realistically perceive and accept the differences.

213

4. Discussion of feelings, especially ambivalent, fearful, and guilty feelings.
5. Further discussion to consider new and different approaches to the new situation. This is especially important when the work is with a family composed of adult patients with adult parents and siblings, or adult children, rather than with adult patients who have young children.

The following case situation represents an example of this type of decision making in a family with decision making processes similar to those of a centripetal-style family, when there has been no social work or other professional intervention early in the process. This is a situation in which one family member had potential for more flexible behavior.

Mr. P was a 33-year-old, dependent single man who lived with his mother. He was part of a close-knit, matriarchal, extended family of Greek origin. Mr. P had end-stage renal disease, and was at the point of either having to have a kidney transplant or going on chronic hemodialysis. The philosophy of the physicians treating the patient was not to involve the patient in the discussion of the selection of the kidney donor. Further, these physicians chose to have minimum involvement in the family's decision-making process, and this also was extended to limiting the social worker's involvement in that process. As general procedure, the physicians informed the family of the results of the tests used to select the family member who would be the best kidney donor. The physicians provided complete and detailed medical information, answered all questions in detail, and prepared both the patient and the family members for the operation. After that, the family was on its own to decide whether someone would donate, and who the donor would be.

In this case, the family's decision-making process was directed by Mr. P's mother, who, along with other siblings, put pressure on the patient's sister, Mrs. V, who was found to be the best match for a living donor transplant. Although Mrs. V was reluctant, she followed the family's wishes and complied with the family's value system and decision-making pattern. There was little room for flexibility and deviation from the norm. Mrs. V seemed to feel that she had no other choice. The family remained very involved with both Mr. P and Mrs. V until the transplantation operation was performed.

Following the operation, the family withdrew much support from Mrs. V, and she felt abandoned and angry. After the operation she began to talk more with the social worker. She expressed that she wished she'd never given the kidney. For the first time, she ventilated her anger toward her brother for being so dependent and toward her mother for doing "everything" for that brother. Further, she began to consider the reality of the implications for her of living with only one kidney.

214

This family rigidly followed its familiar decision-making process emanating from the power structure of the family of origin, with the mother making the decision and the adult siblings assuming and accepting their old roles as their mother's children. This type of situation in a family with characteristics of a mid-range, centripetal-style family requires a different approach than if the behavior were similar to that of either a severely disturbed or a centrifugal-style family. In the centripetal-style family, the coalitions and the power structure are more stable than in either of the other two family types. Families with structures like this are usually less fragile and more able to tolerate change, even under stress. Further, the P family was one in which all the members were adults, and in which separation, although incomplete, had occurred (except for Mr. P).

For these reasons, it was feasible for the social worker to consider attempting to bring about changes in existing coalitions in the P family. In this situation, Mrs. V was the most ambivalent member and was the one who had been physically separated from the original family group. Therefore, she would be the family member the worker could select to intervene with. If the worker could have entered the case earlier (some time prior to the point where the need for the donor decision became urgent), perhaps Mrs. V could have been helped to examine her feelings, especially of ambivalence, disloyalty, and fear of disapproval, and considered the consequences of any decision in light of the reality of her current situation as an adult married woman with children and responsibilities of her own.

Power Structure in the Healthy Family, and the Social Worker's Approach. Families with a power structure similar to that of healthy families permit the greatest ease in decision making. These are families with whom the social worker and physician can communicate openly and freely in sharing information. Once they have the necessary information, the members should be able to make independent decisions with a minimum of emotional support from staff.

The case of the R family provides an example of the decision-making process in a relatively "healthy" family, in which the family's structure permits accommodation to the new situation.

Mr. and Mrs. R had been married for 20 years when she was diagnosed as having Hodgkin's disease. Their marriage had been stable, and they shared many activities together. Mr. and Mrs. R worked well together in relation to decision making. They

215

shared responsibility and supported each other in making important decisions and plans. The children were included in discussions, although the parents appropriately took responsibility for making the final decisions.

This stability continued during the first year following the time the diagnosis was made. However, around the time of the "anniversary" of the occasion of diagnosis, the patient experienced anxiety, agitation, and increased irritation with others (which was assessed by the social worker to be an "anniversary grief reaction" as described by Lindeman, 1965, pp. 7–21). She and her husband began to disagree more frequently, tension increased between them, and she turned to him increasingly to take more responsibility in decision making. She also found it more difficult to be firm in decisions regarding the children.

During discussions with the social worker, the patient was finally able to recognize how much it had upset her to know that she had Hodgkin's disease. In the first joint interview, Mrs. R was able to begin to get in touch with her feelings and talk about them, and both Mr. and Mrs. R were able to look at the areas of change in their lives and begin to make decisions about how they would handle them.

II. PERCEPTION OF REALITY

Two factors were assessed by Lewis et al. (1976) as influencing the accuracy of reality perception. The first was family mythology (a concept they borrowed from A. J. Ferreira), defined as "'a series of fairly well-integrated beliefs shared by all family members, concerning each other and their mutual position in the family life, beliefs that go unchallenged by everyone involved in spite of the reality distortions which they may conspicuously imply'" (Lewis et al., 1976, p. 71). The second concept, timebinding and timelessness, was derived from A. Korzybski's definition of man as a "timebinder," capable of acknowledging the passage of time. The ability to accept and acknowledge life-cycle change, loss and death—incidents which naturally occur over time and are biologically determined—appears to be related to the degree of individuation achieved within the family system.

In evaluating the severely disturbed families they studied, Lewis et al. concluded that they exhibited the greatest disparity between reality and family myth. Family members appeared totally unaware of even the most bizarre behavior in their midst. Myths were held onto steadfastly and appeared to be unchanged and unmodified over time, even when they bore little resemblance to actual behavior. For example, family members expounded the myth that the father was a warm-hearted, generous man, even though he was frequently sadistic in his treatment of them. The authors paint a picture of families who were encapsulated and unaffected by a broader "social reality," so they could maintain their myths "by denial, obliviousness, and careful family teaching." Family members handled the discrepancies between real and mythical behavior by suppressing their own realistic perceptions and developing the ability to live out the shared fantasy. Behavior appeared partially motivated by fear of not being accepted within the family system and of being excluded.

Lewis et al. also found that severely disturbed families had the greatest distortion with regard to perception of time passing. There was a sense of timelessness, in which change was not perceived and the "face of the biological clock" was obliterated.

In both styles of midrange families there were also discrepancies between myth and reality, but there was far less distortion than in the severely disturbed families. Disparity appeared to be most pronounced in the area of sensitivity to feelings. Both types of midrange families seemed oblivious when a member was experiencing emotional pain. The most striking difference noted by Lewis et al. between the centripetal-and centrifugal-style families involved the quality of the core mythology for each. In centripetal-style families, the concern was with acquiring "social power." Therefore, family members were concerned about the appropriateness of their behavior and closely monitored each other's behavior. Centrifugal-style families appeared to view themselves as second-class citizens and behaved in ways which were congruent with that image, even though the behavior was not always "appropriate" (e.g., beating the kids).

Midrange families were found also to distort the reality of passage of time, but they did not need to pretend that time stood still. They were able to accept, although with pain, the realistic, biological changes which occur over time. For example, these families' problems with time were expressed through the parents' competitiveness with their adolescent sons or daughters, whose waxing strength and vitality posed a threat to the parents' own images and forced acknowledgement of the parents' waning strength and vigor.

In healthy families there was less of a gap between family myth and reality. The views these families held of themselves were closely approximated by the objective assessments of outsiders. These families did not strongly need to preserve a mythical image and so did not need to hold rigidly to myths. The myths held by these families (e.g., that mother can't manage money) were more flexibly held and could be relinquished when circumstances changed and required different behavior. Also, the quality of the myths was more "gentle and humorous," and they encompassed the notion that human beings are permitted to make mistakes. Both of these latter qualities appeared to be limited or absent in the family mythology of midrange and severely disturbed families.

With regard to acknowledgement of the passage of time, the healthy family had the greatest ability to accept change. An important implication of this capacity is that the more open people are to acknowledging that there is change, and the less they have to hold on to a sense of timelessness, with its static quality, the greater is their capacity to deal with and enjoy the here and now. They are more able to grasp the reality that time passed is time irretrievable and can enjoy moments for what they are. Lewis et al. comment that when children are not seen as "competitors or crutches" (as in midrange families), they can be enjoyed and "viewed with pride." Members of these families do not have a great need to deny loss but rather are able to take the opportunity to experience the sadness and say goodbye.

Application of Perception-of-Reality Findings to the Medical Hospital Setting

The concepts of family mythology and accuracy of time passage affect the various family types in their interactions with health care professionals in different ways, as indicated in Table 2. These concepts are extremely important ones for health professionals, including social workers, to understand. Frequently the behavior of patients and family members seems clearly "off the wall," and health professionals observe that a family group or member is being "unrealistic" or is "denying." The behaviors which call forth these observations include family members persisting in the notion that they can easily care at home for a relative who is totally bedridden and can't feed himself, or not wanting a patient-relative to return home but not facing the patient directly. Others involve patients who recognize that it is physically impossible to return to their previous living situations but who persist in the conviction that they will return, and construction worker patients who should change their line of work because of illness but who persist in returning to heavy labor. Unrealistic behaviors may also be exhibited by both family members and patients who outwardly do not appear affected by the diagnosis of a serious chronic illness and proceed to make plans for the future.

TABLE 2

Perception of Reality—Timebinding And Family Myths

Family Type (Lewis, et al.)	Family Characteristics (Lewis, et al.)	Family's Behavior In Interaction with Health Care Professionals	Approach of Staff
Severely disturbed	Family members:	Family members:	Staff need to:
	1. Great disparity between reality and family myth.	1. Will not appear to accept and be aware of how reality or illness situation will change and affect lives.	1. Assess accurately and early when a family demonstrates this type of behavior.
	2. Members may appear totally unaware of even most bizarre behavior in family.	2. May pull away from staff if staff attempts to "force" reality on them.	2. Continue presenting and holding to reality.
	3. Myths are held on to steadfastly and are unchanged and unmodified over time.	3. May try to prevent staff from understanding their mythology.	3. Realize that these family members may continue to hold to own myths and deny time even when reality is overwhelming and contradictory.
	4. Family myths will usually not be affected by a broader "social reality."	4. Will not have insight about their discrepancies and will usually not be able to develop it.	4. Handle their own frustration and be prepared when family members make "irrational" decisions.
	5. Family members appear to suppress own realistic perceptions and develop the ability to live out the shared fantasy.		5. Try to determine what the family myths are and, to the extent possible, work with and not against them.
	6. Greatest "time sense" distortion—family members appear not to perceive change or acknowledge passage of time.		6. Resist forcing reality on patient and family members; this will only increase anxiety and intensify rigidity.

219

	The Family:	Staff need to:
Midrange	1. Families will first resist accepting changed situation and need to make illness-related changes, but over time will be able to accept and make changes.	1. Recognize that these families' first reaction to change will be resistance.
1. Members demonstrate discrepancies between myth and reality, but *far less* distortion than in severely disturbed families.		2. Bear in mind that with time, patience, and empathy, these families may move toward acceptance of change.
2. Family members seem oblivious to each other's emotional pain.	2. Families will need help in identifying what their myths and related expectations are.	3. In discussion, help these family members share their myths and expectations, and help them recognize that though myths are hard to give up, life will be easier to manage if they can.
3. The central mythology differs between the two family types:	3. Family members are usually capable of getting in touch with myths, with help from staff.	4. Recognize "worthy" qualities of centripetal family members, convey acceptance when family members can't always live up to their own expectations, and help families realize difficulty in trying to reach unrealistic goals.
a. Centripetal—family members are concerned with "social power" and will closely monitor behavior for appropriateness.	4. Centripetal family members are generally insecure about their own worth, which can intensify holding on to myths and resisting time change.	
b. Centrifugal—family members appear to view themselves as "second class" citizens and behave in ways congruent with that image, even when such behavior is inappropriate.	5. Centrifugal style families frequently behave inappropriately with staff.	5. Convey clear expectations of appropriate behavior in hospital and illness situations, and clearly convey what consequences are if behavior is not appropriate (e.g., family members will not be able to visit patient if they keep shouting).
4. Family members distort time passage but don't	6. Both style families have difficulty accepting the notion that human beings are permitted to make mistakes.	6. Consistently convey that it's all right for people to make mistakes and that making mistakes is part of being a human being.

pretend that time stands still.

5. Family members can accept, however painfully, realistic, biological changes over time.

Healthy	The family will:	Staff need to:
1. Members hold view of selves that closely approximates objective assessments of them by outsiders.	1. Be able to accept suggestions and advice from staff.	1. Have open, joint discussions to discuss changes.
2. Members do not need to perceive a mythical image, so have no need to hold rigidly to myths.	2. Be able to "hear" suggested changes and reasons for changes far more easily than other family types.	2. Gently help these family members give up old expectations in light of new circumstances which require change.
3. Myths are flexibly held and easily relinquished when circumstances change and require different behavior.		
4. Light, gentle, and humorous quality to myths.		
5. Myths encompass the idea that humans make mistakes.		

Frequently when patients and family members behave in these ways, staff respond by presenting them more forcefully with "reality" (e.g., your mother *can't* go home—she could *die* there) and trying to convince them that the illness will cause changes in the future. These responses, however, frequently consolidate rigid, denying behavior.

If social workers are aware of the concepts of family mythology and timebinding/timelessness and use this knowledge to guide other staff, the responses to such patients and family members might facilitate greater acceptance of the changes that have occurred. For example, the myth behind the behavior of family members who are unrealistic about their inability to care for a very sick patient-member may be that they are "towers of strength" who can handle everything. The family members who cannot directly refuse to take a patient member home may hold the myth that society is critical of people who do this. The patient who refuses to acknowledge the reality that he cannot be cared for at home may be trying desperately to hold back time and also to live in accordance with a myth that "my family loves me and therefore will always be there to care for me." The construction worker may deeply believe that physical strength gives him control in a way that emotional strength cannot; further, he may feel very pained and vulnerable if he has to acknowledge that he is losing his strength and growing older. Patients and family members who live as if the presence of a chronic illness will not alter the course of their lives may have a severely disturbed sense of time.

In the above examples, the social worker may accomplish more by attempting to identify the basic myth involved and assessing the degree of strength with which it is held, instead of insisting that the patient or family member acknowledge reality. Then empathy can be expressed for the pain a person who cannot live up to a cherished view of self feels and for the difficulty in trying to change that view.

Reality Perception in the Severely Disturbed Family, and the Social Worker's Approach. An example of the handling of mythology and time passage in a family whose behavior resembles that of a severely disturbed family can be seen in the following poignant case situation. In this case, a middle-aged woman clung to the image of herself as a child and of her mother as her protector.

Miss F was an unmarried, 40-year-old woman who had always lived with her mother. For two years Miss F had known that she had leukemia but never acknowledged it. She presented herself to the world as if she had no idea what was wrong with her, or why she kept returning to the hospital. During the final hospitalization, as she entered the terminal phase, Miss F gave the first acknowledgment of the severity of her illness when she asked the social worker, "Can you believe that I am going to die?" The worker replied, "Yes, because it is not me." Although the response was cryptic, it conveyed two things: yes, we are all going to die; and, yes, it is hard for all of us to acknowledge it.

The woman continued to live, and desperately wanted to return home. Her mother had not been coming to visit her, thus refusing to accept the reality that time was passing and her daughter was dying. The mother also consistently refused to permit Miss F to return home. Finally, for reasons which were never clear, the patient's mother agreed for her to come home the next day, fully knowing Miss F would die at home. Miss F was told, relaxed, and experienced a sense of peace. (Her mother loved and wanted her, and all would be the same as before.) That night, she died peacefully in her sleep.

Reality Perception in the Centripetal-Style Family, and the Social Worker's Approach. The following case example illustrates how a family with structural aspects similar to a centripetal-style family attempts to cope with reality, and the difficulties members have in coming to grips with change and death.

The E's had had a long marriage. At 53, Mr. E developed cancer and had a rapid, downhill course. Mrs. E became quite anxious about raising her mid-teenage son by herself and was quite worried that she would not be able to support herself financially. In a talk with the social worker during her husband's final hospitalization, she expressed great concern about her son, John. He was refusing to do his homework, and he was staying away from home. Mrs. E felt that there were many things John "should" be doing that he wasn't. She also had high standards for herself and was strongly resolved not to "break down" in front of John, even with consistent feedback from the social worker that it was appropriate and "all right" to do so. In fact, Mrs. E clung so tenaciously to this myth that the worker decided it would be less destructive to support it at that time than to try to subject the myth to reality testing.

On the other hand, Mrs. E requested that the social worker speak with John (who was agreeable) alone. She did not want to be involved. Her primary aim was to have John stop the behavior which was unacceptable to her. Although she was not an unfeeling woman, she did not seem to realize that her son might be feeling his own private pain in response to his father's impending death. The worker met privately with John and helped him express his sense of conflict about taking the role of the man of the house into which he felt his mother was pressuring him. The worker was able to strengthen John's perception of reality that he could not, and did not have to, fill his father's shoes. They then discussed ways in which John could comply with some of his mother's wishes for "appropriate" behavior, without having to totally

223

fulfill her fantasy. John seemed to relax, and his behavior did change. This, in turn, enabled Mrs. E to feel less anxious, and she reduced pressure on him.

This family was most concerned with "appropriateness." As Mr. E became too ill to continue to function in his role as leader, Mrs. E perceived herself to be a helpless person. She attempted to deny the reality of the passage of time, marked by the anticipated death of her husband, by thrusting her son into her husband's role.

This case raises two important treatment issues for the social worker to consider in dealing with family myth and reality when one member has a serious chronic illness. First, the social worker needs to identify the underlying myth and evaluate its strength. The strength of the myth is crucial, especially at a stress point such as anticipation of the death of a family member. The worker needs to exercise clinical judgment and consider the total case situation as a basis for deciding whether to try to help a patient or family member begin to give up a myth or to leave the myth intact. In the above case, the worker chose the latter approach in consideration of the rigidity involved, the increased stress in the situation, and the intense anxiety generated in Mr. E when reality was presented.

Second, the social worker needs to decide whether it is possible to work through another family member. Different family members often have internalized the family mythology to varying degrees and often it is helpful to the more "realistic" members to see the worker separately. The worker then can support the accuracy of their perceptions and collaboratively they can come to a decision about the extent of confrontation with the "less realistic" family member(s). These decisions should include an assessment of other factors, such as power structure, degree of individuation of various family members, and ages of the people involved. The most dramatic examples of this type of split occur in situations in which patients and family members are reacting at different rates to the news of a new diagnosis, an exacerbation of the illness, or an impending death.

Reality Perception in the Centrifugal-Style Family, and the Social Worker's Approach. The following example of a family's struggle with a chronic illness represents how tenaciously held family myths can affect treatment of families similar to centrifugal-style families.

224

Mr. Y was a 36-year-old man with a history of violence. He became ill with a degenerative neurologic disease which greatly affected his strength and which interrupted his career as a skilled laborer. His wife, always a dependent person, became an alcoholic. Mr. Y became severely anxious because he felt increasingly vulnerable and "weak" as a man and could no longer live up to his image as a strong man. His basic ability to accept reality, however, was evidenced in his ability to actively participate in treatment, especially physical therapy. Mrs. Y, on the other hand, never quite seemed to believe that her husband was truly ill. She frequently stated, "He could do more if he wanted to." Additionally, although Mr. Y could realistically acknowledge to the physicians that he was ill, it was two years before he could disclose details of his illness to his children, because the illness interfered with his mythical goal to be the strong and reliable parent he never had. His wife also had considerable difficulty in giving up the myth of the strong man who had rescued her from an unhappy family situation and who should be her pillar of strength for the rest of her life.

Mr. Y continued with the social worker and was able to make some changes. Mrs. Y withdrew from interviews with the social worker and refused joint interviews.

If husband and wife or mother and daughter (or any similar combination in the midrange family category) can meet jointly with the social worker or other helping professional, open discussion may make them aware of and sensitive to each other's expectation and areas of pain. This can help them modify expectations, provide mutual reassurance that the other will not leave, and enable them to be more supportive and cooperative with each other. However, in work with families with structure and style similar to that of midrange families, the worker must be aware that as long as each partner feels sharp pain from the hurt of not being able to live up to his or her own myth, each will have great difficulty in being honest with the other, fearing an attack when he or she is vulnerable. If partners are brought together, the worker needs to exercise care in providing a reality base which acknowledges that "no one can live up to his ideals." Attempts also should be made to help these family members be a little more sensitive to one another.

Reality Perception in the Healthy Family, and the Social Worker's Approach. The manner in which a family similar to the healthy-type family handles family myth and the perception of the passage of time can be seen in the following case example. In this case, the couple could make use of open, joint discussion.

Mr. and Mrs. P had been married for 25 years. Both were in their fifties. There were two adult, married daughters and one teenage son living at home. Mr. P

225

developed a severe form of leukemia and was hospitalized almost continuously for one and a half years. Throughout this severe disruption to their lives, both Mr. P and Mrs. P were able to make appropriate role changes. Mr. P did not berate himself for no longer being able to work, although he was appropriately depressed. Mrs. P joked about her own handling of financial matters, which was new to her. She visited Mr. P a great deal, yet did not neglect her child or household responsibilities. She continued to meet her own needs through spending time with friends, socializing, and so on.

The one area that troubled staff was that neither Mr. nor Mrs. P appeared to have acknowledged openly to each other the reality that he could die. However, further assessment indicated that these were people who expressed their feelings very privately. They more easily expressed affection through behavior than verbally. Further, the social worker learned that Mr. P had not been able to discuss his possible death with his wife because he felt he was letting her down. Through discussions with Mr. and Mrs. P individually and as a couple, the social worker was able to influence the mythology and enable them to verbally express their feelings to each other. Before Mr. P died, they had been able to express their caring and concerns, and discuss the future.

Mrs. P further demonstrated her ability to accept the reality of death at the time when Mr. P was actually dying. She stayed in the room and brought other family members into the room in shifts. She encouraged their teenage son to come, also, because she wanted him to see that death was "nothing to be afraid of." After Mr. P's death, although tearful and sad, Mrs. P held a wake filled with beer drinking and good company, "because that's the way he would have wanted it." At no time did she deny the pain of the meaning to her of his dying or his death.

III. AFFECT

In the discussion of affect in family systems, Lewis et al. (1976) define it as including: (1) the mood or feeling tone, (2) the degree to which feeling is expressed, and (3) the quality of empathy which prevails.

The prevailing mood could range from feelings of warmth, tenderness, and hopefulness at one end of a continuum to a host of negative feelings, including hostility, bitterness, apathy and a mixture of anxiety and depression, at the other. The definition of warmth by these authors is important because members of the health care staff often find it difficult to differentiate true warmth from that which masks dependency and possessiveness. Lewis et al. define warmth as follows:

. . . "human warmth is human need, honestly expressed, with a recognition of the limits of the other person." It is a *reaching out* and, therefore, is related to *need*. Many people confuse warmth with "giving"—which often leads to a virtuous

226

sterility and emotional starvation. Needs consciously acknowledged, however, may go awry if they are not clearly expressed—if too opaque or expressed obliquely, disappointment rather than warmth results. Finally, if one's needs are expressed clearly but are unrelated to the other person's capacity for meeting those needs, frustration, anger, and guilt result rather than the possible warm interaction. To apply this definition to family interaction, one may say that a family whose interactions are characterized by warmth is one in which members are able to express their individual needs clearly, with an accurate recognition of the limitations of the others' abilities to meet those needs. (p. 78)

The degree of expressiveness of feeling has to do with the ease with which feelings are verbalized, and also with the types of feelings which are more or less easily expressed. For example, some families find it easier to express angry, retaliative statements than to freely say "I love and care about you."

Empathy is the ability of a family system to be sensitive and responsive to the needs and feelings of its members. Some families are consistently empathic, others vary in their ability to be empathic at different times and in different situations, and other family systems demonstrate little or no ability to respond empathetically to their members.

Lewis et al. cite findings from their own and other studies which reflect differences in affect among the three types of families—severely disturbed, midrange, and healthy. The data indicate differences along a continuum similar to those for the other aspects of family structure previously mentioned. Affect is measured on a continuum showing movement from rigid and closed to flexible and open, thus continuing to reflect the differences in the basic structures of each type of family system.

The study assessed expression of affect in the severely disturbed families to be predominately negative. Feeling tone and predominant mood varied from cynicism, disparagement, and open hostility to depression, hopelessness, and despair. The prevailing atmosphere, laden with negative affect, is reflective of a rigid, closed family structure with limited individuation, in which there is little room for warmth and support.

The mood of midrange families also tended to be negative. However, negative feelings expressed lacked both the qualities of sadism and intense hostility found in the severely disturbed families. In some of the midrange families, the prevailing mood lacked warmth and joy. Additionally, in these families, members were not very sensitive or responsive to each other's needs.

227

In comparison, healthy families were able to openly express kindness, warmth, and caring. There was frequently a mood of hopefulness and pleasure in these families which did not prevail in the other types.

Application of Affect Findings to the Medical Hospital Setting

A family's ability to express warmth, discuss feelings, and be supportive to its members is very important when a member has a chronic illness, particularly during stress points in the course of the illness, when the patient and other family members are especially upset and anxious. There are several reasons why the social worker and other health professionals must be able to take an accurate reading of the family's emotional climate. First, staff need to be able to anticipate how much support family members can give the patient and each other, especially at stressful times, and to anticipate to what degree staff will need to fill this role. Second, staff need to be aware that a family system which fosters expression of negative speech and feelings will not be likely to produce people who are comfortable with warmth and tenderness. Thus, staff need to know what is "normal" emotional expression for a specific family, so they will not anticipate, expect, or try to force behavior that is not natural for that family, especially during times of increased illness-related stress. The social worker often must help staff understand the behavior of these families, in order to reduce the frustration that can be experienced in working with these families.

Additionally, some family systems may not be able to identify their own needs accurately and consequently will have difficulty expressing them accurately. A patient or other family member in this type of family may be most negative and verbally abusive to other family members when she or he is most frightened or upset and therefore most needful of warmth and concern. However, the person may not be able to identify her or his feelings clearly and may not know any other way of communicating them. The hospital-based social worker needs to be able to assess whether these family members are so severely disturbed that they would not benefit from the short-term intervention which could be provided, or whether the family members, with help extended during crises, could learn to identify and express clearly feelings appropriately associated with the illness situation.

The differences in mood, expression of feeling, and quality of empathy among the severely disturbed, midrange, and healthy families, and the ways health care professionals interact with these families, are outlined in Table 3. These differences can be illustrated by comparing the S family, discussed in the section on power structure, with the E and P families, cited in the section on perception of reality. The S family (p. 211) is similar to a "severely disturbed" family, the E family (p. 223) is similar to a "midrange" family, and the P family (p. 225–26) is similar to a healthy family.

Affect in the Severely Disturbed Family, and the Social Worker's Approach. Mrs. S, a separated, asthmatic woman, was raising several children alone, including Ed, who had leukemia.

Ed described his household as one in which people were constantly putting each other down; the siblings derived pleasure from emotionally and physically hurting each other; and fighting was constant. The expression of negative feeling was more the norm than the expression of warmth. Ed knew that his mother was a very needful person and could give very little comfort to her children, and, consequently, he put on a "tough" front. As his leukemia progressed, his "front" got "tougher." Nursing staff recognized the underlying need for support and tried to give it, but Ed could not accept more than mild expressions of warmth and concern. Nursing and medical staff tried to pressure the mother to be more concerned and warm, but she responded by withdrawing even more. The social worker tried to explain the mother's behavior, but the nurses continued to be angry with her. In this situation, staff response may have only served to compound the problems.

Affect in the Midrange Family, and the Social Worker's Approach. Expression of affect in the E family, a family similar in behavior to a midrange family, was not as intense or hostile as in the S case.

Mrs. E did not express intense or open hostility toward her son for not behaving "appropriately." But her affect was consistently depressed, and there were no relaxed or humorous moments (as in the P case, representing a more healthy family). However, two key members of this family, the mother and the son, were able to permit the social worker to be supportive, and the son was able to use her help to become more accurately in touch with, and express, his own feelings.

Affect in the Healthy Family, and the Social Worker's Approach. The Ps, unlike the Ss, did not fight constantly, and when there were arguments, they did not derogate each other.

Although Mr. and Mrs. P initially showed constraint in verbal expressions of sadness and caring, and in open discussions of death, they were able to do so, with minimal assistance from the social worker. An outsider could feel the warmth between them. Another quality the P family system possessed was a sense of hopefulness intertwined with the depressed affect. (Mrs. E never seemed to convey this.)

IV. DEGREE OF FAMILY INDIVIDUATION

The Lewis et al. (1976) study found that severely disturbed families were least likely to encourage the development of autonomy among members. People kept check on each other, boundaries were blurred, and there was little differentiation and individuation. These families had difficulty seeing each other as separate people with separate viewpoints, which prevented negotiation.

Midrange family life also did permit individuation but produced people who were rigid and who had set standards of behavior, thought, and feeling. These families did not seem to be comfortable with accepting their human frailties or expressing feelings honestly. Control was very important. Both centrifugal and centripetal-style families shared an "assumption that man is essentially evil" (Lewis et al., 1976, p. 63). However, families with the centrifugal style seemed to operate on the basis that since no one in the family is good, it is ridiculous to demonstrate behavior that reflects goodness, virtue, or competence. The people in centripetal-style families behaved as if a good person is one who controls himself and hides his less acceptable "animal" self. The midrange families were unable to tolerate ambivalence well and tended to view the world in all-or-nothing terms. Scapegoating both within and outside the family was common.

The healthy families had the highest degree of individuation. These families were characterized by "autonomous interaction that is relatively free of unresolved conflict; a clear, yet flexible family rule system; relative freedom in communication; skill in negotiation in which ambivalence is acceptable and agreement results from inventive compromise" (Lewis et al., 1976, p. 66). Because these family members had the freedom to be themselves, they relied very little on defenses such as denial, projection, blaming, and scapegoating. Further, they were able to tolerate differences among themselves.

TABLE 3
Affect

Family Type (Lewis, et al.)	Family Characteristics (Lewis, et al.)	Family's Behavior In Interaction with Health Care Professionals	Approach of Staff
		The Family	Staff need to:
Severely disturbed	1. Feeling tone and predominant mood varies from cynicism, disparagement, and hostility to depression, hopelessness, and despair. 2. Negative affect. 3. Prevailing atmosphere is reflective of a rigid, closed family structure with limited individuation. 4. Little room for warmth and support.	1. Family probably will not conform to expectations of staff as to "normal" expressions of warmth, tenderness, and support.	1. Understand the "normal" expression of affect in these families. 2. Handle their own sense of "outrage" when these family members do not show feelings in accordance with staff norms (e.g., stay away when the patient family member is near death). 3. Resist trying to make these family members express warmth when it is not "normal" for them to do so.
		Family members may:	Staff need to:
Midrange	1. Mood tends to be negative but lacks sadism and intense hostility found in severely disturbed families. 2. Sometimes, prevailing	1. Not be able to identify their own needs accurately or may need to defend against certain needs (e.g., dependency) and feelings (e.g., sadness). 2. Behave in one way, while	1. Refrain from facing family members with feelings or needs that staff assess to be "the real" feelings, when members may not be able to deal with them. 2. Refrain from taking expression of

mood reflects lack of warmth and joy.

3. Family members are not sensitive or responsive to each other's needs.

actually feeling another (e.g., may reject staff or family members while actually wishing for closeness).

3. Appear very warm and giving, yet underneath may be very much in need themselves and not be able to sustain support to patient.

4. Be able to use help in expressing feelings appropriately and in recognizing needs of other family members.

5. Be erratic in ability to express warmth, tenderness, and support to patient member and each other.

6. Inappropriately get into fights within hospital setting.

need and feelings at face value with these family members.

3. Learn to evaluate when expression of warmth is superficial and "false," so as not to have unrealistic expectations of these family members and not to become angry with them when they do not follow through.

4. Help these family members identify own needs and feelings and become more sensitive to the needs and feelings of other family members.

5. Develop tolerance for erratic behavior of these family members in relation to ability to express warmth and support to patient member and each other.

6. Set limits with these family members re inappropriateness of fighting.

Healthy

1. Able to openly express kindness, warmth, and caring.

2. General mood of hopefulness and pleasure in these families that does not prevail in the other family types.

Family members may:

1. Express feelings in ways staff expect and evaluate as "normal" and appropriate.

2. Be able to experience and sustain normal grief reactions.

1. Staff need to be available to provide support, especially at sad or stressful times.

2. Staff can expect these families to be able to talk about feelings and to be able to benefit from discussions about feelings, with staff.

Application of Individuation Findings to the Medical Hospital Setting

An assessment of the degree of individuation that has been achieved by individual family members is important for several reasons. The degree of individuation in the various types of families, its effect on the family's behavior, and the approach of staff in their interactions in the medical hospital setting are presented in Table 4. First, as the illness progresses, roles and responsibilities change, and it is necessary to understand how difficult it will be for family members to make the changes. Second, it is important to gauge accurately the degree of ambivalence that families can tolerate. The course of any illness in a patient is uncertain, and there are often periods of ambiguity, especially in relation to prognosis or when it is necessary to determine the effects of a particular drug. Third, some individuals and family groups may have had a pattern of recurring illnesses, in which the illness allowed family members a socially acceptable basis for remaining involved with one another by performing nurturing and caretaking functions. Such a pattern is difficult to break.

Individuation in the Severely Disturbed Family, and the Social Worker's Approach. The findings of the Lewis study indicate that families similar to the severely disturbed type are the most difficult for the social worker and the hospital staff to negotiate with. The worker needs to be very patient with these family members, because they have great difficulty taking responsibility. A careful history should be taken to determine whether the patient or a family member has had psychotic episodes. The deteriorating effects of illness normally affect the balance between dependence and independence, but if the individuals in the family are poorly differentiated, then disequilibrium in this vulnerable area can threaten their basic integrity. It is important for the social worker to be able to anticipate the possibility of the occurrence of a psychotic episode during the stress of the illness process in order to take steps to prevent it or to help the family prepare for that possibility.

The following case situation is illustrative of this type of situation. In this case, the potential for breakdown was identified in time to provide intervention.

233

TABLE 4
Individuation

Family Type (Lewis et al.)	Family Characteristics (Lewis et al.)	Family Behavior In Interaction with Health Professionals	Approach Of Staff
Severely disturbed	1. Least likely to encourage development of autonomy among members. 2. Members keep check on each other. 3. Difficulty seeing each other as separate people with separate viewpoints (which prevents negotiation).	Family members: 1. Have difficulty negotiating. 2. Have difficulty taking responsibility. 3. Are most vulnerable to individual and family system disintegration and disequilibrium with illness-related stress.	Staff need to: 1. Anticipate areas of vulnerability/possible breakdown. 2. Provide guidance structure and assistance with reorganization. 3. Mobilize concrete supports and human contacts through appropriate community agencies. 4. Make clear what behaviors are expected and acceptable. 5. Direct involvement and intervention on part of professional.
Midrange	1. Rigid. 2. Set standards of behavior, thought, and feeling. 3. Not comfortable with accepting human frailties. 4. Not comfortable with expressing feelings honestly. 5. Not able to tolerate am-	Family members: 1. Attempt to control and manipulate staff and each other. 2. Have great difficulty making changes. 3. Blame and scapegoat patient, staff, and each other. 4. Will not easily tell staff what they are thinking or feeling. 5. Will have difficulty committing	Staff need to: 1. Understand that these reactions are woven into the fabric of the individual and the behaviors reflect more than simply a reaction to the illness. These are *characteristic* ways of responding to stress. 2. Begin to recognize own angry reactions to these behaviors. 3. In dealing with the need to change

234

bivalence well.

6. Pessimistic view of human nature: "Assumption that man is essentially evil."

   a. Centrifugal-style members operate as if it is ridiculous to demonstrate behavior which reflects goodness, virtue or competence

   b. Centripetal-style members behave as if a good person is one who controls himself and hides his less acceptable "animal self."

7. Scapegoating both within and outside the family.

self to carrying out tasks.

6. Will become very anxious in ambiguous and ambivalent situations but will present as angry, not anxious.

7. Often feel patient "brought this on themselves" and consequently on family.

8. Demonstrate strong notions that patient (and doctor) can control course of illness.

(e.g., role) refrain from the tendency to struggle with these people and avoid and "step outside" of pointless arguments; stay issue focused.

4. Accept the feelings of frustration that family members have toward the ill member and/or his behavior.

5. Accept their frustration at thwarted plans.

6. Acknowledge how difficult it is for them to deal with changes.

7. Clarify that family members are not expected to control the ill person's behavior and vice versa.

Healthy

Family members:

1. Autonomous interaction.
2. Interaction relatively free of unresolved conflict.
3. "Clear, yet flexible family rule system."
4. "Relative freedom in communication."
5. "Skill in negotiation."

Family members:

1. Are most flexible in making role changes required by illness.
2. Demonstrate "normal" and appropriate anxiety.
3. Are able to use discussions with health professionals to deal with anxiety and plan for changes.

1. Physician and other staff should offer specific times to talk with families about anticipated changes and plans.
2. Staff need to offer emotional support (empathy) for stress and anxiety.
3. Staff need to recognize that even the most mature people will regress and

235

6. Tolerate and accept ambivalence.
7. "Agreement results from inventive compromise."

4. Are able to use problem solving.
5. Are best able to tolerate ambiguity and uncertainty.
6. Are able to use anticipation to handle anxiety and prepare for change.

behave irrationally under stress, at times.

Mr. A was a 57-year-old man with leukemia. Mr. and Mrs. A had been married for 30 years. Mrs. A, 55, was completely dependent on her husband. The nurse alerted the social worker to Mrs. A's history. She had had two previous psychotic episodes during which Mr. A spent long periods of time with her, feeding her and talking with her. When he became ill and his death approached, the social worker began preparing Mrs. A for the emotional impact. The worker also helped Mrs. A begin application for social security benefits before her husband died. Additionally, the worker arranged for a contact for Mrs. A in a mental health center in her community where she could go during Mr. A's hospitalization. During the actual dying process, the social worker permitted Mrs. A to discuss her feelings and fears to the degree to which she was comfortable doing so. Mrs. A expressed a wish to cry, but stated that relatives were telling her not to cry. The social worker gave her support and permission to cry, stating that this was a normal response to the death of her husband. Mr. A died, and follow-up indicated that Mrs. A was able to make the transition without having another psychotic episode.

Individuation in the Midrange Family, and the Social Worker's Approach. In the Lewis et al. (1976) study, problems with individuation were manifested in midrange families through problems with control, ambivalence, blame, and scapegoating behavior. In relation to illness, family members like this often harbor feelings of blame toward the ill person for not seeking medical help sooner. Or, they may believe the patient did something to "bring this on himself" (and, consequently, other family members). The social worker needs to evaluate whether these beliefs are present early in contacts with this type of family, because this type of thinking can generate considerable anger toward the patient. The thought that people can control the occurrence or course of an illness by what they do is an example of magical thinking, based on notions of omnipotence. This is a normal reaction to illness for all people, but such a belief is often more overtly expressed and more strongly held in families with problems in individuation similar to those found in midrange families, especially in families who have members with behavior disorders.

Because of the strength both of the feelings and the defenses employed, usually it is not possible to alter either, particularly at points of increased stress. For character-disordered individuals, and for families with the structure which produces these individuals, it is important to understand that these reactions are woven into the fabric of the individual, and the behavior reflects more than simply a reaction to the illness. It is a characteristic way of responding to stress. The most effective approach with these family members is for the social worker to accept the feelings of

237

frustration that family members have regarding the ill person's behavior; accept their frustrations at thwarted plans; acknowledge how difficult it is for them to deal with the changes; and clarify that they are not expected to control the ill person's behavior. The ambivalent, controlling, blaming behavior similar to that of midrange families can be seen in the following example. In this case, the patient's behavior was motivated by fears of dying and of losing his wife.

Mr. R was a 45-year-old South American married man with an emotionally disturbed wife. He had a heart attack, and during the hospitalization kept telling the social worker that he wanted to put his wife in a mental hospital. The social worker accepted the desire at face value, without recognizing the possibility of underlying ambivalence. (Mr. R had lived with his wife continuously for many years and had never "put" her in a mental hospital.) The social worker told the patient that she would look into the possibility of hospitalization for Mrs. R. Almost immediately following the departure of the worker from the room, the patient signed out, against medical advice. When the worker later discussed this with him, he acknowledged that her intended action was very frightening to him.

The poorly individuated person can become extremely frightened of dying when in a situation such as the one described above. The patient may be angry and blame his spouse, but the greater fear is the threat of losing this support. Further, when people like this are very frightened, they often verbally express little need for other people, especially family members (e.g., "put her in a mental hospital"). This overt behavior is designed to push away the person's feelings of increased need for important others, especially at times of acute illness.

Individuation in the Healthy Family, and the Social Worker's Approach. The healthy family type would be the most flexible in making the role changes required by illness. However, families with this mature type of coping also require the support of social workers and other health care professionals in dealing with illness and its effect on the family. Anxiety in these situations is common for all people and families, regardless of their degree of individuation or psychological health.

However, families similar to healthy families are most able to use discussions with the social worker and physician to deal with anxiety and to anticipate and plan for the changes that will come. They can use problem solving to handle anxiety once health care professionals fully define illness-related problems for them. This group of families also are most able

238

to tolerate ambiguity, especially if staff outline for them, preferably in advance, types of uncertainty they can expect and remain available to talk with them at those times. These family members are able to employ the coping behavior of anticipation to handle anxiety and prepare for probable changes.

An example of this type of family functioning can be seen in the following case summary. The family members were secure enough that even change did not threaten their integrity.

Mr. Z was a 47-year-old married man with chronic renal failure who was accepted into a dialysis program. He was able to continue his same line of work, with some time adjustments made to accommodate to the dialysis schedule. His second marriage was stable, and his wife was willing to follow his diet and gave support in many ways. This family required limited input from the social worker in the program. The patient and his wife used the support from the relationship with the physician to make the necessary transitions. The couple was able to explain the illness and its implications to the children. The family was able to handle the accompanying anxiety and make the necessary transitions with a minimum of disorganization.

V. ACCEPTANCE OF SEPARATION AND LOSS

In the study by Lewis et al. (1976), severely disturbed families were found to be the least individuated and the most threatened by change. They had the greatest resistance to separations and the most difficulty accepting loss. They were found to have severe difficulty adapting to changes brought about by the normal life development process, including aging and death.

Midrange families also had difficulty tolerating separation and loss. Parents in these families evidenced their difficulty with separation by maintaining conflict-ridden relationships with their own parents. Children in these families were found to seek new relationships with people who were copies of their parents.

Healthy families were found to have the greatest ability to tolerate separation. Parents in these families had the ability for strong mutual bonding, which indicated their ability to separate from their own parents. Family members in this group had been able to establish identities beyond their immediate family and had individuated to the degree that no one

239

person was viewed as irreplaceable. The degree of acceptance of loss and separation by different types of families and the way staff can facilitate coping in the medical hospital setting are developed in Table 5.

Loss and Illness

The task of dealing with separation and loss is ongoing in adapting to being chronically ill or having a family member who is chronically ill. Losses which arise during illness are numerous and varied.

First, the course of the chronic illness brings constant changes in living which inevitably cause the individual's and the family's life to be different than it was before. Adaptation to the differences in individual and family functioning requires disengagement from the previous roles, styles, activities, or functions, relinquishing them, and adopting new roles and styles. Second, there are literal separations which occur when the patient is hospitalized, sent to a rehabilitation facility, or placed in a nursing home. Third, there are subtle emotional separations which occur when family members can no longer share meaningful activities together, or when there is a shift in the quality of their sharing. Fourth, there are separations from previously held dreams and goals, and the need to come to terms with the reality that the individual's life and the family's life will never be the same. The degree to which the patient and other family members can mourn and grieve a specific loss is very important because people cannot begin to deal with a new set of realities until they have separated from the old. The degree to which the sick person and other family members can give up the old ways of functioning and taking roles will determine the extent to which they can reorganize around new patterns of functioning.

Family Adaptation at Transitional Phases in Illness

The patient and family will experience many losses and deal with many separations during the transitional process from "wellness" to illness. As the transitional process occurs, the patient and family move along a continuum from being well to being sick to being chronically ill and different. Successful transition for the patient and family members involves integrating the illness into their lives and adapting to a new life-style as a different, chronically ill person or one living with a chronically ill person (Feldman, 1974).

240

TABLE 5
Acceptance of Separation and Loss

Family Type (Lewis, et al.)	Family Characteristics (Lewis, et al.)	Family Behavior In Interaction with Health Care System	Approach Of Staff
Severely disturbed	1. Most threatened by change. 2. Greatest resistance to separations. 3. Most difficulty accepting loss. 4. Severe difficulty adapting to normal life developmental process changes, including aging and death.	Family members: 1. Have severe difficulty handling the strong feelings mobilized at the time the diagnosis is made. 2. Often present with strong denial of both affect and cognitive awareness. 3. Have severe difficulty making decisions related to changes.	Staff need to: 1. Gently hold to reality, but resist "forcing" family members to verbally acknowledge diagnosis, illness, changes, etc. 2. Explicitly accept family's difficulty in accepting diagnosis, prognosis, etc. 3. Be able emotionally to tolerate family's tendency to deny, while holding to reality of need to plan.
Midrange	1. Difficulty tolerating and adapting to change, separation, and loss. 2. Adults maintain conflict-ridden relationships with their own parents. 3. Children seek new relationships which are copies of their parents.	1. Family members have difficulty and find it painful to accept changes and loss, but are able to do so. 2. Members evidence strong denial at points of diagnosis, hospitalizations, and exacerbations, but are able to relinquish denial, with help and	Staff need to: 1. Acknowledge difficulty in adjusting to loss and change, but not push; empathy is needed. 2. Give members time to absorb information re diagnosis, prognosis, changes, etc. 3. Relate to the underlying concerns, feelings, issues, and effect of families' behavior; staff should not get

4. Difficulty establishing separate identifies outside own families.
5. Difficulty with the notion that "no one person" is "irreplaceable."

support.
3. For these families, diagnosis and other medical changes threaten their sense of being in control/sense of security, and cause anxiety. Anger, controlling behavior, denial of concern and manipulation and fear may be presented to cover anxiety.

into struggles.
4. Help families maintain some sense of their control at stress points.
5. Identify the emotional as well as the real meaning of the losses to the family, and help them with that aspect.

Healthy

Family members:

1. Greatest ability to tolerate separation.
2. Adults have the ability to separate from their parents and the ability for mutual bonding within their own families.
3. Family members are able to establish identities beyond their immediate family.
4. Family members are able to hold view of "no one person" being irreplaceable.
5. Family members have had previous successes in handling separations.

Family members:

1. Demonstrate flexibility and ability to problem solve.
2. Can most easily get in touch with feelings—they use denial less and it is less rigid.

1. At times of diagnosis, hospitalizations and other illness-related stress points, staff need to:
   a. Help patients and family members recognize the capacities they utilized to handle previously stressful situations.
   b. Enable them to verbalize upset feelings.
   c. Help them channel their energies into problem-solving activities.

242

The starting point for the transitional process is the point at which the diagnosis is made. This is the first major stress point in the course of the chronic illness, because it signals the end of an old way of life for both the patient and the family. There are four successive stress points in the course of any illness which involve separation: diagnosis, hospitalization, discharge, and the transition from sick to different. The effects of each stress point on different types of families, some reactions to separation and change that can be expected, and suggested treatment approaches with each family type will be discussed below.

1. Diagnosis

The beginning of the need for illness-related changes in the patient's and the family's lives occurs when the diagnosis of a chronic illness is made. When the physician shares this information with the patient and family, it marks the beginning of an awareness, usually suppressed, that their lives will never be the same. The uncertainty, anxiety, and fear of the unknown that are generated within the patient and all other family members can be severe. For this reason, people most often utilize denial as the primary mechanism of defense (Verwoerdt, 1966; Feldman, 1974).

When people are poorly individuated, they have more difficulty handling the strong feelings that are mobilized at the time the diagnosis is made and in the period immediately following. The more severe the feelings of fear, anger, and anxiety are, the stronger the need is for the person to defend against them. Thus, the stress point of diagnosis is a crucial one. It is at this point that the family may desperately want help and support from, and closeness to, each other and involved friends and professionals. However, the family members may be unable to accept assistance because of the intensity of their dependency feelings. These dependency feelings are often frightening and unacceptable because they generate strong feelings of helplessness in patients and families. To a greater or lesser degree, most people tend to counter these feelings with behavior that demonstrates their independence and shows they do not need others. The more threatening change is to people, the more they will tend to deny the event which necessitates the change.

Diagnosis in Severely Disturbed Families, and the Social Worker's Approach. Families with characteristics of the type described as severely disturbed have a very difficult time when the diagnosis is made, because

243

they have the most difficulty accepting change and loss. An example of the reaction similar to this type of family can be seen in the S case situation, discussed earlier under power structure and affect.

Ed was diagnosed as having acute lymphocytic leukemia. His mother, Mrs. S, was assessed as having a borderline personality, and her reality testing seemed poor. Ed kept up his tough exterior from the time the diagnosis was made until the night he actually died. He did this partly out of his own needs, and partly to keep up a "front" for his mother, who needed him to be strong. Mrs. S was told the diagnosis and understood it but kept saying repeatedly, "when Ed gets better . . . " During the final stages, when he was dying in the hospital, Mrs. S kept saying "when he comes home. . . . "

In such situations, the major task for the social worker is to continue to present reality to the non-ill family members. Thus the worker gently but steadfastly commented that Ed was not getting better or was not going home. She also stated explicitly that Mrs. S was having difficulty accepting what was happening and this was understandable because of the pain she must be feeling. This was done to help Mrs. S identify reality and to help her make sense out of her need to deny. With Ed, the issue of separation was dealt with in the context of his hospitalizations, by discussing his feelings of loneliness when he was away from familiar people and surroundings. This was the only form in which he could tolerate discussing separation.

Diagnosis in Midrange Families, and the Social Worker's Approach. The midrange families in the Lewis study had difficulty accepting change and loss but were able to do so, even though it was painful. Families with similar separation behavior utilize denial strongly at the point of diagnosis, but they are able to relinquish it more readily than severely disturbed families are.

Families with behavior similar to the centripetal-style family are likely to be more verbal and better able to express themselves than centrifugal-style families. For both midrange types, diagnosis sets in motion forces which threaten these families' sense of being in control. The social worker needs to keep in mind that a great deal of the family's and the patient's energies will go into absorbing the implication of the diagnosis. Providing comfort and assurance of availability are important at this point, but the worker's major goal is to help these families maintain some sense of control over the situation. With families who tend to pull away under stress, the worker

244

should be the initiator. A strong practical approach at this critical juncture involves follow-up telephone calls or letters to see how they are doing and to remind them of the need to stay connected to the hospital and clinic for continued treatment. With both centrifugal-style and centripetal-style families, the worker needs to be aware of the lack of flexibility and vulnerability to loss of control. It is important therefore to reinforce the notion that they will have more control over the situation if the patient takes the prescribed medicines and comes to clinic appointments, and if both patient and family members learn to manage the illness.

The social worker also should be very sensitive to the ways in which illness-related losses will affect the balance of power and control in families with this style of functioning. The Ys, who were described earlier in the section on perception of reality (p. 225), demonstrate how shifts in the balance of power can be very destructive to this type of family system.

Mr. Y's illness progressed to the point that he became weak and lost his job. The loss of job and subsequent loss of income forced the family to apply for public assistance and find lower-rent housing. As Mr. Y lost physical strength, the balance of power between him and his wife changed. Mr. Y became increasingly depressed, and both Mr. and Mrs. Y became increasingly anxious and angry. The frequency of arguments increased, and Mr. Y felt increasingly powerless because he could not be in control in the same way as before.

The social worker's thrust was to help Mr. Y "recoup his loss" through helping him find another type of work through which he could regain his sense of power and self-esteem. This involved helping him redefine his notion of strength so that he could feel strong in a nonphysical type of job. Once this was accomplished, he felt powerful again and was able to learn to exert authority at home in a different way.

In this case the social worker selected a specific focus, with the goal being to restore balance in the power structure. No attempt was made, initially, to restructure the nature of the relationship. In illness situations with midrange families, it is important that the worker's first goal be restabilization. These families are vulnerable when dealing with change, and if two major change processes are operating simultaneously, the family members' circuits can become overloaded. It is more useful to these families if the social worker deals with one major change at a time.

Diagnosis in Healthy Families, and the Social Worker's Approach. The healthy families in the Lewis study were described as having good ability to

245

tolerate separation. However, similar families would also be vulnerable during the period immediately following diagnosis. The major strengths in the healthy family that enable them to cope better with loss and change are their flexibility, their previous successes in handling separations, their ability to solve problems, and the relative ease in which feelings can be made available to them. In such families, therefore, the hospital-based social worker can facilitate adaptation following diagnosis by helping patients and family members recognize the capacities they have utilized to handle previously stressful situations; enabling them to verbalize upset feelings; and helping them channel their energies into problem-solving activity.

The following case provides an example of how a family similar to a healthy type of family handled diagnosis and the illness-related losses which occurred around that time. In this case the couple was able to draw on their many years of shared experience with problem solving.

Mr. B was a 46-year-old married man with four children. He was self-employed and did a variety of household repairs. He developed arthritis and was already very physically limited by the time the diagnosis was made. Following the diagnosis, Mr. and Mrs. B were informed of the serious implications of the illness, and Mr. B began to realize that he could not return to his previous type of work. He was understandably depressed but was in touch with his feelings and was able to talk about them. During his hospitalization, he had conversations with the social worker in which he began to recall and talk about his nonwork-related successes, from which he had derived much satisfaction and which enriched his sense of self-esteem. He and his wife were highly individuated people and secure in their marital partnership. Once financial security was established through eligibility for social security disability benefits, the marriage was not threatened by his hopefully temporary inability to work. The social worker encouraged Mr. B to utilize his capabilities to obtain his high school degree, and he did begin to do this.

The major function the social worker served in this situation was to facilitate the problem-solving process. She accomplished this by allowing the patient to sort out and accept his feelings and look realistically at his strengths, and thereby she helped him move away from feelings of depression so that he could regain a sense of hope.

2. Hospitalization

Hospitalizations are critical stress points which occur throughout the transitional process of moving from well to sick to different. Hospitalization is especially stressful the first time it occurs. It is even more difficult to handle if the diagnosis is made or confirmed during hospitalization, because hospitals can be strange and lonely places. Separation from family, meaningful relationships, and known surroundings can be experienced as anxiety provoking and depressing under normal conditions. It can be an even more difficult experience for the ill person.

Family members can also become increasingly anxious during the separation caused by hospitalization. It is usually difficult for people to deal with and tolerate uncertainty, and there is much uncertainty attached to hospitalization. If hospitalization occurs for the purpose of making or confirming a diagnosis, family members will experience anxiety while waiting for the outcome. This anxiety will be intensified because the patient and family are physically separated and thus deprived of mutual support. Anxiety and frustration are further intensified by having to deal with the new and strange atmosphere of a hospital, with its rules and procedures, and with the feelings of regression and depersonalization hospitalization generates for both patient and family. (For a more detailed discussion of the difficulties patients and families encounter in hospitals, see Verwoerdt, 1966; Jaco, 1972; Moos, 1977.)

The basic problem with uncertainty, and with not knowing "what will be," is that uncertainty is fertile ground for all types of fantasies, wishes, and imagined outcomes. Family members can dream that the hospitalized patient will be "all right," and then be bitterly disappointed and angry when, instead of this, the patient returns home from the hospital with a diagnosis of multiple sclerosis or diabetes, for example. The outcome can be better tolerated if the patient and family suspect a more serious diagnosis than the one actually determined.

The families who have the greatest difficulty in dealing with uncertainty and ambiguity are those in the severely disturbed and midrange categories. Techniques and methods for helping these families deal with these issues, described previously, can be applied appropriately in helping them cope with hospitalization.

Outcomes of hospitalizations not only can dash hopes for good health. They also often cause disappointment and frustration for patients and families who were expecting cures from drugs or other treatments, or who perhaps were permanently paralyzed and had expected to walk. The degree to which people have individuated and can tolerate change is often an important determinant of the degree of acceptance of the diagnosis or prognosis. These factors also affect how family members will cope with the uncertainty regarding expectations of the patient's behavior and functioning after the return home and will affect their ability to plan for discharge.

3. Discharge

A consideration of the family's ability to tolerate change and to accept the changed patient family member is very important at the juncture of preparation for discharge from the hospital. This stress point is one in which the social worker and other staff are likely to encounter great resistance to change from both patient and family, especially with families similar to those described as severely disturbed and midrange. This resistance usually manifests itself in lack of cooperation, refusal to come to the hospital, or refusal to participate at all in the planning process.

There are three important tasks for the social worker to accomplish when dealing with resistance from the patient and the family. These are: (1) to keep in mind the overriding reality that the patient must leave the hospital when she or he no longer needs acute care; (2) to identify the specific separation-related issues which are causing the family difficulty; and (3) to separate these issues from the discharge-planning issues. Implementation of these tasks often takes both considerable diagnostic skill and patience on the part of the social worker. However, the worker who can follow these guidelines may avoid becoming involved in a struggle with patients and families.

Discharge Planning in Severely Disturbed Families, and the Social Worker's Approach. The following is a case example of discharge planning with a family similar to the severely disturbed families in the Lewis study. In this case, a confused, overburdened woman needed much help in her struggle to resist change.

Mrs. N was a very dependent, separated woman in her thirties who had frequent hospitalizations for seizures. As the time for discharge planning approached on one occasion, Mrs. N pleaded that she could not go home without a homemaker. Since there was no reality basis for this, the social worker was unable to obtain a homemaker. Once discharged, the patient refused to take care of herself, and she refused to seek help at a community mental health center. She closeted herself in her home and spent most of her time in bed. She kept one of the children at home with her at all times, because she was "sick." There were no other adults in the home, and the children were young, so there was no one to help care for her. Her own needs and her inability to perceive reality and the needs of her children made it necessary for the social worker to refer the case to a community-based agency with some authority to act on behalf of the children.

Situations like this are frustrating to both the social worker and other health care staff. Often the worker must help staff to handle their anger toward these patients and to understand why people like Mrs. N are unable to readily change their behavior.

Discharge Planning in Midrange Families, and the Social Worker's Approach. An example of discharge planning with a family similar to a midrange family can be seen in the following case example. This family was able to accept help with making changes at the point that the threat of separation becomes real.

Mrs. L was an overweight woman in her 60s who was admitted to the hospital with pneumonia. At home was her 70-year-old husband, who had been ill with emphysema for about a year, had very limited mobility, and required a great deal of care. He refused to go to a nursing home and would not permit a homemaker to come into the home to help his wife. Mrs. L was very angry with her husband but felt that she had to comply with his wishes, because he had always been a "good," reliable husband and had been a good provider for her and their children. She had developed pneumonia by standing in the open door on a windy winter night when she'd opened the door so her husband could get some air. Realistically the wife would go home, but it was obvious that unless the caretaking issue was resolved, Mrs. L would be back in the hospital shortly after discharge.

The social worker's selected goal was to devise a discharge plan to prevent Mrs. L's rehospitalization, while still enabling Mr. L to remain in the home. She met with the father and all the grown children in the family during a home visit. The children expressed anger at their father as the perceived cause of their mother's illness. The worker spoke from authority based on her position in the hospital and her partnership with the physician. She accepted Mr. L's needs but stressed the reality of the need to relieve the strain on his wife. She suggested a homemaker would enable his wife to continue to care for him. This approach relieved the threat of another separation and provided a plan which allowed Mr. L to remain secure at home. Mr. L accepted the plan.

Discharge Planning in Healthy Families, and the Social Worker's Approach. The final case is an example of discharge planning with a family who demonstrated the type of maturity and individuation representative of the healthy families described in the Lewis study. In this case, the couple used support to say goodbye to an aging parent.

Mr. and Mrs. T initiated contact with the social worker for help in placing Mr. T's father, Mr. C, in a nursing home following hospitalization. Mr. C's health had been failing for some time. It was a painful decision for the whole family, but Mr. and Mrs. T helped Mr. C understand the need for placement. Mr. and Mrs. T carried the major responsibility for contacting nursing homes and utilized the social worker mainly to provide support, information, and direction. Mr. and Mrs. T were able to express their feelings of sadness and regret, but were simultaneously able to separate from Mr. C and plan for the change which would take place.

4. The Transition from Sick to Different

Once the crisis of moving from being well to being sick abates and the chronically ill patient and family begin to internalize the diagnosis, they must settle down to the arduous task of "learning to live with" the illness and moving from being sick to being different.

The issues for both patient and family members at this crisis point are to recognize that (1) the patient is different than he or she was before the illness, (2) the family will be different, and (3) there will be specific ongoing changes which the patient and the family will have to make in living with the illness.

The concept of the sick role theoretically defines the mutually expectable behaviors and roles of the sick person, his physician, and others who interact regularly with him. However, recent studies indicate that this theory does not hold in relation to chronic illness behavior (Segall, 1976). The basic problem is that sick-role theory is based on behavior in acute illness, from which people recover. In chronic illness, however, the patient never fully recovers from the illness. The issue is that if the patient and his family view him as sick in the *acute* sense, with the expectation that he will be cured or recover, this notion can encourage holding on to the old self-images and family images.

Further, when the process of relinquishing the old self and family images, goals, and roles is retarded, the transition from being sick to being different is delayed. Only when patient and family accept the reality that the illness *has* caused changes will they be able to shift from old roles and functions which were adaptive and functional prior to the illness but may now be maladaptive and dysfunctional.

250

In essence, patients and families need to go through a mourning process. As succinctly stated by Feldman (1974), "mourning facilitates the structuring of a future-oriented existence, which may not be possible until what has been lost has been grieved for" (p. 788).

Ability of Family Types to Make the Transition from Sick to Different. It is important for the social worker to be aware that mourning is a process which most of the families in the Lewis study had considerable difficulty experiencing. The severely disturbed families were poorly individuated and normally had immense difficulty dealing with change, loss, and separation. Consequently, when illness forces family changes, it would be unrealistic for the hospital-based social worker, with limited time, to attempt to direct similar families in the process of disengagement from the past. Helping families to recognize the need for changes in important areas and to cope with them would be a more productive effort.

At the other end of the continuum, healthy families in the study were found to be the most capable of accepting life's developmental changes, losses, and separations. These patients and families were verbal and able to communicate. There are many indications that in medical settings families similar to this type want help, will either reach out for it, or accept the help that is offered, and will deal openly with feelings of anger, depression, guilt, fear, and hope. This type of person-family unit is best suited for treatment in which the end goal is similar to that described by Feldman (1974):

> Regardless of previous life experience, to be the victim of catastrophic illness poses an awesome reality. The stricken one must accept that life is irrevocably different, and because of that difference, a new meaning and a way of life must be found. . . . To discover a new meaning in life in the face of dissolution of the old meaning, to accept the difference imposed by the illness, and to still maintain one's dignity and worth is the essence of the transition from sick to different. When one has accomplished this, there is no longer a need for illness as a primary life style. (p. 289)

The midrange families in the Lewis study were found to have more difficulty, but they demonstrated they could change, even if they found life's changes "distasteful." Although it would be unrealistic for social workers to expect families with behavior similar to that of midrange families to achieve the same goals as healthier families, these families, particularly those similar to the centripetal type, could utilize appropriate social work

251

help to deal with transitions in the course of illness. Families who cope with separation and loss in a manner similar to the centripetal-style families appear to be best suited for treatment in which the end goal is similar to that described by Shellhase and Shellhase (1972):

> The task involves more assisting the family toward an understanding and acceptance of the realities of the patient's disability. The work of the family is to accommodate itself to the permanence of the disabling condition and to reallocate both the sentiment and substance of family resources to maintain the family intact through such experience. . . . (p. 549)

The same goal could be attempted with families similar to the midrange families with the centrifugal style. However, because of their rigidity and their tendency to pull away from help, the social worker would need to recognize that the goal may not be achieved as readily, if at all. It would be a goal to work toward, over time, and not necessarily a goal to be accomplished.

FACILITATING THE TRANSITION FROM SICK TO DIFFERENT

The approach presented in this section represents my formulation of a method the social worker can use to enable certain types of patients and families make role transitions and to help them with the change process. It is an approach that attempts to alter self-images and family images and to facilitate the mourning process. The basic assumption is that change will occur only when people can grieve and mourn the loss of meaningful aspects of their lives that are no longer possible to experience when chronic illness changes their lives. This approach will be most effective with families similar to the midrange centripetal-style and healthy families described in the study by Lewis et al.

This approach should be principally used at the transitional points following the stressful time of diagnosis. This is important, because denial tends to be very strong following diagnosis. The social worker will not be able to utilize this approach effectively unless the patient or family member can be helped to get in touch with the depression which is usually experienced once the use of denial has been relinquished (Feldman, 1974). It signals the beginning, unconscious acknowledgement that loss has occurred. The key is to move this depression, and the acknowledgement of loss or losses, into conscious awareness and into the verbal sphere, so that the person and family can begin to take active steps toward change.

The following characteristics signal that a patient and family members are beginning to struggle with the transition from being sick to being different:

1. Regardless of socioeconomic group, the person and family are people who usually have accomplished something in their lives. They pride themselves on their strengths and, to a greater or lesser extent, on not needing others.
2. For the most part, they have been able to reach the point where they are not denying the illness or what is happening.
3. They may or may not verbally acknowledge depression, but the depressive affect is apparent.
4. There is sensitivity to feeling critical of self and family, and they may express criticism of health care professionals.
5. They convey a distancing with each other and with health professionals, while at the same time transmitting the wish for involvement and understanding.
6. The patient experiences an undercurrent of not feeling good about self.

In order to help the patient begin to make the transition from sick to different, the following steps are suggested:

1. The social worker needs to recognize that the patient is experiencing a constellation of regressive feelings—helplessness, dependency, loss of control—that are threatening to overwhelm his sense of integrity and self-esteem.
2. The social worker needs to identify for the patient the changes in his life. The methodology is to contrast the time prior to the illness with the period following the illness and highlight the losses, e.g., what the patient was able to do that he can no longer do, his feelings about his competence and other tangible and intangible realities. Concomitantly, the worker needs to generalize and express understanding of the resentment "anyone" would have in this situation.
3. The social worker then needs to acknowledge that people feel good about their accomplishments and feel bad when they can no longer accomplish in the same way. This may make them feel as if they have failed. In essence, the social worker is setting the stage for the acceptance of a new

concept of self, different from before, but still acceptable and not "bad." This approach is designed to deal with resistance that can develop if the person is overwhelmed by feelings of worthlessness. Basically, the social worker is trying to convey: "You, as a sick person, are not a bad person; life is not a matter of all or nothing; your old self was not all good, and your new self is not all bad; it is a matter that you are different, now." The social worker attempts to help the person become aware when he is being too hard on himself, and realize that by holding on to the old notions, he is trying to achieve a goal which is not humanly possible.

4. The social worker then needs to identify the patient's strengths and resources, such as his accomplishments, determination, courage, and continuing wish to provide for his family. Often, because the person is measuring himself by the standards of his "old" self, and because he may be in despair and feeling that his new existence is futile, he will not see these qualities as strengths and may not even want to listen to the social worker. If these signs appear, and if the patient continues to hold on strongly to the old self, it may signal that he is resisting change because of fear of newness, the uncertainty related to being different, and the general anxiety which accompanies change. The social worker needs to determine, with the patient, what his specific fears and concerns are, and, through mutual discussion, subject the fears to reality testing. The social worker also needs to help the patient anticipate and verbally express concerns and ideas about how family and friends will relate to him in this "different" state.

5. The social worker needs to help the patient look at the changes that he needs to make, give support that he will feel better if the changes are made, and underscore the achievements once these are accomplished. There will be some resistance during this process, because no one wants to acknowledge that he won't be "whole" again, and the wish to return to the previous state is strong and recurrent. To help handle the resistance, the worker needs to help the person see that by holding on he will prevent himself from enjoying what he does have and can still have.

6. The social worker needs to collaborate with the patient to identify what still does have meaning for him in his life, and to identify how his life can be restructured so that his sense of purpose and his values can be attached to new areas and new goals.

7. In order to be able to help the patient fully, the social worker needs to think about her or his own notions of perfection and to examine her own feelings in relation to the reality that life does not fulfill anyone's ideals. The

critical issue is to help the patient realize that people cannot control everything that happens to them. People can only manage, direct, and control how they cope with what does occur in life.

The ill person usually will need the opportunity to discuss these issues alone, particularly when the concerns first begin to surface, because they are very painful to express. Very often, because there are such deep feelings of guilt, shame, and embarrassment and general emotional pain, the ill person and key family members may need to talk separately with the social worker before family discussions can be held.

The following approach, similar to that taken with the patient, can be followed with families:

1. The social worker needs to identify for the family the patterns and areas of their lives that are affected.

2. The social worker needs to permit them to express feelings of resentment. This will be difficult because the anger that is experienced is felt in relation to the patient for becoming ill and upsetting their lives. This is disturbing for the family members to express and probably would be destructive of the integrity they are trying to maintain. Family members will be more likely to own feelings of resentment toward an external illness, over which they have no control, which has invaded their lives.

3. The social worker needs to identify for the family the sources of anxiety, frustration, and resentment for all ill people and their families: loss of control, living with uncertainty and unpredictability, and constant change.

4. The social worker needs to discuss these sources in the concrete terms of the members' own lives; what they can no longer plan for; what activities can no longer be shared; what roles have to be taken over by others; what roles can be given over to the ill person.

5. The worker and family need to verbalize the feelings that accompany these losses and place them in the context of what is usual to experience in these circumstances. This both normalizes and educates. Families are often ashamed of their feelings, feel strange having them, and need a standard for what is "all right" to feel in this new circumstance. Discussion of feelings, especially of sadness and annoyance in relation to the role changes that are occurring, can reduce tension and permit greater mutual acceptance, so that there can be specific planning for change.

255

6. In the transactions, the social worker must be emotionally prepared to acknowledge forthrightly the grimness and despair that can accompany these changes and be able to accept verbalizations of these feelings from the patient and family. Attempts to minimize the harshness of the reality of the situation can short-circuit the grieving and the letting-go process.

7. Whenever possible and appropriate, the social worker should try to structure family discussions so that patient and family members can work on troubling issues together, share problem solving, and learn to be responsive to each other as changed people in a new and different life situation. Further, the worker can act as a buffer, serve as role model and negotiator, and create a neutral environment in which family members can feel safe, say things they may be reluctant to say normally, and express feelings of tenderness which might get lost in anger or remain unsaid.

The case presentation of the H family reflects the process of change involved in integrating illness into the family structure. Although work was done both individually and jointly with husband and wife, the segment presented below focuses on the process of Mr. H's movement from sick to different. The general characteristics of the behavior of the H family were similar to those of the centripetal-style families described in the Lewis study.

Mr. and Mrs. H had been married 12 years when Mr. H developed leukemia. They had one six-year-old daughter. Mr. H was perceived by both himself and his wife as the leader in decision making. He had been the main disciplinarian, handled all of the finances, and had been the family's sole support. They had not been separated since they had been married, and Mrs. H was emotionally dependent on her husband. The onset of the illness was sudden, and the diagnosis was made following hospitalization.

The staff became concerned about Mr. H's strong use of denial and heavy reliance on religion and contacted the social worker. The social worker's entry into the family system was based on helping them apply for temporary financial assistance. Initially, the social worker focused on helping Mrs. H take a more independent role, stabilizing the situation, and helping the couple deal with the separation which the hospitalization imposed. Once the situation was stabilized and a new routine was established, the couple was able to talk about some of their feelings in relation to the illness, hospitalization, and death.

In subsequent discussions during periods of rehospitalization, the social worker began to focus on the ways in which Mr. H coped with his illness. She was able to determine that the strong belief in God was motivated by an equally strong fear of separation. Mr. H expressed his belief that, after death, those who had "found God" would be reunited in Heaven. Additionally, Mr. H felt ashamed to express his fears of death and separation and to acknowledge his angry feelings. His image of himself was of a strong man who was in control of his feelings and the situation. It was very difficult for him to acknowledge that he did not have total control and that he felt so "weak" and vulnerable. The social worker assessed that Mr. H would not be able to cope with the illness-related changes (e.g., changes in his work role, the marital relationship, and life-style) until he could accept and cope with these feelings.

The worker helped the patient recognize that he was not a "bad" person because he felt angry, nor was he weak because he felt afraid. She further helped increase his self-esteem by focusing his attention on the aspects of himself which he valued (e.g., his sensitivity to others, his caring feelings for his wife and daughter, and his work accomplishments). As Mr. H demonstrated increasing ability to tolerate anxiety and fear, and to express anger and worry, the worker changed her focus. She then assessed that the patient was ready to confront basic issues related to individuation, separation, and loss. Mr. H began to demonstrate increased ability to cope with uncertainty, take charge of his life, and help his wife prepare for a future without him. His expressions of faith in God became less intense, and he found new satisfactions and meaning in relationships with his wife, daughter, and his father.

The degree of change in the patient's ability to cope with separation was exemplified in a dream which the patient related to the social worker a few months before he died. He had "always" had a fear of being buried, and he had a dream about his funeral. He recalled that the casket moved downward very slowly and moved "all the way down." When the casket reached the bottom, he looked around and "felt better." Then, the casket returned to the ground level. He stated that he did not feel fearful when he woke up.

SUMMARY

The purpose of this chapter has been to present an organized framework which will permit the hospital-based social worker to accurately evaluate and assess families, and to predict the family's styles of coping with and adapting to illness-related problems and changes. The findings of the Lewis et al. (1976) study were used as a basis for comparing families with similar characteristics who are seen in medical settings. The concept of the course of chronic illness was employed to predict the points when there will be increased stress on the coping capacities of the family system. A variety of treatment approaches to be used with different family types at different stress points in the course of the illness were suggested.

REFERENCES

Abrams, R. D. *Not Alone with Cancer*. Springfield, Ill.: Charles C Thomas, Publisher, 1974.

Bromberg, H., and Donnerstag, E. "Counseling Heart Patients and Their Families." *Health and Social Work*, 2:159–72, 1977.

Cohen, P., Dizenhuz, I. M., and Winget, C. "Family Adaptation to Terminal Illness and Death of a Parent." *Social Casework*, April, 1977, pp. 223–28.

Cotter, J., and Schwartz, A. "Psychological and Social Support of the Patient and Family." In A. Altman, and A. Schwartz, *Malignancies of Infancy, Childhood and Adolescence*. Philadelphia: W. B. Saunders Co., 1978.

Feldman, D. J. "Chronic Disabling Illness: A Holistic View." *Journal of Chronic Disease*, 27:287–91, 1974.

Fink, S. L., Skipper, J. K., Jr., and Hallenbeck, P. N. "Physical Disability and Problems in Marriage." *Journal of Marriage and the Family*, February 1968, pp. 64–73.

Jaco, E. G. (ed.). *Patients, Physicians, and Illness*. 2nd ed. New York: Free Press, 1972, pp. 118–30.

Kaplan, D. M., Grobstein, R., and Smith, A. "Predicting the Impact of Severe Illness in Families." *Health and Social Work*, 1:71–82, 1976.

Klein, R. F., Dean, A., and Bogdonoff, M. D. "The Impact of Illness upon the Spouse." *Journal of Chronic Disease*, 20:241–48, 1967.

Lewis, J. M., Beavers, W. R., Gossett, J. T., and Phillips, A. V. *No Single Thread: Psychological Health in Family Systems*. New York: Brunner/Mazel, 1976.

Lindeman, E. "Symptomatology and Management of Acute Grief." In H. J. Parad (ed.), *Crisis Intervention: Selected Readings*. New York: Family Association of America, 1965.

Moos, R. H., and Tsu, V. D. "The Crisis of Physical Illness: An Overview." In R. H. Moos (ed.), *Coping with Physical Illness*. New York: Plenum Medical Book Co., 1977.

Nagi, S. Z., and Clark, L. D. "Factors in Marital Adjustment after Disability." *Journal of Marriage and the Family*, May 1964, pp. 215–16.

Segall, A. "The Sick Role Concept: Understanding Illness Behavior." *Journal of Health and Social Behavior*, 17:163–70, 1976.

Shellhase, L. J., and Shellhase, F. E. "Role of the Family in Rehabilitation." *Social Casework*, November 1972, pp. 544–50.

Verwoerdt, A., M.D. *Communication with the Fatally Ill*. Springfield, Ill.: Charles C Thomas, Publisher, 1966.

Wishnie, H. A., Hackett, T. P., and Cassem, N. H. "Psychological Hazards of Convalescence Following Myocardial Infarction." In R. H. Moos (ed.), *Coping with Physical Illness*. New York: Plenum Medical Book Co., 1977.

CHAPTER **10**

From Divorce to Family Reconstitution: A Clinical View

By JOHN GOLDMEIER

The Family may neither vanish nor enter upon a new Golden Age. It may—and this is far more likely—break up, shatter, only to come together again in weird and novel ways.

Alvin Toffler, *Future Shock*

The changes in the family that Alvin Toffler foresaw may already be upon us! In this chapter clinical intervention with families is related to the societal context within which family breakdown and reconstitution occur. Concepts from the social sciences and the observations of social critics are introduced to help explain the cycle in which forces pushing the family variously toward dissolution or reconstitution constantly interact to influence the treatment process. Formulations related to the concept of social stress are applied to develop an understanding of a number of examples of families in the throes of this type of upheaval. Examples of such stresses which can pose impediments to problem solving also are discussed.

Much of the thinking of family therapists appears to be based on notions

259

of the nuclear family which no longer apply. Attention to the family in which a spouse is absent, or the family in the process of dissolution, has not yet produced relevant theory and practice principles that would be consonant with the tenor of an age in which 45 to 60 percent of all marriages sustain a separation at some point in their existence (Weiss, 1975). Insufficient attention also has been paid to the family in the process of reconstitution, although popular notions relating to the right to "self-fulfillment" are being expounded to explain this increasingly common phenomenon (Quindlen, 1977). Much of the current theory too readily assumes commitment by family members to the preservation of the family unit as originally formed. Further, many family therapists have difficulty in coming to terms with discomfiting notions about family instability. An example is given in Tennenbaum (1968):

> When I first became a therapist, I would consider no possibility of divorce. If I could not help a couple live with their marriage, I would terminate my professional relationship. I would refuse to preside over the liquidation of the marriage. I conceived as my task keeping every marriage going, and if I couldn't I would tally that up as one of my failures and resign. Theoretically, I no longer hold to this position. Many marriages, I have come to feel, are so bad that they are not worth saving; in fact, the continuance is destructive to both, and the partners can salvage for themselves a better life if they had the courage to start fresh. Although I concede the wisdom of such a step, I still find it hard if not impossible professionally to participate in a marital separation. (p. 247)

In order to provide a background for current changes in family structure, the implications of certain demographic factors will be discussed. An appreciation of the influence of these factors is necessary to understand the notion basic to this chapter: Family dismemberment and reconstitution are part of a continuum which must be seen as a feature of the developmental life cycle.

DEMOGRAPHIC IMPLICATIONS

There is increasing evidence that the traditional nuclear family, husband and wife and their mutual offspring, is becoming less and less a feature of modern society. Hirschhorn (1977), in an article tracing the composition of families and the role distribution of their members, notes how people move in and out of various household arrangements (p. 435). From 1950 to 1970 remarriages, as a proportion of total marriages, rose from 21 to 26 percent. By 1970, 1 out of every 5 divorced women remarried within one year after her divorce (Glick & Norton, 1973, p. 302). About two thirds of all divorced women and three quarters of all divorced men now remarry at some point in their lives (Epstein, 1974). The trend toward divorce at a younger age serves to increase the probability of remarriage, which now may occur a number of times. As those who are divorced or separated set up independent households, they contribute toward an appreciable rise in the number of female-headed families. In 1972, 14 percent of all families with children had a female head, representing a 40 percent increase since 1960.

Educational and vocational trends have done much to affect the rate of family dissolution. The importance of education lies largely in the realm of new consciousness for women, while employment and its corollary of financial independence seems to exert a more direct influence on the actual decision to separate. Thus education has generally been seen as contributing to changing views about the traditional female role (Lipman-Blumen, 1975), even though the Carnegie Commission reports that ever since 1900 women have been less likely than men to enter college. This trend continues, despite the fact that women are more likely than men to complete secondary education (Carnegie Commission, 1973). Figures on female participation in the labor force from 1940 to 1970, however, rose from 15 to 41 percent for married women (Waldman & Eaddy, 1974). In March 1973 the percentage of married women with husbands present who worked reached 42 percent (Lipman-Blumen, 1975, p. 68), thereby considerably increasing a wife's option if she wished to leave her husband without remaining financially dependent on him.

The implications of these statistics differ from traditional notions about the relationship between financial independence and divorce only to the extent that more families are now affected. In 1930 it was already known that economic independence and freedom to divorce were closely related (Waller, 1930/1967). Willard Waller, the pioneer sociologist who first presented evidence of this, found that the adjustment process after divorce seemed to be much easier when each of the former marital partners was relatively independent financially. These findings have continued to be supported, most recently in a 1967 study which also found that those who are more affluent are more likely to remarry eventually (Glick & Norton, 1973, p. 302). If the woman had a relatively high personal income her

261

remarriage might, however, be delayed, presumably providing a greater opportunity to find a compatible marriage partner.

These statistics on family dissolution and reconstitution emphasize the pervasive nature of the changes in family structure and the extent of the forces, many of them outside the family, associated with these changes. It was inevitable that, perhaps as a consequence, there would be modifications in the way the family is viewed.

CHANGING CONCEPTS IN FAMILY LIFE

In spite of the fact that divorce is increasingly common, it is still a traumatic experience for most people. Whether because of its disruptive features or because of the stigma still sometimes attached to the divorced person, public acceptance of divorce is by no means universal. While attitudes about it are changing, these changes are slow, and they only alleviate the trauma of divorce to a limited degree. A study conducted by the Roper Organization in 1974 revealed that although more women and men favored divorce in 1974 than in 1970, 20 percent of the women and 24 percent of the men were still opposed. Nineteen percent of the men also thought that couples should stay together because children would be harmed by the separation (Roper, 1977).

Whether or not divorce, as a feature of family life, has gained acceptance, it is clear that it no longer has the finite quality it once had. Social scientists and professionals who work with troubled families (like myself) increasingly see divorce, family breakup, and family reconstitution as a process characterized by stages in the life cycle. This idea seems to be basic, despite differences in how the central conflicts leading to family dissolution are formulated. For example, social exchange theorists see the notion of reward as essential; at some stage in the life cycle one or both of the marriage partners may find that the rewards inherent in continuing a marriage no longer adequately compensate for the emotional investment made. If a more benign balance is not established the forces pushing toward family dissolution are set in motion (see Bagarozzi & Wodarski, 1977; Edwards, 1969). Erikson's epigenetic view of the central conflicts in young and mature adulthood, involving the struggle over intimacy first and generativity later, constitutes another dimension in the way family dismemberment and reconstitution can be viewed (Erikson, 1959). This view seems to guide a recent series of articles on divorce in *The New York*

Times, in which the increasingly powerful forces pushing toward independence were juxtaposed with the equally strong urge toward intimacy (Quindlen, 1977, p. 36). The case examples in the Quindlen article suggest that an optimum balance allowing for the satisfaction of both of these central needs, intimacy and independence, must exist in a satisfying marriage. The loss of a degree of independence may be tolerated in exchange for gains in intimacy or vice versa, depending on the changing orientations of each of the marriage partners as they go through life. However, when neither the need for independence nor the need for intimacy is satisfied, the family inexorably moves toward dissolution. The following case example may be typical:

"I was a fun wife," said Diana McLaughlin, a handsome woman married for 34 years to a merchant marine captain. "I drank with him, I played with him, I jumped in and out of bed, I was a good time. And when he was away at sea I raised four children with no help. I knew toward the end the marriage was disintegrating, but I didn't do anything because I didn't know what to do with myself if I did. I was a very independent type when I got married but after all those years I didn't feel that way. Then two days before Christmas a couple of years ago he came home and told me he wanted to divorce me for another woman." (Quindlen, 1977, p. 36)

This example makes clear that in today's rapidly changing world, theoretical formulations developed and tested in earlier years need to be supplemented. Among such earlier formulations are institutional approaches to the family, the structural-functional hypothesis, interactional and situational explanations, and developmental theories (Christenson, 1967). All of these explanations are premised on family units that are more stable than recent data on family dissolution and reconstitution would suggest. To supplement these theories, it is worthwhile to take cognizance of current social critics whose observations may make up in timeliness and perspicacity what they as yet lack in theoretical refinement.

Alvin Toffler, one of these critics, offers some intriguing formulations of modern family life-styles. For example, he identifies what are described as "stability zones," "marriage trajectories," and the "parallel development" phenomenon (Toffler, 1970, pp. 371–97 and 236–59). People create stability zones, Toffler argues, not to suppress change but to manage it. A stability zone, characterized by a limited number of enduring relationships, can consist, for example, of a stable marriage of 20 years amidst frequent job changes, moves, and other dislocations. On the other hand, a

263

person may have gone through a series of love affairs and through several cycles of divorce and remarriage, all while maintaining basically the same relationship with an employer. Toffler thus argues that for many the marital relationship which has been traditionally seen as relatively enduring may not be one of these stability zones but rather an alliance without such permanence.

It then follows, Toffler goes on, that family life should be seen in the context of marriage trajectories. Marriage viewed this way is a relationship with significant turning points as it matures, if it does indeed mature. Significant turning points are: (1) the trial marriage, which is not legally sanctioned but which may result in a more permanent union; (2) the point where a couple decides to first formalize the relationship and stay together until, at least, the next stage; (3) the end of parenthood, if there are children; and (4) the onset of retirement, which requires the fashioning of a new set of habits, interests, and activities. Toffler sees the third stage as most critical because it is during that time that two mature people, presumably with well-matched interests and at complementary stages of personality development, would look forward to a relationship with a greater statistical probability of enduring. Not all marriages, it is important to note, survive all these stages, so it is necessary to see the developmental phases of the family in new ways.

One of these ways is to pay special attention to the theory of parallel development, as Toffler calls it. This idea (whether or not it as yet qualifies as theory) represents an interesting takeoff from the earlier contributions of the so-called symbolic interactionists (Foote & Cottrell, 1955). In the earlier formulation people caught up in the vast process of interaction are seen as fitting their developing actions to one another, being closely attuned to how their communications are received and interpreted and mindful about how they in turn interpret the communications of others. Toffler qualifies this type of interchange by introducing the idea that the interactions, at least of the marital pair, are dependent to a large extent on their phases of distinct but comparable development. In other words, there is a certain separateness, possibly represented by feelings about independence, intimacy, and personal achievement, which modifies the couple's interactions. When the development of each of the marital partners proceeds on a complementary course, the marriage continues. However, if this development is uneven, the marriage may be dissolved, only to be reconstituted later with a new partner who is seen as more complementary.

The above concepts, grantedly, introduce a temporal element in the understanding of family life. It seems that this is necessary to redress what may be beginning to be an overemphasis on largely systematic factors (see for example, Haley, 1971). In the following section concepts from social stress theory will be used to reconcile both systemic and developmental factors (see Rodgers, 1964) in an approach to coping with family dismemberment and reconstitution.

A CLINICAL APPROACH TO FAMILY DISSOLUTION AND RECONSTITUTION

Family stress theory recognizes that pressures in family life are constant, despite intermittent crises (Burr, Hill, Reiss, & Nye, 1978). The theory also places particular emphasis on the process of separation and therefore is highly relevant in understanding family dissolution. I propose, therefore, that for purposes of clinical intervention, the long period beginning with divorce and ending in family reconstitution should be conceptualized as one long continuum. Clinical interventions at selected points along this continuum can only be meaningful when family dissolution through absence of a spouse, and family reconstitution are seen as central but interrelated segments. To think, for example, of the decision to divorce as a discrete crisis—especially when a crisis is understood as having distinct time parameters (Rapoport, 1966, p. 26) and therefore calling only for short-term intervention—would too greatly oversimplify the complex nature and aftermath of such a decision. In fact, the divorce phase itself may be a long one. Goode, in his classic study of divorce (1965), found that it usually took couples 12 months to file suit after considering divorce, while 33 percent of his sample took 24 or more months to take this step.

A Family Stress Framework

McCubbin, in his work on separation (1977), and Brown, in her study of divorce (1976), identified a cluster of coping repertoires which, it seems to me, must be addressed by clinicians as they follow families from divorce to family reconstitution or as they make contact with a family at some stage in between. In this stress framework, the coping behaviors may be seen as

265

units of attention during the several discrete phases from divorce to reconstitution.

As adapted here, the first major phase is one in which the concerns about divorce are played out. This phase, according to Brown, consists of a decision-making process followed by a restructuring process. In essence, the decision to separate or divorce is made during this phase. In preparation for this step, a major aim for both the family therapist and the couple is usually to have the actual separation proceed as amicably as possible. Then comes the transition to the new nonmarital status, which calls for major focus on the realignment of roles. The second, or middle, phase is that between divorce and remarriage. During this phase coping is directed at maintaining family or personal integrity in the face of family dissolution. Additional steps in this phase consist of the attempt to reconnect with the past and to establish independence in the present. In the third phase, the reconstitution phase, coping again reverts to the decision-making process, this time involving the prospective spouse, and this is again followed by the restructuring of relationships within the reconstituted marriage. The various phases and basic coping tasks can be represented as in Figure 1.

FIGURE 1
Coping Tasks in the Divorce, Family Dissolution, and Family Reconstitution Phases

Phase One: The Divorce Process
1. Decision to divorce or separate.
2. Restructuring of roles and relationships in preparation for and immediately following divorce.

Phase Two: Family Dissolution
1. Seeking resolutions to feelings of being separated.
2. Reducing anxiety.
3. Establishing autonomy and maintaining ties.
4. Maintaining family and personal integrity.
5. Establishing independence through self-development.

Phase Three: Family Reconstitution
1. Decision to remarry.
2. Restructuring roles and relationships to include the new spouse and, possibly, the new spouse's family members from the prior marriage.

Timing of Interventions

Those who work with families must be prepared to intervene at any point during the long and stressful period encompassed by the three phases in the stress framework. However, such intervention does not necessarily call for weekly, ongoing contact with the client for an indefinite period. Contact may be episodic and when called for. The administrative device of a case closing, usually occurring after a period of intensive contact, should not stand in the way of a more open-ended type of intervention. In fact, there is evidence that many clients do, indeed, see their contact with helping professionals as open-ended. For example, family agency statistics reveal that 20 percent of family agency clients reapply for service later (Beck & Jones, 1973, p. 181). It is suggested that the service must be adapted to the situation at hand, and this calls for flexibility and a judicious use of time in appointment scheduling. A simple choice between long-term and short-term modalities of intervention (see Reid & Shyne, 1969) does not appear to be the answer.

In a previous study of family agency practice (Goldmeier, 1976), I made an effort to explicate the alternatives open to practitioners under such a more flexible arrangement. The point made was that scheduling should be planned rather than either being rigidly set for one appointment weekly or allowed to proceed in a haphazard fashion. There are four basic choices, which may be varied or alternated, concerning intervals between a series of interviews and the frequency of interviews. The choices are (1) the variable-interval–variable-frequency schedule, (2) the variable-interval–fixed-frequency schedule, (3) the fixed-interval–variable-frequency schedule, and (4) the fixed-interval–fixed-frequency schedule. The fourth is the traditional type of schedule, involving regular weekly appointments. It does not, in my experience, meet the needs of the great majority of clients during the protracted phases of the divorce–family dismemberment–family reconstitution continuum.

An example of the variable-interval–variable-frequency schedule might be to see the family weekly during the divorce phase; intermittently during the dissolution phase, for specific problems in coping as identified; and regularly again at the point of family reconstitution. A fixed-interval–variable-frequency arrangement might be made in a situation where a stressful event, such as a court hearing, a move, or a job change, can be predicted with some certainty, although the impact of the stress cannot. The client

267

comes in on these occasions, and, depending on the degree of stress, the frequency of visits may vary. The variable-interval–fixed-frequency arrangement may be appropriate when the occurrence of stressful events cannot be predicted. The client comes at intervals when the need for service is felt, as during a particularly stressful peak in the divorce phase, and a fixed series of appointments, perhaps three or four each time, is offered. Adaptations of the above types of schedules may also be made for particular persons or subunits in a family, when additional individualized help to overcome special hurdles becomes necessary. Such help may be given on a collateral basis, while a different schedule is followed with the family unit as a whole.

The following case situation, from my practice, illustrates these principles as they are applied during the phases of coping with divorce, separation, and remarriage. The example highlights contact with the client at variable intervals and at fixed or variable frequencies during the almost four years the case was active.

Mrs. A, a 36-year-old mother of three children, requested an appointment for what she called a "marital problem." She described her husband as inattentive. He was unwilling to take seriously her efforts to go back to school or work, refusing to even recognize the possibility of an impending divorce. They had married when Mrs. A was 18. Mrs. A had not until now seriously questioned her right to basic satisfactions in her marriage or in an occupation.

At the beginning, the couple was seen jointly for three interviews. After these appointments, the husband, an engineer, decided to discontinue, sensing a lack of determination on his wife's part to proceed with divorce at this time. His assessment was essentially accurate, as Mrs. A was suffering from a sense of inferiority which made it difficult for her to act.

A new contract was then made with the therapist, calling for monthly interviews with Mrs. A alone. These interviews were to help her develop self-confidence and clarity about what it was that she wanted. The interviews continued for about a year. During that time Mrs. A decided to work full time and see how this would work out. After this experience, she decided that she did want a divorce, a decision which became increasingly firm despite the husband's taunting and some very practical considerations which often discouraged her. These considerations—frequently overlooked in divorce counseling—included her desire to retain her house, to minimally disrupt the lives of her children, and to obtain the most favorable legal settlement possible. The latter, she hoped, would occur if the husband decided to move out in preference to her leaving. In the year during which Mrs. A was seen once a month she seemed to gain in self-esteem and self-confidence. This time was apparently needed to help her gain convictions that she could hold a job and be self-reliant. She also needed support as she negotiated with her husband, who likewise needed time to fully appreciation the situation. The husband at about that point went on to see another therapist.

After this came a two-month period of more frequent appointments. This was during the period of stress emanating from the actual divorce and her coping with separation (the end of Phase One and the beginning of Phase Two). She came through these phases quite well, as did the children, who were seen a number of times with her.

Following this, there was no further contact until about 18 months later when Mrs. A came in again for three interviews to discuss remarriage. Remarriage had been discussed before. The subject had first come up during the divorce phase, when there had been an affair with another man. This time Mrs. A again needed to clarify her ideas a little further. Her decision was not to marry now.

About three years after she first came in to request help, Mrs. A called on the phone to inform the therapist about her impending marriage to a person she had met more recently and had now known for about six months. Although additional appointments were offered, she declined them. She seemed confident about her decision and was preparing herself for her new role as a wife and as mother to her new spouse's child as well. It seemed that Mrs. A. had been able to productively use the help provided her during the divorce and dismemberment phases, and, so far, she seemed to be able to renegotiate the family reconstitution phase without further professional help.

This example is illustrative of the use of time in a treatment situation involving divorce, family dissolution through divorce, and remarriage. A fixed-interval–fixed-frequency schedule was used early in the decision-making phase of the divorce process. With the need to allow time for Mrs. A to arrive at her decision and to acquire self-confidence and a degree of financial independence, appointments were changed to a fixed- and then variable-interval schedule covering about two years. The design of interventions in a case of this type will be illustrated in a subsequent example.

Design of Interventions

The interventions along the divorce–family dissolution–family reconstitution continuum to be discussed fit under the rubric of a systems approach, but go somewhat beyond it incorporating also a developmental view of family life. Ample references to a number of systems approaches can be found in a rich literature on the subject (see, for example, Minuchin, 1975).

Because treatment may be infrequent and less intensive when stress is relatively manageable, there is reason to be especially clear about focus and goals at these times. Kressel and Deutsch (1977) address this issue by suggesting clusters of therapist activities or strategies which have been found useful for couples in the process of divorce. Three types of strategies are identified, two of which, labeled contextual and substantive, consist of quite active interventions. The third type, called reflexive, is mainly relationship building and is especially useful for eliciting diagnostic data in the initial encounter. Though originally explicated for a situation of divorce, the strategies are equally applicable when divorce has occurred and on through to the family reconstitution phase.

The reflexive type of interventions consist of the following therapist activities: (1) building trust and confidence through supportive statements and questions which help the therapist understand the situation: (2) conveying impartiality to the individual, the couple, or the whole family, while at the same time genuinely sharing observations as necessary to establish a contract for ongoing work: and (3) piecing together specific information and observations, vague cues, and personal hunches stemming from the therapist's own reactions. All these activities not only help in assessing and reassessing coping strengths and weaknesses but also lay the groundwork for continued involvement in therapy.

Contextual interventions are largely geared to the resolution of feelings, while substantive interventions tend to develop skills. Examples of contextual interventions include: (1) reduction of the level of emotional tension by clarifying the impact of feelings like anger or fear that are frequently associated with a past or potential marriage partner; (2) shifting the focus from other to self and, especially during the divorce phase, from accusation to reflection; and (3) structuring the sessions so that members of the family can be seen separately or together, and weekly or at intervals to enhance communication.

There is a necessary connection and some overlap between contextual interventions which specifically address feelings so as to free up the client for purposive action and substantive interventions which attempt to develop skills. Interventions which may be seen as substantive include: (1) activity designed to enhance the client's skill in communicating; (2) helping the client recognize and deal with frequently evident patterns of behavior which, while supposedly designed to "save" the marriage or end a state of separation, actually sabotage such change; (3) helping a spouse of either sex develop skills in dealing with tangible matters such as parenting, especially when some stepchildren are living in the home and others are living with a former spouse; and (4) helping the client become adept in enlisting the skills of other family members who can help out. To an extent these skills can be taught in family interviews by simply supplying the client with information. However, efforts must also be made to facilitate communication so that skill deficits in any of these areas can be assessed and then addressed.

As much of the intervention in all the phases revolves around decision making, attention must be devoted to following through. Techniques that enhance following-through have both contextual and substantive qualities. Helping the client follow through requires a focus on the norms of equity and reasonableness necessary to create an atmosphere conducive to dealing with such problems as property settlement and child custody. Collateral activity on behalf of the client, such as mediation with a lawyer during the divorce phase or referral to a singles group during the separation phase, when the single person's need for affirmation is especially great, may also be necessary for follow-through.

A frequently neglected tool is the multiple-family interview. This type of interview may involve two reconstituted families, each composed of a former marriage partner, who may wish to identify and deal with impediments common to the optimum functioning of both families (Goldman & Coane, 1977). I have encountered this type of situation a number of times with adolescents who run away to rejoin the "lost" parent long after a divorce has taken place. Both former spouses and their reconstituted families may need to adopt a consistent stance helpful to the adolescent.

An example illustrating the design of such interventions follows. The case focuses on a period of intensive work during the divorce phase, followed into the separation phase.

Mr. B telephoned in obvious distress, requesting help because his wife had left the family and had moved to a motel. He wanted someone to talk to his wife to "make her see" what she was doing. There were three daughters, one 18 and about to graduate from high school, one 16, and one 12. The youngest child was a boy of 10. Mr. B was employed as a foreman for a large manufacturer. Mrs. B, after a number of jobs which she had difficulty keeping because the regular hours of employment interfered with the irregular demands of a family, was now finally working in real estate and doing quite well. At the therapist's insistence, the couple came in together for the first interview. They came without the children.

271

During the first interview the couple was encouraged to express their dissatisfactions with each other and what few satisfactions could be elicited. Mrs. B revealed herself as an articulate person who repeatedly said that she was "tired" of catering to the needs of everyone, that she now had the self-confidence and economic base to make a change and was determined to do so. Mr. B seemed to be a somewhat dependent person who had had a drinking problem intermittently, yet had been steadily employed by the same firm for the past 12 years. There was no "other" man or woman in the lives of either at the time, although both had had extramarital relationships previously. The latter type of information, often important in divorce counseling and frequently not shared in the presence of the children and spouse, came out in later interviews when husband and wife were seen separately.

The children were seen together with the parents for the second interview and separately as a unit a few sessions later. The oldest daughter was assuming a leadership role in the family and was ambivalent about this. She acted as mother to her youngest siblings and made proposals to her parents to influence them to delay a decision about divorce until they could reflect on it with less vindictiveness. The 16-year-old daughter talked mostly about losing her friends if she would move, and the younger children were simply very confused and upset.

Activity during the first three or four interviews was mainly of the reflexive type. Diagnostic material was obtained by alternating interviews at appropriate intervals and frequencies with different parts of the family system and the family as a whole. A working liaison with all family members was established and, in the process, diagnostic formulations were made. An essential finding was that there was no severe pathology in this family. Rather it appeared that family members, especially Mrs. B, were, in the Toffler sense, on different life trajectories from which there was apparently no turning back.

The contextual interventions with this family, mainly occurring between the fourth and tenth interviews but present also early and later, had to do with decision making about the permanence of the separation and the prospect of divorce. After the therapist encouraged the expression of feelings that were barely below the surface, there was considerable working through of guilt, fear, and anger on the part of everyone concerned. For instance, the older daughter was angry about finding herself in the position of mediator. Mrs. B, while distressed about the aftermath of her leaving the house, became increasingly determined to go through with plans for a divorce yet felt guilty. When she had resolved her guilt sufficiently she was helped in following through on a decision to take an apartment. The finality of this move seemed to diminish much of the stress in this family and this, in turn, freed up the coping energies of both spouses as they tried to reconstruct their lives. The distress of the children was also alleviated markedly because weekend visits with their mother, including the establishment of even a part-time presence in her apartment, reintroduced some stability into their lives.

Subsequently more substantive interventions emphasizing skills, especially in assuming new roles, became the primary goal. The parameter for work here was the reality of the separation between the spouses, and the intermittent separation from the children, who continued to live with the father. Focus was particularly on the father and the two oldest daughters, who were now beginning to protest. If the children were to continue to follow through on their desire, expressed earlier, to stay together with the father in the house where they had grown up, some readjustments would have to be made. The institution of some regularity in the weekend visits with the mother in her apartment helped somewhat. However, the major outcome of substantive interventions was a more equal distribution of housekeeping and child care roles.

As the case went into the sixth month, with appointments differentially scheduled for different units of what was once the nuclear family, the mother engaged a lawyer to finalize arrangements for the divorce. With knowledge acquired in her real estate work, she handled this very well; however, the father needed help in learning to cooperate to the extent that his own interest was protected. Opportunity was provided for the father, as part of the treatment goals, to acquire competence in dealing with these kinds of very practical problems. Both contextual and substantive interventions were prominent during this phase.

After the decision to divorce and when the separation had became final, family interviews involving both spouses ceased. Individual contact, however, continued, although less frequently. The four siblings were also seen less often as a unit and more often with the father. Altogether, interviews were spaced over a period of about six months while the case was active, after which time the equilibrium of the members of the remaining family unit seemed to have become reestablished. Regular interviews stopped at that point, but the path was left open for mother, father, or any of the siblings to return. It was anticipated that this might occur during a period of family reconstitution.

IMPEDIMENTS TO PROBLEM SOLVING IN THE DIVORCE, FAMILY DISSOLUTION, AND FAMILY RECONSTITUTION PHASES

In clinical practice there has been a tendency to underestimate what Helen Perlman once called the therapy of action (Perlman, 1975). This type of therapy can be conceptionalized in psychodynamic terms as counseling and environmental intervention designed to strengthen the ego for the kind of coping discussed earlier in this chapter. A therapy of action can also be seen as helping clients to undertake agreed-upon tasks or behaviors which contribute to problem solving (Reid, 1977; Schwartz & Goldiamond, 1975). When movement toward problem solving has been slow it is often because the importance of active interventions has been insufficiently appreciated. Interventions where the therapist takes considerable initiative will be described in this section, in the context of the impediments to the client's coping which they are designed to address.

It is possible to understand and identify some of these impediments on the basis of practice wisdom, some still developing and as yet unformulated. Many are attributable to what may be a temporary cognitive block on the part of the client which makes it difficult to communicate and to think logically and in cause-effect terms (see Kelley, 1955; Delo & Green, 1977). Others are primarily affect related, stemming from strongly felt emotions that impair the ability to act. The major impediments I have encountered in the course of many years of practice will be discussed as features of the various phases of the divorce to family reconstitution continuum.

Impediments in the Divorce Phase

Guilt. It is important to recognize that there seldom is equal motivation for divorce for both marriage partners. Guilt seems to be one of the major dynamics which can delay a decision either to work on the marriage or to divorce. The guilt seems to take two forms, one best described as intrapersonal and the other emanating largely from external sources. The guilt generated intrapersonally has to do with remorse and a feeling of failure about not having succeeded in the marriage or not having tried hard enough. The feeling is often heavily laden with self-reproach, to the point that depression is present or threatened. It therefore must be understood, resolved, or at least accepted by both spouses before the family dissolution phase, in which bouts of depression stemming from loneliness can only compound the problem.

The guilt that is largely external in origin may be prominent in situations where another man or woman is involved. Research has shown that the presence of alternative sources of satisfaction, such as the possibility of remarriage after divorce, may be a significant factor in the disruption of a current marriage and may hasten the divorce process (Levinger, 1966). Yet at certain points during the divorce phase this type of external pressure can also be so guilt-producing that the client becomes overwhelmed and is unable to move to either end the affair or continue with plans to seek a divorce or separation. When this occurs the underlying feelings must be recognized and dealt with.

274

Feelings of guilt are best elicited by the reflexive type of intervention described above. Sometimes, however, this process requires time. Appropriately spaced individual interviews with each spouse may be preferable, because joint sessions, if used exclusively, may be so replete with accusation, blame, and recrimination that the resolution of guilt feelings at the root are barely possible. Educative types of interventions, either contextual or substantive, are also useful when there is a disabling mind set attributable to guilt. For example, "staying together for the sake of the children" is a rationalization sometimes used to avoid dealing with guilt stemming from largely intrapersonal problems. Depending on client readiness, this dynamic can sometimes be dealt with on a cognitive level. For example, the family therapist may share the knowledge that children from happy marriages may, indeed, be better adjusted than children from divorced marriages, but then, the children of divorced parents are happier compared with the children of parents whose marriages are intact but unhappy (Udry, 1974).

Fear. When coping behavior is impaired during the divorce phase the reason may often be fear. Although fear may be quite pervasive, two rather specific sources in the immediate environment should be ruled out or dealt with. One is the fear of physical violence, sometimes involving an assaultive spouse. The other is the fear that one or the other spouse would hurt him or herself, even commit suicide, if abandoned. Both of these types of fears may be quite real in that the feared event could quite easily happen. The rationale for an exploratory focus on these two specific fears goes beyond the preventive thrust of ruling out imminent danger. For one or both marriage partners a possibility exists that the couple may be unable to consider separation out of the need to sidestep the issue of violence entirely. Often the mere thought of violence can so immobilize a person that little that is either constructive or destructive can be done. The therapist, by conveying at the very least acceptance of the feeling, may be able to free both clients to cope more realistically.

There are many gradations of violence towards others, ranging from temper tantrums, during which furniture or more dangerous objects can be thrown, to outright assault. The literature on the latter phenomenon, particularly child abuse or wife abuse, has received much prominence in recent years (see for example, Martin, 1976). On one extreme is the wife batterer, who has been described, perhaps in somewhat general terms, as "a man with low self-esteem and poor coping skills who is unable to express his feelings easily" (Higgins, 1978). Reflexive interventions are usually insufficient to deal with this type of situation. Direct action of the substantive kind is often required of the therapist, such as making arrangements for an immediate move out of the house by one of the marriage partners or a child. In this type of case, the possible fear of the husband that he would lose control, and that of the wife or children that they could be hurt, are of equal importance.

Fortunately, not all situations of violence are as extreme. Still they must be dealt with. An example follows:

Mrs. W had been seen in weekly sessions initially and then less often. She came in because of uncertainty about whether to leave her husband, who did not want her to leave. The husband, as is common with men who are impulsive and prone to violence, refused to come in. After discussing a number of problem areas, it was found that Mrs. W's mixed feelings about separating took the direction of wanting to remain in the marriage every time the husband had temper tantrums of the kind where dishes would be thrown against the wall. It was necessary for a three- or four-month period to elapse for this reaction in Mrs. W to become apparent to both Mrs. W and the therapist. The issue of violence and Mrs. W's realistic fear of it could then be dealt with. Looking at the history of the husband's outbursts and Mrs. W's provocations and reactions, a more realistic appraisal of the hazards involved was then made. Mrs. W eventually began to understand that her pattern of caving in under the threat of violence was counterproductive, and after a more reasoned consideration of the risks involved, the move toward separation was eventually made.

As for examples of fear of harm to self, these situations also appear to be much more common than is generally supposed. In the following case example a spouse did not wish to terminate the marriage but became depressed because the other partner threatened to leave. During the initial stages of exploration, the couple could not openly face the fear of a possible suicide attempt by the depressed marriage partner. The case example illustrates how the therapist can elicit such a fear, at the same time clarifying the treatment contract:

Mrs. R somewhat coldly responded to her husband, initially during the second joint interview, that she wished to work with him to continue the marriage and resolve their marital problems. That had been the explicit contract made during the first session, but events during the week had suggested that this seemed to be a smoke screen. Later in the second interview, Mrs. R indicated that she wanted to end the marriage. Faced with the incompatibility of these goals, Mrs. R then said that she feared that were she to leave, her husband would take an overdose of pills, as he had once done earlier in their marriage. Her way out of this dilemma, she admitted, was to seek a connection with a therapist primarily to allay her fear about leaving him and to provide him with a source of support later.

This statement, though brutally frank, seemed to remove a weight from both of the spouses as well as the therapist. The husband, perhaps recognizing some positives in his wife's attitude which had hitherto seemed either totally unfathomable or negative, suddenly seemed to be much more ready to accept his wife's decision and his own need to decide on the course of his life. The therapist also could be much clearer about his contract with the family, and he could better address and weigh the risks involved. As it turned out, the wife did leave, and the husband continued in therapy for a period of time after the separation.

Loneliness in the Family Dismemberment Phase

The feeling of loneliness can best be described as a desire for interaction that is blocked (Znaniecki, 1969), although the strength of this desire may vary from person to person, from time to time. There cannot be much doubt that the family dissolution phase, after the original spouses have separated and before the family reconstitution phase, is the most likely time when feelings of loneliness are especially oppressive. As noted by Weiss (1973b), of all the negative feelings of the newly separated, none is more common or important than loneliness (p. 23). Only a minority fail to suffer from it and even those who most keenly desired the end of the marriage often find the initial loneliness excruciating (Hunt, 1966, p. 25).

The feeling of loneliness can be an impediment to learning again how to cope with a single life or single parenthood. It can result in a number of reactions, the possibility of which the therapist should be aware. Primary is the paradoxical search *for* loneliness characteristic of the person who has become drained by the demands of a conflict-fraught marital relationship. As one social critic has observed:

Looking at the growing numbers of persons proclaiming happiness from the solitude of private burrows, you wonder whether we are becoming a race that is simply afraid of people or whether we are finding such joy in self-love that it can only be spoiled by human contact. . . . The distaste for the messiness of human relationships is not new of course. Nowadays, Americans come to New York to be alone, and the drift toward loneliness is nowhere better illustrated than in changing sexual customs. A recent report in the *New York Times* tells of spreading "asexuality" among New Yorkers. Increasing numbers of persons, it states, are finding that abstinence from sex develops into atrophy of sexual appetite, which makes it easy for them to live contentedly without sex. (Baker, 1978)

277

While this is one type of response to a situation of loneliness, the opposite, a frantic search for relationships that may be both superficial and fleeting, can occur also. The essential feature that underlies both types of reactions, recoil from people or frantic search for human contact, sexual or otherwise, is that neither approach seems to be satisfying in the long run. At best, these reactions are temporary expedients or protective devices that deny the reality of the pain of loneliness. The therapist, working with the person who has been married but is now separated, must be alert to indications of client readiness to change either of these patterns. Sometimes this readiness can be hastened through encouragement, but more often it has to run its course. In this connection, it is worthwhile to differentiate among clients whose orientation suggests that a single life or single parenthood is the life-style of choice, and those in the majority, as the demographic data presented earlier suggest, for whom separation is a phase or interlude between marriages.

In helping the client pursue a more balanced and considered search for companionship, the prospect of reconstituting a family with another partner should certainly be given attention and perhaps even encouraged. The argument to do this is compelling because evidence has been accumulating that, at least from the standpoint of physical and emotional health, those whose life-styles are oriented away from relative isolation may have taken a more adaptive path. For example, the association between the incidence of schizophrenic episodes and living alone has been recognized in research (Weinberg, 1966–1967), and in practice familylike peer-support groups are a prominent feature of current efforts to rehabilitate the mentally ill (Fisher, Nachman, Keller, & Vyas, 1978; Goldmeier, Shore & Mannino, 1977). In terms of physical health, evidence that the lack of human companionship adversely affects the incidence of heart disease and cancer is even more dramatic (Lynch, 1977).

There are very cogent reasons, therefore, for the therapist to be quite active in the separation phase, and the substantive type of intervention is especially appropriate in this regard. Substantive interventions imply that the therapist has a point of view about problem resolution, in this instance the need for social support. Consequently, referral for this type of help should be considered as an integral part of any helping strategy, supplementing reflexive and contextual interventions.

The following is an account of the outcome of one such referral. The referral was for a peer-group activity, Parents Without Partners. The

278

referral mitigated, though in itself it did not resolve, the separated person's sense of alienation:

> Both men and women sometimes found that contribution to the organization through administrative or planning roles supported their own sense of worth. Leaders referred to this phenomenon by saying, "The more that you put into PWP, the more you get out of it." There were at least three ways in which individuals benefited through their contribution to the organization and so facilitated further participation. A woman who was chairman of a dance committee remarked that it was only because she was in charge that she had the courage to attend. Second, the effective management of an organizational task reassured members of their general competence, a quality that the failure of their marriages had led many of the separated and divorced to doubt. And finally, successful completion of an organizational task was rewarded by both formal and informal praise, which contributed to increase self-esteem. . . .
>
> Most members, even those who had voluntarily ended their marriages, experienced loneliness prior to joining PWP. It was widely believed in the organization that hope of respite from loneliness was the reason most members had joined the organization. But the friendships among women and colleagial relationships among men that PWP sponsored seemed only to mitigate, not to dispel loneliness. (Weiss, 1973a)

Impediments in the Family Reconstitution Phase

Although there are many sociological and psychological studies of marriage, of the family, of children, and of divorce, there are few studies of remarriage and almost none of stepchild-stepparent and step-sibling relationships (Duberman, 1975, p. 1). Yet it has been estimated that there are about 8 million reconstituted American families and that there are some 7 million children living with a stepparent (*Time*, September 8, 1969, pp. 67–68). Thus there is still little to guide either the family therapist or prospective members of reconstituted families, other than to observe the adjustment of those who have already remarried. It is reasonable to assume, therefore, that the greatest impediment to a decision to remarry would very likely be uncertainty about what to expect. This uncertainty is increased when there are children from previous marriages who may decide, often somewhat impulsively, that they want to live either in or away from the reconstituted family unit. As for the decision to remarry

279

under such circumstances, in at least one study, 41 percent of those contemplating remarriage had to make this decision basically unsupported, and sometimes even opposed by close or extended family (Duberman, 1975, p. 121).

It follows that support and encouragement to make a decision in favor or against remarriage should be a basic strategy undergirding all other interventions during this phase. Thus, not only should reflexive techniques be used, so as to be as responsive as possible, but contextual and substantive help must be provided for situational problems that particularly affect reconstituted families. Among the problems that can be targeted in a situation of family reconstitution, the following are likely to be meaningful to family members:

1. The intended or actual family arrangement may be categorized as deviant by society. One way this may be reflected is in concern on the part of family members about different last names. Yet overhasty name changes can be counterproductive, and it may be more appropriate to help family members learn to accept this aspect of reconstituted family life. Fundamental to this issue are psychological factors largely reflecting a child's sense of identity and legal factors having to do with adoption and child support.

2. A conscious effort must be made by the reconstituted family members to establish themselves as an entity. Knowledge of this primary task should serve as a general focus for meaningful problem solving.

3. The relationships between stepchild and stepparents and among step-siblings and children from previous marriages are often fraught with conflict. A period of role transition and role reequilibration must usually elapse before family members can learn to live with each other in a reasonable harmony. The focus must certainly be the marital relationship itself. Findings in both research and practice point to the marital relationship as central in its effect on how step-siblings get along with each other (Duberman, 1975, p. 105).

If the family therapist is prepared to anticipate and help with stumbling blocks to family reconstitution such as those discussed above, the course of adjustment in this final stage of the divorce to family reconstitution cycle should prove to be a little less difficult than it otherwise might be.

SUMMARY

This chapter has considered an increasingly apparent phenomenon of many modern families, their cyclical movement through phases from a primary state including the original marriage partners and their mutual offspring, to divorce and separation, and then to a state of reconstitution with different marriage partners. Movement through these phases can be conceptualized to reflect different stages of development in the marriage partners and that there are different stresses in each phase that have to be addressed. The focus has been on differential helping strategies and their timing. A number of common obstacles to the resolutions of problems posed by passage through the respective phases have been discussed.

It is clear that clinicians can no longer rely solely on the concepts and techniques developed with the primary, nuclear family as a model. This chapter should serve to stimulate further inquiry into an area of family practice that has until now received only scant attention.

REFERENCES

Bagarozzi, D., and Wodarski, J. "Social Exchange Typology of Conjugal Relationships and Conflict Development." *Journal of Marriage and Family Counseling*, 3:5360, 1977.

Baker, R. "The Search for Loneliness." *The New York Times*, May 13, 1978, p. 23.

Beck, D. F., and Jones, M. A. *Progress on Family Problems*. New York: Family Service Association of America, 1973.

Brown, E. M. "Divorce Counseling." In D. H. Olson (ed.), *Treating Relationships*. Lake Mills, Iowa: Graphic Publications Co., 1976.

Burr, W., Hill, R., Reiss, I., and Nye, I. *Contemporary Theories about the Family*. Vols. 1 and 2. New York: Free Press, 1978.

Carnegie Commission on Higher Education. *Opportunities for Women in Higher Education*. New York: McGraw-Hill, 1973.

Christenson, H. T. (ed.). *Handbook of Marriage and the Family*. Chicago: Rand-McNally & Co., 1967.

Delo, J. L., and Green, W. A. "A Cognitive Transactional Approach to Communication." *Social Casework*, 58:294–300, 1977.

Duberman, L. *The Reconstituted Family: A Study of Remarried Couples and Their Children*. Chicago: Nelson-Hall Co., 1975.

Edwards, J. M. "Familiar Behavior as Social Exchange." *Journal of Marriage and the Family*, 31:518–27, 1969.

Epstein, J. *Divorce in America: Marriage in an Age of Possibility*. New York: E. P. Dutton & Co., 1974.

281

Erikson, E. H. "Identity and the Life Cycle." *Psychological Issues,* Monograph 1. New York: International Universities Press, 1959.

Fast, I., and Cain, A. C. "The Stepparent Role: Potential for Disturbance in Family Functioning." *American Journal of Orthopsychiatry,* 36:485–91, 1966.

Fisher, T., Nachman, N. S., Keller, N., and Vyas, A. "Cooperative Apartment Program of a Family Agency." *Social Casework,* 59:279–86, 1978.

Foote, N. N., and Cottrell, L. S., Jr. *Identity and Personal Competence: A New Direction in Family Research.* Chicago: University of Chicago Press, 1975.

Glick, P. C., and Norton, A. J. "Perspectives on the Recent Upturn and Remarriage." *Demography,* 10:301–14, 1973.

Goldman, J., and Coane, J. "Family Therapy after Divorce: Developing a Strategy." *Family Process,* 16:267–77, 1977.

Goldmeier, J. "Short-term Models in Long-term Treatment." *Social Work,* 21:350–55, 1976.

Goldmeier, J., Shore, M. F., and Mannino, F. V. "Cooperative Apartments: New Programs in Community Mental Health." *Health and Social Work,* 2:119–40, 1977.

Goode, W.J. *Women in Divorce.* New York: Free Press, 1965.

Haley, J. (ed.). *Changing Families: A Family Therapy Reader.* New York: Grune & Stratton, 1971.

Higgins, J. G. "Social Services for Abused Wives." *Social Casework,* 59:226–71, 1978.

Hirschhorn, L. "Social Policy and the Life-Cycle: A Developmental Perspective." *Social Service Review,* 51:434–50, 1977.

Hunt, M. *The World of the Formerly Married.* New York: McGraw-Hill, 1966.

Kelley, G. A. *The Psychology of Personal Constructs.* Vol. 2. New York: W. W. Norton & Co., 1955.

Kressel, K., and Deutsch, N. "Divorce Therapy: An In-Depth Survey of Therapists' Views." *Family Process,* 16:413–43, 1977.

Levinger, G. "Sources of Marital Dissatisfaction among Applicants for Divorce." *American Journal of Orthopsychiatry,* 36:803–7, 1966.

Lipman-Blumen, J. "The Implications for Family Structure of Changing Sex Roles." *Social Casework,* 57:67-69, 1975.

Lynch, J. L. *The Broken Heart: The Medical Consequences of Loneliness.* New York: Basic Books, 1977.

Martin, D. *Battered Wives.* San Franscisco: Glide Publications, 1976.

McCubbin, H. I. *Integrating Coping Behavior in Family Stress Theory.* Papers presented at the National Council on Family Relations Annual Meeting, San Diego, Cal., October 1977.

Minuchin, S. *Families and Family Therapy.* Cambridge, Mass.: Harvard University Press, 1975.

Nye, F. V., White, L., and Frideres, J. "A Preliminary Theory of Marital Dissolution." Unpublished papers read before the National Council on Family Relations, Minneapolis, Minnesota, 1966.

Perlman, H. H. "In Quest of Coping." *Social Casework*, 56:213–25, 1975.

Quindlen, A. "Self-fulfillment: Independence versus Intimacy." *The New York Times*, November 28, 1977, pp. 1 and 36.

Rapoport, L. "The State of Crisis: Some Theoretical Considerations." In Howard J. Parad (ed.), *Crisis Intervention, Selected Readings.* New York: Family Service Association of America, 1966.

Reid, W. J. "Process and Outcome in Treatment of Family Problems." In W. J., Reid and L. Epstein (eds.), *Task-Centered Practice.* New York: Columbia University Press, 1977.

Reid, W. J., and Shyne, Ann W. *Brief and Extended Casework.* New York: Columbia University Press, 1969.

Rhodes, S. L. "A Developmental Approach to the Life Cycle of the Family." *Social Casework*, 58:301–11, 1977.

Rodgers, R. A. "Toward a Theory of Family Development." *Journal of Marriage and the Family*, 26:262–70, 1964.

Roper Organization. *The Virginia Slims American Women's Opinion Poll.* Vol. III, *A Survey of Attitudes of Women on Marriage, Divorce, the Family and America's Changing Sexual Morality.* Washington, D.C.: DeHart and Broide, 1977.

Schwartz, A., and Goldiamond, I. *Social Casework: A Behavioral Approach.* New York: Columbia University Press, 1975.

Tennenbaum, S. *A Psychologist Looks at Marriage.* New York: A. S. Barnes & Co., 1968.

Toffler, A. *Future Shock.* New York: Random House, 1970.

Udry, J. R. *The Social Context of Marriage,* 3rd ed. New York: J. B. Lippincott Co., 1974.

Waldman, E., and Eaddy, B. J. "Where Women Work: An Analysis by Industry and Occupation." *Monthly Labor Review*, 97:3–13, 1974.

Waller, W. *The Old Love and the New.* Carbondale, Ill.: Southern Illinois University Press, 1967. (Originally published, 1930.)

Weinberg, K. S. "Forms of Isolation Relative to Schizophrenia." *International Journal of Social Psychiatry*, 13:33–41, 1966–1967.

Weiss, R. S. "The Contribution of an Organization of Single Parents to the Well-being of Its Members." *Family Coordinator*, 22:321–26, 1973 (a).

Weiss, R. S. *The Experience of Emotional and Social Isolation.* Cambridge, Mass.: M.I.T. Press, 1973 (b).

Weiss, R. S. *Marital Separation.* New York: Basic Books, 1975.

Znaniecki, H. L. "Loneliness: Forms and Components." *Social Problems*, 17:248–61, 1969.

Part III

The Social Work Agency

Part I presented theoretical perspectives relative to family functioning, and Part II suggested social work strategies for intervention with selected populations of families with problems. While only these limited populations were addressed, extrapolations can be made to work with a wider variety of families with different backgrounds and problems. The unifying theme of Parts I and II is emphasis on the family as a system, with interactions between the subsystems of the family and between the family and the social worker. It also reflects the interrelatedness of the family's problems and its problem-solving efforts.

An important part of effective family treatment is the context in which the social worker provides the necessary services. Many social workers and practitioners are successfully engaged in family treatment in private practice, but the context we consider here is the social work agency. Part III focuses on the role of the agency and its staff in planning and providing treatment to families.

This section endeavors to bring the social work agency more directly into the treatment process by presenting various aspects of agency operations that impact on service delivery to families as clients. Among the issues addressed are treatment within the interdisciplinary agency; colleagial

284

involvement and responsibility in treatment; the responsibility of agency administration; and implications for training social workers to engage in treating families.

Part III is not intended to be an exhaustive presentation of social work agencies. We believe it is important to supplement our approach to family treatment with at least a brief look at the context in which the treatment is offered, however. In this way we hope to increase awareness of the mutual responsibilities of social workers, agency administrators, and other staff members in engaging the family as the unit of treatment.

CHAPTER 11

The Agency and the Worker in Family Treatment

Unless families seek private practitioners for the solution of their problems, agencies provide the setting for their contact with the social worker. In many instances, such as the hospital or school setting, the family could not get the services it needs outside of an agency context. Were it not for its need for other services, it might not of its own initiative seek contact with the worker.

A multitude of factors in the relations between family members and workers come into play because of the agency context for family treatment. Of central interest among these many factors is the way the agency conceptualizes the problems of individuals and families that come to its attention. A corollary and closely related factor is the congruence (or lack of it) between agency views and worker views of the client and the family. These views have consequences for the way the agency organizes itself for services to the family, and consequently also to the way the worker engages with the family when they are referred.

These conceptions of agency impact on family treatment have clear implications for the kind of training needed by social workers. They imply that if workers are to "think family," the agency must provide them with support. All staff, not only those in direct contact with the family, need

286

orientation and training in order to "think family." Without such orientation, staff and agency practices may impede or prevent effective work with the family.

THE IMPORTANCE OF THEORETICAL CONCEPTUALIZATION OF FAMILY PROBLEMS

At the core of agency impact is the way in which the problems brought to the agency by individuals are defined. Two basically different conceptualizations are possible. One orientation sees the problems as resident in the individuals. The other, which we have presented, sees them as resident in family relationships and in the family's relation to the external world.

Working from the individual orientation, helping systems have readily understood that physical or mental illness, delinquency or crime, and the loss or gain of a spouse, parent, or child are problems for the individuals who present them. They are the ones who have the problems and need to cope with them. In many instances this problem definition has been utilized even if the problem has been defined by someone, be it family member or person in the community, other than the individual who supposedly has the problem. Diagnostic procedures are designed to illuminate the problem the individual has, and diagnostic staff are recruited accordingly. Treatment procedures are oriented to work with one individual, and staff with skills in individual treatment are recruited.

This orientation may run into difficulty when the individual who supposedly has the problem does not accept the idea that it is his problem but sees it rather as a problem that others, especially family members, impose on him. Individually oriented agencies have responded to such client positions in two ways. Either the client's view is seen as a distorted perception of others, or the problem is viewed as lying in the way the individual responds to family behavior. Family members are not included in treatment and sometimes are specifically excluded. Workers are not permitted time for contact with family members. The treatment focuses on changing the client's perceptions, or on changing his ways of coping with the family. The need for change in the family is not recognized. While some of these clients may be able to accept such a redefinition of their problems, others will participate in treatment only to convince the helper of their views. Or they may discontinue treatment.

Agencies oriented to treating individuals, however, sometimes see the

287

need to "do something about the family" of a primary client or patient. The family is seen as having a detrimental effect on the patient, creating anxiety, frustration, or rage in the patient, allowing no relief and providing no support. Frequently, in this view, "family" does not mean the entire family but refers primarily to a parent or spouse. A separate worker is assigned to help that family member with his or her problem, or the same worker might see the other family member at a separate time. The problem created by the family member is not seen as "appropriate" for service in the agency serving the identified primary client and is therefore sent to some other agency or another department or branch of the same agency. These separate workers may see the value of consultation among themselves about what is happening in the family, but their good intentions are often foiled by lack of time or their supervisors' lack of understanding of the need for such consultation. Family members may be divided up between agencies for individual treatment. Treatment is for the patient *and* for the family. Another possible consequence of this view is that it can prompt hostility toward the family by agency staff, who see them as at fault. This can result in a need to defend the patient to the family.

This orientation is not, in our view, a family systems conception of the situation. The "patient *and* the family" view, as contrasted to "the family *as* the patient," attends to the effects of the family on the patient but gives insufficient attention to the effects of patient on family and their continuing efforts to influence each other. It also seems to be a dyadic view which does not account for the participation of third persons and alliances that may arise.

We have taken pains in this book not to define family systems treatment as the use of conjoint family sessions. Nevertheless, it does seem possible that the greater use of individual sessions is associated with the position that the problem resides in the individual or separately in client and family members.

If problems are defined by the agency as problems in family operations, as they have been in this book, very different agency procedures follow. There is insistence that other members of the family participate in the diagnostic process and in some or all of the treatment. Different diagnostic procedures are used. Home visits and whole-family interview sessions for observation of family interactions serve as the basis for assessment. These take the place of a lengthy social history or psychological or psychiatric examinations. Current transactions are more important than historical developments and psychological introjects.

When the problem is presented by the individual or the family as a family problem, family assessment procedures pose no difficulty for the family. The procedures seem ultimately sensible to them. When the individual who presents his own or someone else's problem as a problem of the individual is confronted with the family orientation of the helping system, however, the encounter may be experienced as an affront. This can easily give rise to hostility and uncooperativeness toward the helping system. Consent to participate will come only when the individual is convinced of the relevance of the family's participation and its use to him.

Social workers are prepared to cope with such hostility and resistance when they and the agency have a thorough grounding in family systems theory. They must be able to see readily the ways in which the family system impinges on the problem-solving ability of the person presenting the problem. Several brief examples will illustrate the issues.

A mother and her 14-year-old daughter were seen on a walk-in basis at a community mental health clinic. The mother complained that her daughter was not investing herself in her school work and was only doing passing work, when she could be doing much better. Also, her daughter neglected her household responsibilities and had to be constantly prodded to do them. Both home and school problems resulted in frequent conflict between mother and daughter. Mother's request was that the clinic find out what was wrong with her daughter and change her.

In this instance the social worker did not agree that the problem presented was the problem of the 14-year-old daughter alone, though her lack of cooperation and apparent stubbornness would in some agencies have been defined that way. In that event efforts would have been made to interest the girl in individual or group treatment and to offer, but not push upon the parents, the "opportunity" to be seen. Instead, the social worker expressed concern about the difficulty that the mother and the father were having in gaining their daughter's cooperation, suggesting that all three needed to be seen in order to understand and solve the problem.

While the mother expressed some awareness of the need for her to be involved, her resistance was expressed in terms of her husband's unwillingness to be involved. She felt that he saw the children as her responsibility. Though this left her feeling unsupported in child-caring responsibilities, she saw no way of gaining his cooperation. At this point she had given up on her efforts to involve her husband. Her agreement to try to bring him for the following appointment was seen as an attempt to reengage him. While the focus remained on the presenting problem, there was also the simultaneous emphasis on changing the family system and its way of coping with the problem.

This brief case description includes only the initial impact on the family. But even in the initial efforts to work on the problem there is a redefinition of family roles, of the images that family members hold of each other, and of the means they use to negotiate and communicate about their problems. The focus on the roles, expectations, and images of family members and their effort to communicate about and change them is also central to the continuing treatment process.

Unintentional consequences may arise in the family system even when all parties concerned—agency, client, and family—initially agree that a given person has the problem. In the following example all three systems defined the problem as resident within the individual. Unfortunate consequences arose because they did not define it as a family problem.

A middle-aged, married male was admitted for psychiatric hospital treatment on the basis of complaints of severe depression and inability to work. In his conversations with hospital staff, the patient began to air negative feelings about his marriage and to express a wish to proceed for a divorce. The hospital staff had experienced the wife as extremely managerial and dominating and had observed that the patient was upset after his wife's visits, being more depressed and manifesting a great deal of body twitching. Given their view of the problem as one individual coping with a difficult relationship, they accepted as realistic the patient's efforts to distance himself in this relationship. They saw this distancing as crucial and valid treatment in his recovery from depression. They supported him by limiting his wife's visiting and by encouraging consideration of divorce.

The wife's response was to employ their adolescent son to tell both his father and the hospital staff how much the father was needed in the family. The wife also got her minister to talk to the hospital chaplain about how she was being deprived of the opportunity to visit her husband. Finally, she cruised the hospital grounds in a car, waiting for her husband to leave the ward so she could visit him.

While it is evident that the hospital staff saw themselves as helping the individual patient to cope, it is also clear that they did not anticipate the impact on family relationships of a change in the identified patient. They were unrealistic in the amount of or kind of separateness achievable in this instance and in their means for achieving it. The wife clearly had not counted on distancing as a consequence of the help that she wanted from the hospital for her husband. Relieving depression did not mean to her this kind of a change in their relationship. The wife's response was to attempt to change the hospital system rather than permit change in the relationship.

A "family is the patient" response on the part of the staff to this problem would have engaged both husband and wife in solving the problem of the depression, recognizing that some alteration in husband/wife roles and expectation of each other might be necessary to the achievement of that goal. Awareness of the transactional qualities of the relationship would have led the staff to see that the patient's withdrawal behavior was a stimulus for the wife's managerial behavior, and vice versa. The focus would have been on their transactions, and this would have resulted in a different experience for both patient and spouse.

In a case discussed in considerable detail, Hoffman and Long (1969) give a vivid picture of the way in which agency orientation can have a profound effect on family relationships. When family income exceeded allowable levels in the public housing project in which a couple was residing, the housing worker suggested that the husband seek to have himself declared disabled because he had been having alcohol-related employment and health problems. Such a move would reduce family income and allow them to remain in the housing project. However, it would also alter the husband's status with his wife, leaving him feeling even less powerful in the relationship than he already felt and encouraging the wife's unilateral decision-making and control efforts. Efforts on the part of a family worker to reduce the husband's helplessness by getting treatment for his alcoholism revealed the wife's wish to keep her husband numbed and helpless by alcohol and medication. It was just easier for her that way. The family worker engaged the spouses in efforts to solve specific marital relationship problems, which altered the pattern of dominance and submission in the relationship. The authors' report does not indicate how the housing problem was finally resolved, but it does indicate that the husband was able to take initiative in returning to employment after the balance in marital relationships began to change.

Hoffman and Long's example demonstrates the interrelationships among agency practices, problem impact, and family process. The housing worker's suggestion did not take these interrelationships into account and would have left the husband as a nonfunctioning family member. In our view the social worker was family systems oriented in attending to the way in which the family system was organized and went about solving its problems. Systems thinking enabled a ready awareness of the effects of agency policy on family relationships. The individual orientation of various agencies and the confusions between agencies interfered with family problem solving rather than enhancing it. Treatment for the family in this instance was effected by reregulating the behavior of external systems.

CONSEQUENCES OF MIXED THEORETICAL POSITIONS

When individual treatment orientations exist side by side with a family orientation in a given agency, or during a time of changeover from one orientation to the other, cases such as the one just described may become more complicated. A given worker may hold to an individual problem definition in contrast to the agency's family orientation, or vice versa. Staff disagreements may arise over philosophy and procedure. An individual-problem-oriented intake worker may tell client and family of the need for individual treatment, and a family-oriented continuing worker may at a later point have difficulty engaging the family. Staff may be confronted with the same difficulties in solving the problem of how to deal with the client that the family group faces in solving its problems.

Staff therefore need to agree on a common value or theoretical perspective about families. They must find ways of resolving their differences if they are to function and agency service is to be effective. Otherwise client or family contacts with staff will produce different interpretations of the problem, inconsistent treatment, confusion instead of help, and frustration of the family's own efforts at problem solution. These difficulties, and others, have led Haley (1975) to the facetious suggestion that agencies should not shift to a family treatment orientation. Foster (1965), using experience in a medical hospital, makes the more positive suggestion that the social worker has a specific dual role in the midst of such difficulties. The first is to enable the resolution of staff differences. The second, which follows from the first, is to make it possible for agency system and family system to work together. In order to do this in the hospital setting, the problems of the patient in the family and the problems of the family need to be taken into account. Similarly, in a school system situation, Freund and Cardwell (1977) demonstrate that conjoint work with school problem children, parents, and school personnel is useful in resolving adolescent school problems.

There is therefore a need for clarity and consistency in the theoretical perspective in both worker and agency. In an agency that is family systems oriented, procedures, starting at intake, are utilized to engage the family as a group in the assessment and treatment process. All staff who have contact

292

with any member of the family are sensitive to the way in which family relationships affect work on the family problem and to the way in which a particular staff person's interventions influence family relationships. Time is available to meet with members of the family other than the identified problem person, either separately or as a group with the patient. Solutions to problems that other family members are having are seen as relevant to the solutions of the problems of the person for whom agency contact originated. There will be less likelihood of dividing the family up between agencies or workers.

SPECIAL PROBLEMS OF INTERDISCIPLINARY AGENCIES

Social workers are not always the ones that determine agency policies, and thus they are not totally in control of the decision about whether or how to engage the family in treatment. This is true in psychiatric, medical, school, and residential settings. The family-oriented worker, therefore, not wishing to stand alone or to leave families unassisted, may have to take a position of advocacy for the family and for a family systems view. The worker's primary approach in this regard is to orient other staff members or disciplines to the needs of the family and to the way in which agency procedures interfere with or support the family's own efforts at problem solving.

This orientation is likely achieved initially on a case-by-case basis (see Chapter 9; also, Foster, 1965), but it may require more systematic training. Beyond this, it may entail considerable effort to change agency procedures and budget to allow more time for work with family members and to minimize the referral of family members to other agencies. And it may entail considerable worker effort to moderate staff reactions to family members or to lessen differences among staff members about how to intervene in the transactions between client and family members.

SPECIAL PROBLEMS OF MULTIPLE-PROBLEM FAMILIES

A variety of forms of intervention is needed for multiple-problem families (e.g., child abuse, problem poverty, and alcoholism families) due to their relatively closed nature and their isolation from the larger community. A one-worker-to-family relationship which emphasizes talking appears to be insufficient for their needs and provides only limited support

293

and access to the larger community. More contact hours per family and the possibility of home visits need to be made part of the agency repertoire. Doing with, being with, going with in relation to everyday activities and specific needs of the families are important aspects of worker activity. The simultaneous provision of information, ideas, and access are all conditions of contact which enable family members to relate to the worker, the agency, and other available services in the community, and to each other in a new and meaningful way.

Agency willingness and capacity to relate to such family systems on these terms is predicated on the kind of understanding about modes of operation that has been put forth in this book. Where agencies persist in seeing such families as unmotivated, additional services and different modes of engaging the families will not be available, and the families will continue to be viewed as hopeless and hard to reach. A change in agency thinking and operations is required before change in the families will be possible. Such a change in the agency may not guarantee success with the family, but it will make it possible or more likely.

Where agencies have continued to define problems as problems of individuals rather than of families, the tendency to divide families up among agencies has persisted. The adult with problems is seen at one agency, the children at another, and workers from still other agencies providing special services are also involved. Each worker in each separate agency sees only part of the problem and gets only an individual member's report of what is happening. Decisions are made with or about the family member that do not take into account the reactions of, or consequences for, other family members.

At a minimum, all workers involved with the family should confer enough to come to a common understanding of the family's structure and process. This understanding should reveal the effects the family has on individual capacity and performance, the effects of individual performance and capacity on family operations, and the changes required in the family's process and structure if performance is to change. One worker must be enough of a case manager to be in regular contact with all the workers involved and keep them abreast of needs and changes. Additionally, case conferences involving all workers are imperative. Joint meetings between family members and their various workers serve to promote the exchange of information, improve communication, and facilitate decision making in the family. Multiple-service agencies that can provide services to all family members are better able to promote such interaction than single-service agencies serving only one family member. The crucial factor, however, is not where the service is provided but whether case analysis is done on a family systems basis.

IMPLICATIONS FOR TRAINING WORKERS

A family-oriented way of conceptualizing presenting problems in agencies has implications for training and staff development. Social workers need to have knowledge of the way family systems work and of the ways in which problems and external systems affect the workings of the family and the individuals in it. Based on this theoretical understanding, they need to have skills which will guide family members in more constructive approaches to problem solving and which will involve them jointly in the problem-solving effort. These needs clearly should influence the training of the worker who meets the family.

Where there is unanimity between the agency and the worker about this way of viewing the problems of individuals and families, the worker and the agency support each other in the provision of services. Where other staff members are at odds with the worker, some effort must be made to orient or train other staff members, including those who are not in direct contact with client and family. Liddle and Halpin (1978) note that various amounts of attention have been invested in this aspect of training. Their comprehensive review of training for and supervision of family treatment discusses theories and modes which can be applied in these efforts.

A family systems approach is not merely the addition of a treatment technique such as conjoint family interviewing (though that technique may be utilized) to another conceptual base and set of skills. It is a different way of thinking about presenting problems. Knowledge about intrapsychic dynamics and skills in individual treatment is, therefore, not always a prerequisite for engaging families. Workers who have no knowledge of individual dynamics often learn just as easily about the way families work, and they need not face the problem of having to dispense with previous learning. Workers who shift from thinking about individual dynamics to the family orientation sometimes have just as much to learn about family dynamics as those who have no knowledge of individual treatment.

The individual-treatment orientation of many social work students and staff members accounts in part for the persistent lack of family contact in agencies. Levande (1976) notes that

> . . . many social work students are hesitant about becoming involved with the family as a whole as the designated client. Part of this reluctance may stem from having a theoretical frame of reference which provides understanding of the individual as the unit of treatment, but having only a limited knowledge when confronted with the possibility of conceptualizing the family system or any of its sub-systems as the unit of intervention. (p. 295)

The view of Beck and Jones (1973) that the family service field in general does not utilize a truly family-centered approach to family problems fits with these observations.

This brief discussion of training for social workers has not considered means, modes, or content. Rather, it has emphasized the need for training to develop a different conceptual approach, centered on the family system. Such an approach is a prerequisite to the worker's willingness to attempt to engage whole families, as well as a requirement for the successful engagement of families. Sager, Masters, Ronall, and Normand (1968) report that after workers received training in family systems theory, the rate of engagement of families in treatment increased markedly.

Schools of social work are increasingly offering classroom training in the understanding and treatment of family systems. Skilled supervision in the field is often unavailable, however, because supervisors themselves lack the necessary conceptual base and experience. For the time being, therefore, continuing education courses and in-service training are needed for workers who wish to move in this direction. Both of these forms of training are open to workers, regardless of the kind or level of previous training. Thus, paraprofessionals, persons with bachelor's, master's, and doctoral degrees, and persons with training in psychiatry, nursing, psychology, guidance, and social work all can acquire family treatment skills.

In some instances, as Haley (1975) has noted, this has resulted in a blurring of the distinctions between professional backgrounds and levels of education. Since prior training often is less relevant in the family systems approach, the emphasis on family treatment puts staff members in a different relationship to each other. This creates or at least opens the possibility of staff rivalries and conflicts equalling those of the family, particularly between those of different disciplines but also between workers and supervisors. In such circumstances the awareness and training of persons at supervisory and administrative levels are as important in the implementation of family treatment efforts as are those of the workers who have direct contact with the family.

REFERENCES

Beck, D., and Jones, M. "Progress on Family Problems." New York: Family Service Association of America, 1973.

Foster, Z. P. "How Social Work Can Influence Hospital Management of Fatal Illness." *Social Work*, 10:30–45, 1965.

Freund, J. C., and Cardwell, G. F. "A Multifaceted Response to an Adolescent's School Failure." *Journal of Marriage and Family Counseling*, 3:59–66, 1977.

Haley, J. "Why a Mental Health Center Should Avoid Family Therapy." *Journal of Marriage and Family Counseling*, 1:1–14, 1975.

Hoffman, L., and Long, L. "A Systems Dilemma." *Family Process*, 8:211–34, 1969.

Levande, D. I. "Family Theory as a Necessary Component of Family Therapy." *Social Casework*, 57:291–95, 1976.

Liddle, H., and Halpin, R. "Family Therapy Training and Supervision: A Comparative Review." *Journal of Marriage and Family Counseling*, 4:77–98, 1978.

Sager, C., Masters, Y., Ronall, R., & Normand, W. "Selection and Engagement of Patients in Family Therapy." *American Journal of Orthopsychiatry*, 38:715–23, 1968.

Index

The Book Manufacture

Family Treatment in Social Work Practice was typeset, printed and bound at Parthenon Press, Nashville. Cover design was by Jane Rae Brown. Internal design was by the F.E. Peacock Publishers art department. The typeface is Caledonia with Ultra Bodoni display.